The Best Places
To Kiss
In The Northwest
(and the Canadian Southwest)

What the press is saying about *The Best Places To Kiss:*

" '*The more intimate you are with a given place, the more intimate you can be with each other.*' I thoroughly agree with this passionate guide book."

Seattle Times

"*I've mentioned this 'romantic travel guide' several times, but the latest edition is still fun, selective, provocative and imaginative.*"

The Province

"*No matter how distant or exotic the destination, you will find it in this beguiling book.*"

The Toronto Star

"*This travel series will help you plan your next vacation, using your heart as a guide. There's even a listing of great outdoor locations and a miscellaneous category—for places you can kiss anytime.*"

First for Women

"*Never has a travel book had so much heart-stirring fun cover-to-cover.*"

Santa Rosa Press Democrat

"*If you need a place for that special occasion, you are sure to find what your hearts need inside.*"

Oakland Tribune

"*Our hearts went pit-a-pat when we received our kissing guide.*"

The New Yorker

"*More delightful travel hints abound in The Best Places To Kiss. Be sure to include this one in your travel collection.*"

San Francisco Examiner

Other Books in THE BEST PLACES TO KISS... Series

The Best Places To Kiss In Southern California $10.95

The Best Places To Kiss In Northern California $10.95

The Best Places To Kiss In And Around New York City . . .$10.95

The Best Places To Kiss In New England **(Spring 1993)** . .$12.95

The Best Places To Kiss In Hawaii **(Spring 1993)** $12.95

Any of these books can be ordered directly from the publisher.

Please send a check or money order for the total amount of the books, plus $1.50 for shipping and handling per book ordered, to:

Beginning Press
5418 South Brandon
Seattle, Washington 98118

Or for charge card orders call (206) 723–8857

The Best Places
To Kiss
In The Northwest
(and the Canadian Southwest)

A Romantic Travel Guide
Fourth Edition

by
Paula Begoun & Stephanie Bell

Beginning Press

Art Direction and Production: Lasergraphics
Cover Design: Design Source
Typography: Lasergraphics
Editor: Miriam Bulmer
Contributors: Elizabeth Janda, Miriam Bulmer, Patrick Kent,
and Sheryl Druxman
Printed in the United States by: Publishers Press, Salt Lake City, Utah

Copyright 1993 by Paula Begoun
Fourth Edition: February 1993
1 2 3 4 5 6 7 8 9 10

Best Places To Kiss™
is a registered trademark of Beginning Press
ISBN 1-877988-07-3

This book is distributed to the U.S. book trade by:
Publisher's Group West
4065 Hollis Street
Emeryville, California 94608
(800) 788-3123

This book is distributed to the Canadian book trade by:
Raincoast Books
112 East Third Avenue
Vancouver, British Columbia V5T 1C8
CANADA
(604) 873-6581

Publisher's Note

Travel books have many different formats and criteria for the places they include. We would like the reader to know that **this book is not an advertising vehicle.** As is true for all the *Best Places To Kiss* books, none of the businesses included here were charged fees, nor did they pay us for their review. This book is a sincere effort to highlight those special parts of the region that are filled with romance and splendor. Sometimes these places were created by people, as in restaurants, inns, lounges, lodges, hotels, and bed and breakfasts. Sometimes these places are untouched by people and simply created by G-d for us to enjoy. Wherever you go, be gentle with each other and gentle with the earth.

We Would Love to Hear From You

The recommendations in this collection were the final decision of the publisher, but we would love to hear what you think of our suggestions. Your feedback assists greatly in increasing our accuracy and resources for information. Please feel free to write Beginning Press if you have any additional comments, criticisms, or recommendations. We would also love to hear about a new place we have yet to discover. Please write: **Beginning Press**, 5418 South Brandon, Seattle, Washington 98118.

Special Acknowledgment

To Avis Begoun, for her extremely creative and romantic original idea for this book.

Dedication

Kissing is a fine art. To our partners, who helped us hone our craft.

> *"As usual with most lovers in the city, they were troubled by the lack of that essential need of love—a meeting place."*
> Thomas Wolfe

TABLE OF CONTENTS

> *"For a moment each seemed unreal to the other... then the slow warm hum of love began."*
> F. Scott Fitzgerald

THE FINE ART OF KISSING

The Fine Art of Kissing, Northwest Style

We admit a strong bias in our feelings about the Northwest. Without question this area provides the best kissing territory anywhere in the continental United States and Canada. This is the fourth edition of *The Best Places To Kiss In The Northwest* and it is the best one yet. Our research was more enthusiastic and our criteria more restrictive. If we're going to recommend a place for romance, we want to be sure your hearts and lips will be satisfied.

Beginning Press still publishes *The Best Places To Kiss In Northern California, The Best Places To Kiss In Southern California, and The Best Places To Kiss In New York City. The Best Places To Kiss In New England* and *The Best Places To Kiss In Hawaii* will be available in the spring of 1993. After all this lip-chapping research, we find it even easier to rave about the Northwest.

You will simply adore this glorious part of the world. More than any other area in the United States, the Northwest has a splendor and peacefulness that is apparent in almost every one of its localities. And along with the beauty of nature's handiwork, the people here have a style and attitude that are quietly conducive to intimacy and affection. Northwesterners know a secret: the more intimately acquainted you are with the earth, the more intimate you can be with each other. In short, it is not only better to kiss here, it is sheer ecstasy.

You Call This Research?

This book is the product of earnest interviews and careful investigation by our staff, but we also include feedback from readers and several researchers who report to us on a regular basis. Although it would have been nice, and from our viewpoint even preferable, kissing was not the major research method used for selecting the locations listed in this book. (And you thought this was the hottest job in town, didn't you?) If smooching had been the determining factor, several inescapable problems would have developed. First, be assured, we would still be researching and this book would be just a good idea, some breathless moments, random notes, overused credit cards, and nothing more. And, depending on the mood of the moment, many kisses would have occurred in a lot of places that do not meet the requirements of this travel guide (which would have been fun, but not productive). Thus, for both practical and physical reasons, a more objective approach had to be established.

How could we be certain that a particular place was good for kissing if we did not indulge in such an activity at every location? The honest, though boring, answer is that we used our reporters' instincts to evaluate the magnetic pull of each place visited. Standard criteria of cleanliness, beauty, hospitality, architecture, comfort, quality, uniqueness, and professionalism were the most important considerations. Then, if during our visit we felt a longing for our special someone to share our discovery, we considered that longing to be as reliable as a thorough kissing evaluation. In the final analysis, we can guarantee that once you choose where to go from among the places listed, you will find some amount of privacy, a beautiful setting, heart-stirring ambience, and (generally) first-rate accommodations. Once you get there, what you do romantically is up to you and your partner.

How Important Is Location?

You may be skeptical about the idea that one location is more romantic than another. You may think, "Well, it isn't the setting, it's who you're with that makes a place special." And you'd be right. But aside from the chemistry that exists between the two of you without any help from us, there are some locations that can facilitate and enhance the chemistry, just as there are some that can discourage and frustrate the magic in the moment.

For example, a tender embrace and an impassioned kiss at the grocery store might be, for some, a rapturous interlude. But the other shoppers and the kids running down the aisle and the preoccupied clerk who dropped your eggs can put a damper on heart-throb stuff for most of us, even the most adoring. Yes, location isn't everything, but when a certain type of place combines with all the right atmospheric details, including the right person, the odds are undeniably better for achieving unhindered and uninterrupted romance.

With that in mind, here is a list of the things that were considered to be not even remotely romantic: a place described as rustic that had olive green or orange carpeting (especially if it was mildewy or dirty);

anything overly plastic or overly veneered; a restaurant or area with an abundance of neon (even if it was very art-deco or very neo-modern); most tourist traps, particularly those with facilities for tour buses; overpriced hotels with impressive names or locations but mediocre accommodations; discos; the latest need-to-be-seen-in nightspot; and most places that encourage visits by families and children.

Create A Romantic Attitude

Above and beyond unromantic locations, unromantic behavior can negate the affection potential of even the most majestic surroundings. These are mood-killers every time: any amount of moaning over the weather (if you don't think rain and mist are romantic, you shouldn't be in the Northwest); creating a scene over the quality of food or service, no matter how justified; worrying about work; getting angry about traffic (even if it makes you miss a ferryboat); incessant backseat driving, no matter how warranted; and groaning about heartburn and other related symptoms, no matter how annoying.

Romance Ratings

The three major factors that determined whether a place would be included here were:
1. Surrounding splendor
2. Privacy
3. Tug-at-your-heartstrings ambience

Of the three determining factors, "surrounding splendor" and "privacy" are fairly self-explanatory. "Tug-at-your-heartstrings ambience" can probably use some clarification. Ambience, by our definition, is not limited to four-poster beds covered with down quilts and lace pillows, or tables decorated with white tablecloths and nicely folded linen napkins. Added to all that there must be a certain plushness or other engaging features that encourage intimacy and allow for continuous affectionate discussions. For the most part, ambience was rated according to degree of comfort and number of gracious appointments, as opposed to image and frills.

If a place had all three of the qualities listed above, its inclusion was automatic. If one or two of the criteria were weak or nonexistent, the other feature(s) had to be really incredible before the place could be recommended. For example, if a breathtakingly beautiful viewpoint was situated in an area inundated with tourists and families on vacation, the place was not included. On the other hand, if a fabulous bed and breakfast was set in a less-than-desirable location, it was included if, and only if, its interior was so wonderfully inviting and cozy that the outside world no longer mattered.

◆ **Romantic Note:** The Northwest is inherently romantic, but it is also a huge geographic area. Often we found ourselves in an area with magnificent scenery but few amenities of any kind, let alone romantic restaurants and inns. We were in a predicament: should we ignore a magnificent area because it doesn't have any facilities that can be recommended wholeheartedly, or should we relax our standards a bit and find decent (though not necessarily irreproachable) places where you can lay your heads down after a day of blissfully touring the countryside? We decided on the latter, and consequently you will read many entries that read something like "This isn't romantic but ..."

Kiss Ratings

If you've flipped through this book and noticed the miniature lips that follow each entry, you're probably curious about what they represent. Most other travel guides use a star system to rank the places they write about; for obvious reasons, we have chosen lips. The rating system notwithstanding, all the places listed in this book are wonderfully special places to be; *all* of them have heart-pleasing details and are worthwhile, enticing places to visit. The tiny lips indicate only our personal preferences and nothing more. They are a way of indicating just how delightfully romantic we found a place to be and how pleased we were with the service and environment during our visit. The number of lips awarded each location indicates the following:

Romantic Possibilities

   ❤   *Very Romantic*
   ❤❤ *Magical*
   ❤❤❤ *Irresistible*
   ❤❤❤❤ *Sublime*

Cost Ratings

There are also ratings to help you determine whether your lips can afford to kiss in a particular restaurant, hotel, or bed and breakfast (almost all of the outdoor places are free of charge or there is a minimal fee for parking and entrance). The price listing for overnight accommodations is always based on double occupancy (otherwise there wouldn't be anyone to kiss). Eating establishment prices are based on a full dinner for two, excluding liquor, unless otherwise indicated. Because prices and business hours change, it is always advisable to call ahead to each place you consider visiting, so that your lips do not end up disappointed.

Restaurant Rating

Very Inexpensive	Under $15
Inexpensive	$15 to $25
Moderate	$25 to $40
Expensive	$40 to $80
Very Expensive	$80 and up

Lodging Rating

Very Inexpensive	Under $70
Inexpensive	$70 to $85
Moderate	$85 to $115
Expensive	$115 to $155
Very Expensive	$155 to $200
Unbelievably Expensive	$200 and up

What If You Don't Want To Kiss?

Some people we interviewed resisted the idea of best kissing locales. Their resistance stemmed from expectation worries. They were apprehensive that once they arrived at the place of their dreams, they'd never get the feeling they thought they were supposed to have. They imagined spending time setting up itineraries, taking the extra time to get ready, making the journey to the promised land, and, once they were there, not being swept away in a flourish of romance. Their understandable fear was: what happens if nothing happens?

Having experienced those situations more than once in my life, I empathize, but I'm prepared with solutions. To prevent this anticlimactic scenario from becoming a reality, and to help you survive a romantic outing, consider these suggestions: when you make decisions about where and when to go, pay close attention to details; talk over your preferences and discuss your feelings about them. For some people there is no passion associated with fast pre-theater dinners that are all but inhaled, or with walking farther than expected in overly high, high heels, or with finding a place closed because its hours have changed. Also keep in mind the difficulties of second-guessing traffic patterns. My strong recommendation, although I know this can be tricky, is not to schedule a romantic outing too tightly or you will be more assured of a headache than an affectionate interlude.

A few miscellaneous suggestions: do not discuss money, family, or the kids; keep your eyes on what's on your plate, not on his or hers; if you have a headache, take some aspirin now and not later; and regardless of how good-looking the person at the next table is, remember that such distractions are never considered to be in romantic good taste. How different factors might affect your lips, not to mention your mood, is something to consider before you head out the door, not after.

In spite of all that, it is important to remember that part of the whole experience of an intimate time together is to allow whatever happens to be an opportunity to let affection reign. Regardless of what takes place, that is what is romantic. For example, do you remember the incredibly impassioned scene in the film *Ghost*, where Demi Moore is working at her pottery wheel with wet clay and Patrick Swayze sits downs behind her and begins kneading the form sensuously at the same time she is? Fervently the wet clay splatters all over the place as they embrace in lustful lovemaking. Well, how romantic would it have been if Demi had started complaining about having to clean up the clay, washing the clay out of her hair, or getting the clay in her mouth while they kissed? Or remember the scene between Kevin Costner and Susan Sarandon in *Bull Durham*, where he throws his full cereal bowl against the wall, cleans the kitchen table with a sweep of his arm, and then picks Susan up and throws her passionately on the table? Well, how romantic would that have been if Kevin had started complaining about the broken china in his hair and the spilled milk running down his arms? Get the idea?

So, if the car breaks down, the waiter is rude to you, your reservations get screwed up, or both of you tire out and want to call it a day, you can still be endearing and charming. It really only takes an attitude change to turn any dilemma into a delight.

The Most Romantic Time To Travel

The Northwest is truly so spectacular, it's hard to imagine any time of the year or the week that would not be romantic. Each season and hour has its own special joy: winter skiing, fireplaces on a chilly day, the warmth of summer, mesmerizing fall sunsets, the rebirth of nature in the melting wet spring. Even in overcast conditions, if you prepare properly there is no reason to postpone investigating the splendor that hovers around every turn in the Northwest. So don't be one of those couples who wait until summer to travel and then decide not to go because it might be too crowded. Oh, and about the rain—it does. Enough said.

"You know I'd rather be lost in love than found."

F. Scott Fitzgerald

British Columbia

VANCOUVER ISLAND

Vancouver Island is accessible by ferry for car and foot traffic from the following ports: Anacortes (one and a half hours north of Seattle), Port Angeles (on the Olympic Peninsula), Tsawwassen (30 minutes south of Vancouver), Horseshoe Bay (in West Vancouver), and Westview (on the Sunshine Coast, north of Vancouver). The Victoria Clipper, a foot-traffic-only ferry, docks in the heart of downtown Victoria after a two-and-a-half-hour passage from Seattle. There is also a passenger-only ferry from downtown Vancouver to Victoria. For information on fares and schedules, contact the British Columbia Ferries, (604) 669-1211; Washington State Ferries, (206) 464-6400; Port Angeles Black Ball Transport, (206) 457-4491; or Victoria Clipper, (206) 448-5000. Be aware that during peak travel times you can find yourselves in line for a long time. Trial by ferryboat is one of the hazards of summer or weekend travel.

Traveling to Vancouver Island is an unconditional romantic must, simply because it has everything that two people in love could want to share. This huge land mass is resplendent with deep forests, an English-style city, miles upon miles of wilderness, rugged coastlines, bustling fishing communities, sandy white beaches, rustic lodges, quaint bed and breakfasts, magnificent bed and breakfasts, and a mountain range that spans its nearly 300-mile length.

The north-central section is mostly uninhabited and thus full of untouched mountain terrain, wildlife, and pristine scenery. The eastern coastal areas are marbled with long lazy beaches, densely forested hills, and verdant meadows. The central west coast is entirely wilderness except for the congenial fishing villages of Tofino and Ucluelet. Along the southwestern coast, near the towns of Sooke and Metchosin, the unspoiled wilderness is again apparent in rocky beaches and extensive forestland.

The city of Victoria, on the southern tip of the island, presents a stark contrast to the rest of the island. The capital of British Columbia, it is distinguished by lavish gardens, charming tea rooms, old-world architecture, plus a multitude of tourist traps and scores of tourists. Actually, much of Victoria's English style is self-consciously marketed to attract visitors. Victoria is still an intriguing city, just not the provincial town you might be expecting.

◆ **Romantic Note:** Canada has a 7-percent Goods and Services Tax (GST) in addition to a hotel tax. Most places will warn you about these extra charges, but if not, be aware that it can be a hefty addition to your bill. The GST portion of your accommodation bill and some purchases are refundable directly from the government if you are not a resident of Canada. Most places provide the required forms and information explaining how you can submit your receipts for reimbursement.

◆ **Romantic Warning:** The Island Highway, which runs the length of the entire island from north to south, can be agony to travel. Being the only main thoroughfare to get anywhere on the island, it gets dreadfully crowded and, unfortunately, not everyone wants to go as fast as you do.

Port Hardy

Outdoor Kissing

CAPE SCOTT PARK and SAN JOSEF BAY,
Port Hardy
(604) 248-3931

Just south of Port Hardy, follow the poorly marked logging road for 28 miles. At the end of the road, you'll pass a government-run meteorology station as you proceed to the parking area at the head of the trail. A very short climb reveals the path.

Cape Scott is on the northwestern tip of Vancouver Island and feels like the end of the world. It is accessible via a miserable, dusty gravel-and-stone logging road. The park is not all that far from Port Hardy, but because of the road's condition you'll need longer to get here than you'd think from looking at a map. You will be ecstatic that you underwent the ordeal; this park is the epitome of wilderness.

At the beginning of the hiking trail, you make a dream-like transition from the gravel-pit road to a land filled with the elfin spirits of nature. A flat walkway of wood planks is the only sign of civilization you're likely to see all day; you are guaranteed privacy.

From the trailhead, you meander for two miles past trees draped in moss and streamered with sunlight, to where the path opens onto an enormous sand-laden horseshoe bay called San Josef, which you can claim exclusively for yourselves. The waves breaking on the beach fill the air with a rhythmic pounding. The U-shaped bay is bordered by forested hills where very few people have gone before. At the end of the trail be sure to mark where you leave the trail or it will be tricky to find that spot again.

◆ **Romantic Note:** Because Cape Scott is so remote, acquire a detailed map and complete information from the visitor center in Port Hardy before you head out there. If you plan on backpacking, the need to be prepared for adverse weather conditions cannot be stressed enough. Weather here can be severe and excessively wet, bordering on torrential.

Campbell River

Hotel/Bed and Breakfast Kissing

PAINTER'S LODGE, Campbell River ❤
1625 MacDonald Road
(604) 286-1102
Moderate to Expensive

Just north of Campbell River, turn right on MacDonald Road and follow the signs to Painter's Lodge.

It's between 5 A.M. and 9 A.M., and you're in a rocking boat, in the rain, out in the middle of a cold channel of water, with no fish in sight. Romance is probably the last thing on your mind. Yet half the battle is *considerately* sharing what the other person thinks is romantic, no matter how wrong he or she might be, and there are those who kiss best after they've landed a king or two.

Painter's Lodge is an angler's delight and has been for more than 60 years. Canadians and Californians flock here to test their patience and skill. Due to a fire a few years back, the lodge has been entirely rebuilt, and the result, for the most part, is elegant and attractive. Some of the accommodations are still hotel basic, but the rooms in the main lodge are really quite nice. None of that matters when the agenda is hooking a coho or king salmon, but it's generally disappointing for more intimate activity. However, the glass-enclosed fireside lounge, with its huge stone fireplace and comfortable seating, is a prime place to revitalize yourselves for another go-around after a few hours spent fighting off the dogfish and weeds.

Dinner in the main restaurant, framed by the same floor-to-ceiling windows as the lounge, is surprisingly lovely, with china, linens, formal service, and impressive menu selections. The food is good, although, given the effort of the staff, it should be great.

STRATHCONA LODGE, Campbell River
Highway 28
(604) 286-8206
Moderate

Just north of Campbell River, take Highway 28 west for 30 miles to the lodge.

You arrive at Strathcona Lodge after driving along a winding mountain road into the core of Vancouver Island. This lodge is like no other lodge on earth! The red hewn-log buildings are set at the edge of a crystal-clear mountain lake encircled by an astounding collection of snowcapped peaks. Strathcona is, without question, a visual paradise. There are no other facilities around for miles, and that sort of isolation has an enchantment all its own.

The staff here is dedicated to introducing all who venture into this realm to the mysteries and excitement of the outdoor magic of Strathcona Park. They offer guided instruction for any mountain and water activity you could wish for: kayaking, rappelling from cliffs, glissading down glaciers, wildlife hiking, canoeing, fishing, sailing, and camping. The lodge's brochure lists a rare selection of packaged challenges for all ages and skill levels. (Even if you are not staying at the lodge, the park is a magnificent area to explore on your own. The vistas and countryside are exquisite.)

You may be thinking yes, that all sounds great but not necessarily romantic, unless you're dating Paul Bunyan. But after you have explored the lodge and the rustic cabins around the lake, wandered into the wilderness for a breathtaking hike, and enjoyed the three hearty family-style meals served daily, you will be convinced that this is an extraordinary place for outdoor-loving couples. Your outdoor fantasies will be fulfilled at Strathcona Lodge.

Courtenay

Restaurant Kissing

LA CREMAILLIERE, Courtenay
975 Comox Road
(604) 338-8131
Moderate to Expensive

Call for directions.

This is probably the most romantic restaurant on the entire island outside of Victoria. Its decidedly intimate atmosphere is tempered by enough comfort to make it relaxing. The superior French cuisine that is served has a distinctive Northwest flair. Service is efficient and polite, with attention to paid detail. The fresh local oysters dabbed with a flawless hollandaise and the flavorful house pâté are both delicious appetizers. For a main course, try the filet mignon or lamb, swimming in smooth, rich sauces. Dessert selections change with the mood of the chef and are worth every decadent bite.

THE OLD HOUSE RESTAURANT, Courtenay
1760 Riverside Lane
(604) 338-5406
Inexpensive to Moderate

As you approach the town of Courtenay, heading north along Highway 19, turn west at the first major intersection, which is the 17th Street Bridge. Then immediately turn right again onto Riverside Lane, the road just before the river. The restaurant is the first house on your left.

As you drive up to the eye-catching rustic mansion that is The Old House Restaurant, you'll be impressed by its rugged architecture and its garden setting. Willow trees and thick green lawn fill the backyard, where outdoor dining is accompanied by the flow of the Powell River.

(The nearby log-processing factory is often in full swing during lunchtime, but it wasn't as much of a distraction as I'd feared.)

The interior is divided into several very pretty rooms, each one dominated by a beach-stone fireplace framed by a wood mantel. Antique furnishings and leaded glass windows reflect warmth and gentility. The food is quite good; the service, for the most part, is attentive and efficient, though sometimes strained when the place is busy. Unusual fresh ingredients along with more standard items are the hallmarks of the kitchen. Pumpkin pasta, smoked goose, quail, and venison are a few of the rare finds on the interesting menu.

Outdoor Kissing

MOUNT WASHINGTON, Courtenay
Box 3069
(604) 334-4744
Inexpensive

Call for directions.

If you're in an adventurous mood, drive 25 minutes northwest from Courtenay to the chair lift that takes you to the ski slopes of Mount Washington. During the off-season (June 5 through September 5), as you dangle above the golden land, you can study the scenic Comox Valley, the Strait of Georgia, and the Beaufort Mountain Range. During ski season, numerous runs boast great skiing and amazing scenery. It isn't Whistler, but the lines are a lot shorter.

Parksville

Hotel/Bed and Breakfast Kissing

BEACH ACRES RESORT, Parksville
1015 East Island Highway
(604) 248-3424
Moderate to Expensive

Just off Highway 19, look for signs on the east side of the road, a few miles south of downtown Parksville.

South of Parksville, along a lovely stretch of beach bordering Craig Bay, with resplendent views of the mountains, a condominium/rental explosion has taken place. Large signs shout at you from the highway. Some properties have mowed down every tree in sight, and in places it looks like a mainland suburb. Luckily, there are still places where you can find a sense of country authenticity and respect for the environment. Beach Acres Resort is such a location, and the beachfront cabins (in the process of being refurbished) are rustic and delightful. Brick fireplaces (you have to purchase the wood), large windows, full kitchens, separate living rooms, patios, and separate (small) bedrooms make for a cozy home away from home. Unobstructed vistas are what make this place special, and the beach at low tide goes on forever.

TIGH-NA-MARA, Parksville
1095 East Island Highway
(604) 248-2072
Inexpensive to Moderate

Just off Highway 19, on the east side of the road, a few miles south of downtown Parksville.

For excellence in resort accommodations, setting, views, and dining facilities, Tigh-Na-Mara could be the best place along the northern coast of Vancouver Island. There is much here to praise. The log cabins, clustered among pinery and red-barked trails, have roomy interiors with broad stone fireplaces that keep things glowingly warm. Even better are the newer suites that lord over the shoreline. These units were created with lovers in mind. The sliding glass door to your private deck opens onto a ringside view of the water. Inside, the extensive cedar-paneled living room has a fireplace; you'll also find a hot tub, cathedral ceilings, and a silky comforter for the queen-size bed.

The restaurant, set in a log mansion with a country-polished interior, is a fine place to enjoy a meal. The service is cordial, although with all the conferences going on it can get abrupt and slow. Still, the food is reliable and sometimes very good.

◆ **Romantic Warning:** The cabins and rooms at Tigh-Na-Mara are set mostly in the woods; as a result, the interiors tend to be a bit on the dark side. It's really not a problem—unless you were counting on a bright sun-filled room. Also, because many of the rooms have space for up to six, Tigh-Na-Mara attracts a lot of families, especially during summer vacation.

Restaurant Kissing

HERON'S RESTAURANT, Parksville
240 Dogwood Street, at the Bayside Inn
(604) 248-8333
Moderate

Just off the East Island Highway on the east side of the street in the town of Parksville.

The Bayside Inn is just an OK hotel with some great views, but its restaurant is a three-tiered showcase with a sweeping view of the water and mountains. If it weren't for the view, there wouldn't be much incentive to dine here; the food is decent, but could easily be better. Breakfast and cocktails and appetizers at sundown are the best.

MACLURE HOUSE INN, Parksville
1015 East Island Highway
(604) 248-3470
Moderate

Just off the East Island Highway, on the east side of the road, a few miles south of downtown Parksville.

Probably one of the last places you would look for a romantic restaurant would be in the middle of a rustic resort complex, in back of the main office and laundry facilities. Nevertheless, here it is and it is enchantingly intimate and gracious. Originally built in 1921, the Maclure House Inn has been handsomely renovated to retain all of its original charm. Although the surroundings are unflattering, the stucco-and-wood exterior is inviting. The dimly lit interior is bathed in the amber glow of a crackling fire that is reflected on the polished dark wood molding and paneling. Windows draped in lace frame the distant view of the water and mountains.

Lunch and dinner are both worthwhile. The hot Camembert cheese rolled in almonds and served with a fresh plum sauce was a flavorful combination, and the classic Caesar salad had exactly the right proportions. The all-you-can-eat tiger prawn feast was a little disappointing; the prawns were on the small side, although unexpectedly fresh and moist. Raspberry torte for dessert was almost too rich, but we "suffered" through it anyway.

Tofino

From Highway 4 at Parksville, head west 75 miles across the center of the island to the water. Where the road dead-ends, follow the signs north to Tofino.

The 75-mile trip west on Highway 4 across the central mountains of Vancouver Island takes you to the remote side of the island. For the last few miles of this panoramic drive, the rocky coast chaperones you as you descend to sea level. When you finally reach road's end, the highway splits: one road forks north to Tofino, the other south to Ucluelet. Both towns are basically fishing villages and whale-watching ports of call. They also pride themselves on being noncommercial places where you can charter boats for fishing and water tours. But for heart-stealing pursuits, Tofino is your destination.

Tofino is what a small town should be: unpretentious, with amiable, unruffled streets and neighborhoods set like small constellations along the volatile, rocky oceanfront and the marinas of the calm inner bay. Every corner of it provides an escape from the madding crowd (although the townspeople can be somewhat colorful, they are as far from madding as you can get). Several waterfront resorts line the shore along the main road into Tofino and have unobstructed views of the beach and ocean. In town you'll find a few basic shops and casual restaurants. Nothing here gets in the way of the scenery. Get close, kick back, and discover that you're in a place where time floats by to a melody you can learn to hum together.

◆ **Romantic Note:** The tourist season here is so brief and intense (mostly in July and August), and the best accommodations so difficult to come by then, that you may want to consider a less popular season for your visit to this area. Try fall or winter and you will think the two of you have the place to yourselves.

Hotel/Bed and Breakfast Kissing

CHESTERMAN'S BEACH
BED AND BREAKFAST, Tofino
1345 Chesterman's Beach Road
(604) 725-3726
Moderate

From Highway 4 turn west on Lynn Road and follow around until it becomes Chesterman's Beach Road.

Oceanfront bed and breakfasts are a treat, for two predictable reasons. First, the proximity to the ocean is enthralling; second, the delectable morning meal is enhanced wonderfully when an endless shoreline happens to be the backdrop. As you sit on the deck you can feel the breeze lift the sea air all around you. The cool mist tingles against your cheek, and as you sip hot fresh coffee the steam briefly warms your face. After breakfast, a sentimental stroll hand-in-hand through the surf can be a wonderful midmorning treat.

Chesterman's offers three rustic units: a large cabin with a private yard; a multiwindowed second-story room with a balcony; and a charming two-bedroom suite on the lower level. All have private entrances. Each of these units is a viable option for a romantic sojourn in this part of the world, especially since all you need is each other and endless majestic scenery.

CRYSTAL COVE BEACH RESORT, Tofino
1165 Cedarwood
(604) 725-4213
Inexpensive

Just before the town center, on the west side of the road.

Set on a quiet inlet next to McKenzie Beach, the nine log cabins here are rustic and quite lovely. Complete with stone fireplaces, full kitchens, windows that offer remarkable views, cozy interiors, and separate living rooms, they are well worth an extended stay. The one negative—and it could be a sizable deterrent—is that 40 campsites and RV hookups lie just behind the cabins. Off-season it isn't a problem, but during the summer it can lose some of its charm, depending on your feeling about campers.

OCEAN VILLAGE BEACH RESORT, Tofino
555 Helleson Drive
(604) 725-3755
Inexpensive to Moderate

On the Pacific Rim Highway, two miles south of Tofino; look for the sign on the west side of the road.

There is nothing fancy about the 24 cedar cabins that make up the accommodations of Ocean Village, but the view, location, and privacy are another story. Eight of these units are individual huts stationed in a row on McKenzie Beach, and these are by far your best bet. Each of these private residences has a sliding glass door that opens to the sand, wind, and waves. Opportunities for beachcombing, whale watching, hunting for seashells, building sand castles, playing in the surf, or listening to the waves lapping against the shore are within inches of your door. This place may not be fancy, but who needs fancy when you have a front yard like the one at Ocean Village?

PACIFIC SANDS, Tofino
1421 Pacific Rim Highway
(604) 725-3322
Inexpensive to Moderate

On the Pacific Rim Highway, two miles south of Tofino; look for the sign on the west side of the road.

Purists won't be happy with this sprawling new suburban-type development. The three modern cedar buildings, which rise up three stories over the shoreline, are actually quite attractive and offer the most elegant accommodations in the area, but they aren't what you would call quaint or rustic. In fact, they are rather upscale and refined. Set on a stretch of magnificent coastline, practically every unit has a spectacular view. The top units offer the most panoramic view, but the advantage must be weighed against carrying your luggage up three flights of stairs. Pale green interiors, sliding glass doors that open to private balconies or patios, wood-burning fireplaces, small but complete kitchens, televisions, comfortable living rooms, and separate bedrooms create a lovely little apartment setting. The older section offers similar accommodations, more rustic but also more spacious, and the top floor here even has soaring cathedral ceilings. A handful of rustic cabins sit adjacent to the property, and these are probably the most purely romantic and relatively secluded spots.

SPINDRIFT, Tofino
1373 Chesterman's Beach Road
(604) 725-2103
Inexpensive to Expensive

From Highway 4 turn west on Lynn Road and follow around until it becomes Chesterman's Beach Road.

Any of the homes residing directly on the rugged ocean shores of Tofino is envied for its treasured location. Spindrift is a newly built, blue-gray wood-frame residence dwelling on just such a corner of forested sand. Inside, the cozy common living room with hardwood floors, floor-to-ceiling windows, and an efficient fireplace is an ideal spot for guests to watch the daily tidal procession change the shoreline's appearance. Three attractive, immaculate suites are available. Two units, without the luxury of a sweeping view, have small kitchens, cozy dining nooks, private entrances, and, particularly the room on the second floor, plenty of room and a peekaboo glimpse of the water. But the Pacific Suite is the one that would fill any kissing requirements you could want in such a remote destination. Vaulted ceilings, fireplace with raised hearth, antique double bed, huge soaking tub, glorious towering windows that frame the spectacular view from every corner of the room: you simply cannot find better in Tofino. As you would expect, the price tag is steep, and there's a two-night minimum during the summer, but it is well worth the expense.

Restaurant Kissing

BLUE HERON DINING ROOM, Tofino   💋
634 Campbell Street
(604) 725-3277
Moderate

At the Weigh West Marine Resort, on the east side of the road, just south of the town center.

Dine at this casual restaurant surrounded with windows, and watch the comings and goings at a busy sport-fishing marina. Almost every table has a ringside perspective of the area. Clayoquot Sound can be still and calm or bustling and exciting, depending on how many spring (king) salmon have been caught. Don't expect an intimate repast here, just fresh fish, passable pasta, and a dazzling outdoor view of Tofino. Breakfast is particularly interesting when the morning fishing boats return with the early catch.

ORCA LODGE RESTAURANT, Tofino
1254 Pacific Rim Highway
(604) 725-2323
Moderate to Expensive

Just outside of the town center, on the east side of the road.

Assuredly the best dining experience in Tofino is to be found in this gray frame building set in a forested wayside off the main road. The small, casual dining room is subtly lit, and an appropriately large wood-burning fireplace radiates a cozy glow. The fresh seafood, particularly the king salmon served with a light pesto sauce and the prawns, is excellent, and the servings are generous. The scallops are succulent but a bit paltry in comparison to the other dishes. Focaccia bread is served along with a saucer of balsamic vinegar and extra-virgin olive oil for Italian-style dipping. By the way, the veal here is the best you will find for miles (and I mean miles) around.

WICKANINNISH RESTAURANT, Ucluelet
Highway 4
(604) 726-7706
Inexpensive to Moderate

Fifteen miles south of Tofino, on Highway 4, look for signs on the west side of the road that will direct you to the restaurant and interpretive center.

This is not your typical kissing place. Wickaninnish is the name of an outstretched beach with hundreds of weathered logs strewn like tooth-picks along the shore. A large wooden building with the same name houses an information center, a museum of Native Canadian culture, and a restaurant, and sits on the edge of the sandy shore. The information center and museum, together known as the Interpretive Centre, are educational points of interest but hardly romantic, unless you want to kiss an artifact. The restaurant, on the other hand, is exceptionally romantic, particularly during off-season, when the tourists are home waiting patiently for summer.

The restaurant is encircled by windows that showcase the beach and the ever-changing moods of the sea. Threatening winter storms, dramatic high tides, and motionless summer days make for a scene that is at one moment languid and silent, and the next violent and thundering. Regardless of what excitement nature is providing, the Wickaninnish

Restaurant will serve you gracious meals while you sit back and watch the show.

◆ **Romantic Note:** After lunch, weather permitting, Wickaninnish is a perfect place to hike along the beach or through the woods behind the building. When you're done, return to the restaurant and drink a toast to the day you shared together.

Outdoor Kissing

HOT SPRINGS COVE ADVENTURES, Tofino
320 Main Street
(604) 725-4222
Expensive

Hot Springs Cove Adventures is one of many boat charters that can take you to Hot Springs Cove. Call for reservations and directions to the marina where you meet the boat.

Coastal wilderness is normally accessible only to those who own a seaworthy vessel that they can navigate along remote, often dangerous shores. But those people fortunate enough to find themselves in Tofino can take advantage of the daily round-trip boat excursions to Hot Springs Cove—and what a trip it is! After leaving the marina, you travel for an hour and a half amid the exquisite scenery of Clayoquot Sound as you head north for Shelter Inlet. Once you dock, you must hike for a bit through lush forest until you see the steaming mists of the cove. The warm, cascading water spills over rocky formations into a series of natural pools. As you soak away the last bits of tension in your neck and shoulders, lean back and watch the ocean waves crash onto the nearby shore. This natural shower is bound to be one you'll never forget.

◆ **Romantic Note:** You have to bring your own water or drinks to the cove, because water supplies are limited and at times nonexistent. Should you desire to stay overnight and treat yourselves to an early-morning rinse in the springs, there are campgrounds a short distance from the dock and there is also the newly built **HOT SPRINGS COVE LODGE**, (604) 725-2215, (Inexpensive). The six self-contained housekeeping units here will make you feel as if you're homesteading, except for the satellite-fed TV in your room. This touch of civilization seems out of place up here, but no one says you have to turn it on. We threw a blanket over ours and were thoroughly pleased with our entire stay.

LONG BEACH,

Just off Highway 4, on the west side of the road, as you head north toward the town of Tofino.

Located between Tofino and Ucluelet, Long Beach offers an abundance of everything that restless surf-lovers could want. This area is defined by rocky cliffs, smooth white-sand beaches, old-growth rain forest, and wooded picnic areas. Several hiking trails run adjacent to the shoreline. The romantic possibilities are many: you can relax, walk along the extensive beach, hike through the forest bordering the shore, or seek the water for a salty frolic. An amazing number of surfers will be out trying to catch a wave at many spots along the beach, which can prove quite entertaining.

OCEAN PACIFIC WHALE CHARTERS, Tofino

(604) 725-3919
Moderate

Call Ocean Pacific for reservations and directions to the marina where you meet your boat. The height of the whale migration season is in March and April, though whales reside here in all seasons.

Take it from a skeptic: whale watching is romantic. Imagine yourself and your loved one staring out from your open Zodiac at the cliff-lined Pacific Ocean and at forested islands haloed in shades of deep, verdant green. The coolness of the morning air swirls around you and you squeeze each other close for protection against the chill. You both slowly scan the calm blue water and your thoughts are filled with the vastness before you. Then suddenly, in the distance, breaking the stillness of a sun-drenched winter day, a spout of water explodes from the ocean surface, followed by a giant, arching black profile. After an abrupt tail slap, all is stillness once again. Believe me, even if you're not sitting next to someone you care about, you're likely to grab the person nearest you and yell, "Wow, look at that!"

Maybe it's the excitement of knowing that such an immense, powerful creature can glide so effortlessly through the water with playful agility and speed. Or it could be the chance of "connecting" with a civilized mammal that knows the secret depths of an aquatic world we can only briefly visit and barely understand. Whatever the reason, the search is one you need to share with someone special. Together you can contemplate what to anyone's way of thinking is surely a miracle.

Ladysmith

Hotel/Bed and Breakfast Kissing

YELLOW POINT LODGE, Ladysmith
Rural Route 3, Yellow Point Road
(604) 245-7422
Moderate to Expensive

Call for reservations and directions.

This popular B.C. getaway is well known for several reasons: its remote location, its extensive beachfront and secluded coves bordered by 180 acres of forest, the attentive staff, the laid-back ambience, hearty meals, and a huge seaside saltwater swimming pool. You can truly relax here; this is a real Canadian West Coast getaway.

The lodging choices are eclectic. The best ones for romantic interaction are the new timber-framed cabins that line the shore, tucked among pines and hidden from view. There are more rustic accommodations scattered around the extensive property in assorted price ranges; the ones in the lodge and the cabins that share baths are the least desirable but still comfortable. While you are here, there is no need to do anything more strenuous than deciding what to wear to the three family-style meals and the three teas served daily in the handsome main lodge, which are part of the price.

Restaurant Kissing

CROW AND GATE, Ladysmith
Rural Route 3, Yellow Point Road
(604) 722-3731
Inexpensive

About three miles north of Ladysmith, on the Island Highway, turn right on Cedar Road and then turn right again at the second turnoff to Yellow Point Road. Travel for one mile to the restaurant, on the right side of the road. Signs along the Island Highway will help guide you.

Nestled among the rolling meadows and tall pines of the countryside, protected by a rose arbor and spiced with rustic appeal, the ambience of another era is alive in an English-style pub called the Crow and Gate. The setting of this cottage, on the pastoral east coast of Vancouver Island, provides a refuge to weary, hungry travelers looking for a place to have dinner and mellow out. Here you'll find restful pleasure as you take your tea or ale at a table near the stone hearth and let the evening linger on. The food is traditional British fare, with the accent on fresh, hearty, and friendly. So snuggle close together and watch the embers flicker and glow in the dimly lit room as you wait for the innkeeper to fetch your afternoon or evening meal.

Duncan

Hotel/Bed and Breakfast Kissing

FAIRBURN FARM COUNTRY MANOR, Duncan
3310 Jackson Road
(604) 746-4637
Moderate

Open seasonally; call for directions.

It is essential for those of us who live in cities to reconnect with the earth every now and then, to restore the soul and the capacity to love. Fairburn Farm offers just such an opportunity. This is authentic farm life, shared with the Archer family and their six children. All around you is one of the most beautiful rural settings imaginable: rolling green hills, flawless forested grounds, sweeping fields, abundant vegetable gardens, and brilliant flowers.

The accommodations are definitely on the rustic side, but they only add to the atmosphere of this authentic rural destination. Built in 1884, the home is still as it was back then, with only what you might call necessary changes. There are six guest rooms; the three best have private bathrooms that, believe it or not, include a Jacuzzi bathtub. The other rooms are more family oriented and have detached private baths. Breakfast in the morning is a hearty affair that helps bring you even closer to embracing the total experience.

If the restaurant has extra seatings for lunch or dinner, Fairburn Farm is a must for gourmet country-food lovers who find themselves near the town of Duncan. Almost all of the food served is produced or raised on the farm, including the lamb, veal, chickens, vegetables, fresh-churned butter, stone-ground wheat bread (from wheat grown on the farm), real maple syrup tapped from the trees, and homemade jams. Meals like this soothe and satisfy in a way store-bought fare never can.

GROVE HALL ESTATE, Duncan
6159 Lakes Road
(604) 746-6152
Moderate

Call for reservations and directions.

A cattle grate will shake your car as you drive through the gate and down a long driveway lined with ancient oak trees. Something stupendous is waiting at the end of this grand entry: a magnificent turn-of-the-century Tudor mansion set on 17 acres of gardens, sweeping lawns, and accessible lakefront. Inside, every corner and each detail is intriguing and unique. The interior is a renovated masterpiece filled with amazing antiques. The ground floor holds a luxurious living room, a stately billiards chamber that has to be seen to be believed, and a formal dining room with a view of the lake, where an appropriately regal breakfast is served each morning. The exotic, sensuous guest suites are upstairs. The Singapore Room has a huge, handcrafted Chinese wedding bed with a view of the lake and gardens. The Indonesia Suite, with its own sitting room, has art pieces and batiks from that part of the world and a private balcony overlooking lake and garden. The Siamese Room has—you guessed it—twin beds and a private balcony set above the gardens.

If there is a flaw in this picture-perfect retreat, it can only be the shared bathroom facilities, though three are available and each is lovely. In my opinion, this is a small sacrifice to make for the memories you will create at Grove Hall Estate.

SAHTLAM LODGE, Duncan
5720 Riverbottom Road
(604) 748-7738
Inexpensive to Expensive

From the Island Highway turn west onto Old Lake Cowichan Road, and then left on Riverbottom Road to the lodge.

In some respects this is a fairly ordinary lodge with some comfortable rooms and rustic cabins located along a surging river embraced by lofty pines. A nice Northwest setting, but not necessarily intimate or distinctive. What is different and worth a closer look are the "Tent Bedrooms" located away from the main building on the banks of the river. These unique, safari-style accommodations are a cross between roughing it and camping in style. The platform tents, with shingled roofs and walls of mosquito netting and canvas, complete with bedroom furnishings, hurricane lamps, and a welcoming bottle of champagne, are as unique as they sound. They are available mid-May through mid-October only. It isn't plush, and the bathrooms are a distance away, but these unusual accommodations really make for some great snuggling.

Breakfast is not included in the price of your room, but is available in the lodge's restaurant. It is nothing much to speak about, because the kitchen doesn't have its heart in it. That's because the emphasis here is on dinner, when a gourmet procession of taste delights is presented in a four-course culinary production. International cuisine is skillfully prepared from seasonal menus. Smoked salmon tortellini, creamy carrot soup served with fresh maple bread, and lemon pork with sautéed apples and lentils may be one evening's repast. Another might be roasted corn and garlic bisque, spring rolls with caramelized chutney, and seafood lasagne. Hearty eating and kissing is definitely what you can expect from your stay at Sahtlam Lodge.

Restaurant Kissing

THE QUAMICHAN INN, Duncan
1478 Maple Bay Road
(604) 746-7028
Expensive

Call for directions.

What a shame you can't eat charm, because this is one charming location for dinner. Set on a knoll overlooking the Cowichan Valley, the restaurant occupies the lower level of a handsome Tudor home. There are three cozy dining areas here, each with a glowing fireplace. The eclectic menu offers mostly fresh local meats; some items are excellent but, sad to say, some are only mediocre. Salads come covered (not tossed) with bottled dressing and prepackaged Parmesan cheese. Sauces are the strong point here, and are light and tasty. Be clear about how you like your dish cooked and you will find yourself pleased with your meal. It's still a good place for a celebration, with a few cautions.

◆   **Romantic Note:** The inn has bed-and-breakfast rooms upstairs, but they are fairly tacky. The restaurant smells and sounds too easily travel upstairs.

Cowichan Bay

Restaurant Kissing

THE MASTHEAD RESTAURANT, Cowichan Bay
1705 Cowichan Bay Road
(604) 748-3714
Moderate

From the Island Highway, turn east onto Cowichan Bay Road and drive to the restaurant.

The Cowichan Bay marina is a picturesque spot, with fishing vessels coming and going and views of the forested hills across the water. Fresh fish, the kind that jumps from the boat onto your plate, can be found at this attractive dockside restaurant. A white, slightly weathered frame building with blue trim houses the dining room (open for dinners only). Inside, everything is white linens, candlelight, and polite service. The succulent oysters, king salmon, and halibut are served with French flair and can be remarkably good.

Mill Bay

Hotel/Bed and Breakfast Kissing

DEER LODGE MOTEL, Mill Bay
2529 Island Highway
(604) 743-2423
Very Inexpensive

Just north of Mill Bay, on the Island Highway, on the east side of the road.

Deer Lodge is an interesting place to include in this collection of special romantic locations. Some of it is exceptionally tacky and some of the rooms smell of cigarette smoke, but the spectacular views and the size of the rooms make it a consideration. If you are traveling north along the Island Highway, this is a good stopping point. The rooms in the new addition are the best, with fairly nice furnishings and enchanting views from large windows that look out to the water and the mainland. Some of the older rooms have fireplaces, sitting areas, complete kitchens, and, of course, views. All of the units are set facing away from the main road, with a manicured lawn and gardens sweeping down the hillside to the water just beyond. There is also a bed-and-breakfast section here. The three bedrooms don't have views, but the common room warmed by a huge brick fireplace has a spectacular one.

PINE LODGE FARM BED AND BREAKFAST, Mill Bay
3191 Mutter Road
(604) 743-4083
Inexpensive

Call for directions.

A 25-mile pilgrimage north of Victoria brings you to serene country-side encompassed by welcome quiet. This eight-bedroom manor has an impressive white pine exterior and an interior that is equally fascinating in its handsome detail and presence. The spacious sitting room has an enormous beach-stone fireplace and is surrounded by a second-floor balcony. Unfortunately, the rooms aren't as impressive as the sitting room and they can be dark (as can the rest of the house), but they are comfortable and outfitted with antiques of superior workmanship. The rooms with a peekaboo view of the fields, the Strait of Georgia, and the islands are ideal. Breakfast is a last-you-all-day enterprise prepared with fresh eggs and homemade preserves.

There is also a cabin on the grounds that has a full kitchen, an outdoor hot tub on the wraparound deck, and a fireplace. This unit is homey and really quite wonderful. Generous breakfast supplies are provided for your own preparation.

◆ **Romantic Note:** The owners have converted the barn into a museum that showcases an amazing array of antique farm implements, horse-drawn carriages, clothing, and tools. It is worth a stay just to be given a tour of this outstanding collection.

Malahat

Hotel/Bed and Breakfast Kissing

THE AERIE, Malahat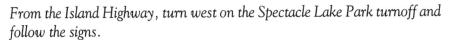
600 Ebadora Lane
(604) 743-7115
Expensive to Unbelievably Expensive

From the Island Highway, turn west on the Spectacle Lake Park turnoff and follow the signs.

Robin Leach, from the television show *Lifestyles of the Rich and Famous*, had just finished two days of filming here when I arrived at The Aerie, which should give you a fairly good idea of what you can expect here. No? Well, what about the fact that the owners are building a helicopter pad to whisk the aforementioned rich and famous from the mainland to this extravagant, magnificent villa, out in the middle of nowhere, for an ultimate, reclusive getaway? If that still doesn't form a vivid picture for you, let me try again. From the moment you approach this sparkling white, expansive, multiterraced, grandiose lodge with its 180-degree glorious, scintillating views of the mountains, water, inlets, and islands, you know to expect luxury. And whether you're here for dinner or a night's stay, luxury is exactly what you get.

Every inch is filled with exotic, oversized (bordering on cavernous) furnishings. You can get lost in the armchairs, and the ornately carved mirrors, four-poster beds, and buffets are almost too opulent. Many of the rooms have sexy Jacuzzi tubs, private decks with outrageous views, leather sofas, marble end-tables, and other sensuous appointments. Do I need to mention the ultra-thick down comforters; the sea green, black, and pale rose color scheme; the vaulted ceilings; or the impressive local artworks gracing the walls? And get ready for this: the dining room has a 14-karat gold foiled ceiling. If you can't kiss here, it's only because you're too busy getting accustomed to the sumptuous surroundings instead of puckering.

The superlative dinners are enhanced by an awesome vista. The pheasant in a delectable almond crust and roasted duckling with a geranium glaze are exceptional and artfully presented. One more point: this is a bed and breakfast, and the breakfast is equal to everything else around you.

Victoria

As much as possible, this book avoids big tourist draws, and without question, Victoria is a sprawling center of tourist activity. But Victoria's charisma is hard to ignore, even in summer when the crowds swell beyond romantic tolerance. The famous Empress Hotel, stately Parliament buildings, Butchart Gardens, the parks, the historical museums, the wax museum, the cozy restaurants, and the Edwardian-style shops—combined with a thriving harbor and marina flanked in the distance by the Olympic Mountains—make the city an Anglophile's nirvana. And it can be particularly wonderful off-season. It may even make you feel lustfully regal.

◆ **Romantic Warning: THE BLACK BALL FERRY TRANS-PORT**, (206) 457-4491, which runs from Port Angeles to Victoria, is a traveler's worst nightmare. This is one of the most inadequate ferry runs in the world. During peak season you have to get your car in line at least 12 hours in advance. That's right, *12 hours*. And Port Angeles is not a particularly romantic destination, worthy of a 12-hour stayover.

One alternative way to reach Victoria from the Olympic Peninsula is to leave your car in Port Angeles and walk on the Black Ball Ferry or take the passenger-only **VICTORIA EXPRESS**, (604) 361-9144 or (206) 452-8088. A second alternative, if you must have wheels, is to take the Port Townsend ferry, (206) 464-6400, to Whidbey Island and continue north on Interstate 5 for two hours to the Tsawwassen ferry terminal (this ferry docks in Sidney, about 20 minutes north of Victoria). Other options are listed at the beginning of this chapter.

Hotel/Bed and Breakfast Kissing

ABIGAIL'S HOTEL, Victoria
906 McClure Street
(604) 388-5363
Moderate to Very Expensive

On McClure, off Vancouver Street.

A brief retreat into the past seems to give the heart a rest from the stresses and strains of modern times. There are many ways to experience the pace of days gone by. One way is to travel to the mountains, where civilization hasn't taken root. Another is to visit a place like Abigail's and slip into dreamy, sophisticated comfort. This dazzling country-style inn is one of the finest accommodations in Victoria. Every nuance of comfort has been added (except an elevator to take you and your luggage up to the third floor).

Abigail's is a classic Tudor mansion that has been renovated into a modern inn, finished in pastel shades of rose and green. Each room is designed with only two things in mind: romance and pampering. Features include private spa tubs, wood-burning fireplaces, plush carpeting, antique washstands, and thick goose-down comforters. In the morning, you and your true love will enjoy a generous, gracious breakfast (the jalapeño-cheese biscuits are great). Of course, the most expensive rooms are the most luxurious, but they are worth it. If you have a special occasion to celebrate, or can make up one, this is an ideal place to come.

◆   **Romantic Note:** Abigail's, the Beaconsfield Inn, and Humboldt House (reviewed elsewhere in this section) are all owned and managed by Humboldt Hotels, a small, privately owned company.

ARUNDEL MANOR, Victoria
980 Arundel Drive
(604) 385-5442
Inexpensive to Moderate

From Island Highway, turn west on Admirals Road. Just after the bridge turn right on Arundel Drive.

Ten minutes north of the town center is this lovely 1912 heritage home set on a grassy knoll overlooking Portage Inlet. This Victorian-style bed and breakfast has all the appropriate, engaging details, including handsome antiques, silver service, English china, and a gracious innkeeper who makes gourmet breakfasts (salmon-stuffed crêpes with béarnaise sauce is a favorite). Ask if lemon preserves are available; if so, spread some over the fresh-baked muffins or fresh fruit crêpes for a taste treat. The five guest rooms upstairs are quite spacious and exceedingly comfortable; all have private baths (one is detached). The rooms with private decks overlooking the water are the best.

THE BEACONSFIELD INN, Victoria
998 Humboldt Street
(604) 384-4044
Expensive to Very Expensive

Many inns claim old-world charm, but few can live up to the term. The Beaconsfield succeeds, and offers a haven to ease city-tired spirits. Its Edwardian splendor is intermingled with contemporary touches; the glass-enclosed entry features black-and-white tile and liberal foliage. Past the foyer, the common rooms and halls are paneled with rich, dark mahogany. Upstairs and down, many of the 12 rooms have large spa tubs, charming sitting areas, wood-burning fireplaces, and interesting touches such as stained glass windows, beautiful crystal chandeliers, and extremely handsome comfortable furnishings. Of particular interest is the Garden Suite, with its own patio and separate seating area. A full breakfast is served in the Beaconsfield's kitchen, which has limited space, and you must reserve your breakfast seating (due to lack of space), but the presentation and attention to detail make this a small distraction and hardly worth noticing.

BEDFORD HOTEL, Victoria
1140 Government Street
(604) 384-6835
Expensive to Very Expensive

The hotel is three blocks north of the Empress Hotel on Government Street.

The Bedford is no ordinary large hotel. It has all the trappings of one, such as room service, luggage handlers, a reception desk, and, yes, even elevators, but there the similarities stop and the heart-stirring differences begin. The rooms are striking and modern, in tones of forest green and burgundy, and the bathrooms were built for two people to enjoy together. Some of the rooms have huge tiled shower stalls with two jets, others have spa tubs, still others have fireplaces, and a few have everything, including a view of the Inner Harbour and a deluxe complimentary breakfast. Afternoon tea is available in the hotel's charming mezzanine-level restaurant for $11.95. For an uptown getaway, the Bedford will fit your requirements and then some.

◆ **Romantic Warning:** The courtyard rooms have no views, and because they look directly across to the other units it is necessary to keep your shade pulled if you expect to have any privacy at all. This is not the best situation on a hot summer day.

DASHWOOD SEASIDE MANOR, Victoria
1 Cook Street
(604) 385-5517
Moderate to Very Expensive

On Cook and Dallas streets.

The brochure says this is Victoria's only seaside bed-and-breakfast inn, and that much is true. The stellar location—across the street from the Strait of Juan de Fuca with the mountains of the Olympic Peninsula in the distance—is indeed spectacular, and almost every room has a view. Even without the view, many aspects of this Tudor mansion make it extremely desirable. The rooms are huge, with kitchens and separate seating areas; two have large fireplaces and others have Jacuzzi tubs. Unfortunately, despite this grand description, much of the bed and breakfast is in pressing need of renovation. Carpets are threadbare or stained, wooden baseboards are deteriorating, some of the beds sag, and the bathroom fixtures are somewhat tacky. If the price tag weren't so steep, the Dashwood would be a real find, but this is a kissing option only in the off-season, when the rates drop to the moderate range.

THE EMPRESS HOTEL, Victoria
721 Government Street
(604) 384-8111
Expensive to Unbelievably Expensive

You can't miss it in the town center, near the marina on Government Street, between Humboldt and Belleville.

The words "Empress Hotel" and "Victoria" are usually uttered in the same breath. The classic, exalted Empress, with its elaborate, palatial elegance and pivotal location, has always epitomized this European-style city. But long-time patrons who have not been to Victoria lately will remember a somewhat haggard hotel that was begging for some physical attention. Well, over the past few years, Canadian Pacific Hotels and Resorts spent $45 million bringing this place up to speed, and if you want to know how to spend that kind of money, this is an outstanding example of how to do it right.

Every detail has been seen to and the result is unequivocally spectacular. There is the opulent **PALM COURT**, with its $50,000 ceiling that must be seen to be appreciated; the formal, architecturally grand

EMPRESS DINING ROOM; the handsome, eminently comfortable **EMPRESS LOUNGE**; the charming **GARDEN CAFÉ**; and the unique **BENGAL RESTAURANT**, casual only in comparison to the other dining spots here. All are stupendous. You won't be surprised to learn that these public areas feel like a museum, complete with gawking tourists. Still, you would be remiss if you didn't visit the Empress and linger awhile over tea and crumpets or a sherry and dessert. As for an overnight stay—the least expensive rooms are fairly small, though beautifully appointed, but as you move up in price the rooms increase in size. Is it worth it? Well, if you can afford the steep tariffs, why not?

THE HATERLEIGH, Victoria
243 Kingston
(604) 384-9995
Moderate to Expensive

On Kingston just off Pendray.

Arched entries and lofty ceilings, handsome light oak paneling and matching moldings, fill this attractive, casual Victorian bed and breakfast. It is located near the south side of the harbor, in a rather ordinary neighborhood setting. Inside, the rooms are spacious and everything is appropriately Victorian and beautifully renovated. Six unpretentious rooms in a variety of configurations occupy the first and second floors. Four rooms have large, two-person Jacuzzi tubs; all have high arched ceilings, tall windows, separate seating areas, leaded glass windows, lace curtains, and views of the mountains and water. All the rooms are exceedingly comfortable, but the best ones are the Secret Garden, the Kingston Suite, and Day Dreams. In the morning, a full breakfast is served in the formal dining room.

HOLLAND HOUSE, Victoria
595 Michigan Street
(604) 384-6644
Expensive to Very Expensive

Call for reservations and directions.

The outside gives little hint of the gorgeous, superior comfort that awaits you inside this continental-style inn. The bright interior is filled with the owner's striking modern art collection. A gourmet breakfast is served every morning in a quaint dining room with French doors that look out to the garden. Each guest suite is beautifully furnished. All have elegant baths; some have fireplaces, canopied beds, and cozy sitting nooks. Holland House is designer heaven.

HUMBOLDT HOUSE, Victoria
867 Humboldt Street
(604) 384-4044
Expensive

On Humboldt near Vancouver Street.

Owned and managed by the same company that runs Abigail's Hotel and the Beaconsfield, Humboldt House proves indelibly that this group knows how to create superior country inns that ooze elegance and style. Discover the sensual pleasures of this renovated Victorian home.

No staff is present at the house: guests check in at the Beaconsfield and have almost the entire place to themselves. Now that's real privacy. The pink frame building is set in a less-than-desirable corner of Victoria, but inside everything is perfect for romance. Each of the three rooms has a well-stocked fireplace, large Jacuzzi tub, colorful furnishings, down quilts, ample space, large windows, and plush fabrics and linens. A distinctive feature is a small two-way butler's pantry, where a picnic basket is placed every night with enticing breakfast treats for your morning repast. Romance here is guaranteed.

JOAN BROWN'S BED AND BREAKFAST, Victoria
729 Pemberton Road
(604) 592-5929
Inexpensive to Moderate

On Pemberton near Rockland.

Ms. Brown has skillfully transformed this vintage mansion into an attractive and endearing place to stay in Victoria. The stately home has high beamed ceilings, seven fireplaces, stained glass windows, formal English gardens, polished wood floors, the original wood staircase, comfortable furnishings, and a mixture of room sizes. The larger rooms, particularly the ones on the ground floor, are the most beautiful. Of the nine rooms, four have private baths and five have shared facilities. The bathrooms are fairly ordinary, but the fabrics and furnishings make this

English-style bed and breakfast exceptional. A generous full breakfast is served in the formal dining room under a striking crystal chandelier.

LAUREL POINT INN, Victoria
680 Montreal Street
(604) 386-8721, (800) 663-7667
Expensive to Unbelievably Expensive

From Government Street, turn west on Belleville Street, then turn right on Montreal Street to the hotel.

Why would you want to spend time in Victoria at a fairly ordinary-looking modern hotel when there are all sorts of provincial, English-style accommodations to choose from? Because Laurel Point Inn has some of the sexiest, most ultra-slick suites in the city. The south wing only (the older north wing has boring, average hotel rooms) has spacious one-bedroom and studio suites with peach marble entries and bathrooms, Jacuzzi tubs, slick (although sparse) blond wood furnishings, shoji-style sliding doors that close off the bath, and tall ceilings. The high point is the wraparound floor-to-ceiling windows, which open to an enormous balcony that overlooks a glorious view of the city and harbor (and the mountains if you ask for the rooms with a view of the outer harbor).

Whether or not you stay at the inn, consider having a cocktail in the glass-enclosed **COOK'S LANDING** lounge, with its in-your-lap view of the Inner Harbour. The two restaurants here are just OK, not really worth a special visit.

OAK BAY BEACH HOTEL, Victoria
1175 Beach Drive
(604) 598-4556
Inexpensive to Unbelievably Expensive

Call for directions.

Long-standing reputations, even undeserved, sometimes never die. The Oak Bay Beach Hotel is well known and often booked. Its august setting, overlooking the open waters of the strait and the mountains in the distance, is impressive, and from the outside the half-timbered Tudor mansion is striking. Yet inside, only a handful of the rooms have been plushly renovated, and they are the most desirable; the others are amazingly second-rate and in serious need of refurbishing. In fact, the third-floor rooms with the highest price tag, best views, and the ones that require the most restoration are, according to management, a last priority for repair because they are always booked. Be careful about which room you request and you can experience a rich Edwardian escape at the Oak Bay Beach Hotel.

◆ **Romantic Note:** One of the best places in town for breakfast or high tea is the hotel's **TUDOR ROOM**: very English, very posh, and very good, plus the views are wonderful.

OCEAN POINT RESORT, Victoria
45 Songhees Road, between Esquimalt and Sonhees
(604) 360-2999
Expensive to Unbelievably Expensive

From Government Street turn west on Esquimalt. Cross the harbor bridge and get into the right-hand curb lane. Follow this to the hotel access road and look for signs to the hotel.

If you haven't heard of this stellar, sparkling new hotel complex, you will. You can't miss it when you arrive in Victoria. Encompassing almost the entire north shore of the Inner Harbour, this massive, contemporary building stands directly opposite the Empress. These two grand dames chaperone the harbor in opposing styles. Where the Empress represents European enchantment and tradition, Ocean Point represents a fresh taste of Beverly Hills. Amenities include a spa (also available to the public) that offers body wraps, massages, aroma therapy, facials, herbal cosmetics, a glass-enclosed swimming pool, and a steep price tag. Everything here is ultra-sophisticated and ultra-plush, with a strong concentration on service; the management and staff take a personal interest in their guests.

Far away from the tourist crowds, the lobby lounge is a plush spot for harbor watching and a quiet tête-à-tête. **THE VICTORIAN RES-TAURANT** is destined to become the finest restaurant in the city. Presentation and quality are both outstanding. Fresh walnut sourdough bread; a light, flavorful potato-leek soup with smoked cod; and superb halibut with garlic-chive cream were all sheer perfection. The three-layer white, milk, and Belgian chocolate mousse was as smooth as silk and almost melted my teeth.

You're wondering about the rooms? Well, except for the suites, they are just nice, relatively upscale hotel rooms. However, if money's no object, go for the designer suites. These exquisite, impeccably furnished retreats have outstanding views, Jacuzzi tubs, private decks, and plush furnishings.

PRIOR HOUSE BED AND BREAKFAST, Victoria
620 St. Charles Street
(604) 592-8847
Moderate to Expensive

On St. Charles Street near Rockland.

Few bed and breakfasts can rival the grandeur of the Prior House. You will renew your love for each other *and* fall in love with your surroundings. This 8,500-square-foot Edwardian mansion is filled with warm comforts. Two plush living rooms with fireplaces, light oak paneling, stained glass windows, and carved stone terraces that look over meticulously groomed lawns and garden are on the main floor. The rooms on the second floor offer a selection of lavish furnishings, wood-burning fireplaces, Jacuzzis, French doors that open to private balconies, views of the mountains and water, and plush seating areas. Three of the rooms are particularly spacious, with the most romantic being the Windsor, Arbutus, and Lieutenant Governor's suites. The Governor's Suite has a bathroom the size of most rooms, with a substantial green faux-marble Jacuzzi tub. On the ground floor is a garden apartment, entered through a stone archway with a private brick patio; its full kitchen, two bedrooms, and living room with a tile fireplace are thoroughly lovely. Although the apartment can be a tad on the dark side and you can hear occasional footsteps upstairs, it is still engagingly cozy.

A light but proper high tea is served in the afternoon and a full breakfast is presented in the formal, chandeliered dining room.

SWAN'S HOTEL, Victoria
506 Pandora Avenue
(604) 361-3310
Moderate to Expensive

On Pandora Avenue near Wharf Street.

This former apartment building has been converted into a rather appealing hotel. The rooms are still apartments, with full kitchens, separate dining areas, living rooms, oversized windows, cathedral ceilings, televisions, and phones. There are 40 units in three configurations—studios and one- and two-bedroom units—but the studios and one-bedroom lofts are the most romantic. One drawback: except for the local artwork adorning the walls, the rooms lack warmth and coziness. Nevertheless, these are still distinctive, spacious rooms in which to set up temporary housekeeping while touring Victoria, and the location is great.

◆ **Romantic Note: SWAN'S PUB** is a handsome, raucous place for beer and steak, but the rooms over the pub can be noisy, so avoid them unless you plan on being out all evening. **SWAN'S CAFÉ** is a lovely little restaurant with some good casual dining in a wood-and-brick setting. When the doors are shut, you won't even know the pub exists.

Restaurant Kissing

THE CAPTAIN'S PALACE RESTAURANT, Victoria   ❥
309 Belleville Street
(604) 388-9191
Inexpensive to Expensive

Across the street from the ferry dock and to the left, you will see Heritage Village. The Captain's Palace is next door.

If you haven't already gotten your fill of Victoriana, venture into The Captain's Palace for an opulent turn-of-the-century of tea, dessert, or snack. The lavish appointments that accompany a taste of sherry or an attentively served breakfast include stained glass windows, frescoed ceilings, stately marble-and-wood fireplaces, crystal chandeliers, antique furnishings, and a sweeping stairway with a carved banister. Having said all of that, I must mention that The Captain's Palace is expensive and the food isn't up to the standards of some of the less ornate dining establishments in town. Instead, plan an off-hour visit to enjoy the romantic setting.

◆ **Romantic Warning:** The Captain's Palace is also a bed and breakfast, with rooms located above the restaurant and in a building next door. These rooms could be wonderful if care and proper attention were given, but at present they are somewhere between opulent and tacky, leaning closer to tacky.

CHEZ DANIEL, Victoria
2524 Estevan
(604) 592-7424
Expensive

On Estevan near Cadboro Bay Road.

Hunter green ceilings, rose and pink trim, crisp linens, and flickering candlelight set the mood for traditional French dining. Considered one of the best French restaurants in Victoria, Chez Daniel lives up to the high expectations. Simple but elegant dishes such as veal Madeira and roasted duck with chestnuts are superior. The table d'hôte menu is reasonably priced and offers an impressive sampling of the kitchen's best efforts.

CHRISTIE'S, Victoria
1739 Fort Street
(604) 598-5333
Inexpensive

From Government Street, turn east on Fort Street to the pub. It is on the right.

While in Victoria, to be certain you experience a genuine English holiday, you must spend time in a pub, even if you don't drink beer. Christie's is one of the most beautiful Victorian-style, albeit modern, pubs in the area. The fish and chips and shepherd's pie are some of the best in the town, and the smoke level rarely gets out of hand. There is an outdoor patio with heated wood benches that surround a propane-generated fire pit.

HIGH TEA, Victoria
What a thoroughly English, utterly civilized way to spend a late afternoon together. And no other town in North America offers this age-old ritual with quite the style, dedication, and abundance as Victoria. The presentations differ as does the price. Some places offer traditional white gloves and silver service, while others provide a more eclectic display on floral-patterned china; most range in price from $8 to $14 per person depending on your surroundings. But the basics are always the same: fresh fruit, dainty finger sandwiches (held with the little finger up), creamy pastries, fluffy Devonshire cream, and tea properly steeped in a china teapot kept warm in a cushioned tea cozy.

The best of the best for savoring high tea in Victoria are: **BLETHERING PLACE**, 2250 Oak Bay Avenue, (604) 598-1413 (quaint traditional Tudor building); **CRYSTAL GARDENS**, 713 Douglas Street, (604) 381-1213 (tropical garden setting); **THE EMPRESS HOTEL**, 721 Government Street, (604) 389-2727 (stunning, well-touristed tea room); **OAK BAY BEACH HOTEL**, 1175 Beach Drive, (604) 598-4556 (Edwardian-style formal dining room); **JAMES BAY TEA ROOM**, 332 Menzies Street, (604) 382-8282 (charming Tudor-style home and interior); **THE DINING ROOM**, at Butchart Gardens, (604) 652-4422 (garden elegance); and **OCEAN POINT RESORT**, 45 Songhees Road, (604) 360-2999 (formal white-glove service with views of the harbor).

LA PETITE COLOMBE, Victoria
604 Broughton
(604) 383-3234
Moderate to Expensive

On Broughton between Government and Douglas streets.

Restaurants don't get much sexier than this. You can enjoy truly exquisite French cuisine in sultry and lavish surroundings. The walls are a dark shade of eggplant, scarlet chairs are placed around linen-draped tables, and elegant sconces are suspended from arched mirrors that reflect a burnished light onto this dramatic interior. There are only a handful of tables in the small dining room, which adds to the intimate ambience.

REBECCA'S RESTAURANT, Victoria
1127 Wharf Street
(604) 380-6999
Moderate to Expensive

On Wharf Street near Yates Street.

This causal, quietly elegant restaurant, popular with local young urban professionals, is gaining a respected reputation for excellent Canadian Southwest cuisine. Exposed brick, high-backed chairs, and a whitewashed-wood bar (which can overflow into the dining room) make this a handsome setting. Our fusilli with fresh charbroiled tuna, capers, and lemon, and a rich banana-curry soup were splendid. A large glass showcase along the edge of the restaurant displays the incredible takeout selections, for at home or an outdoor picnic. The desserts are always heavenly.

Outdoor Kissing

THE BUTCHART GARDENS, Victoria
800 Benvenuto Avenue
(604) 652-4422
Inexpensive

Take West Saanich Road to Benvenuto Avenue and follow the signs to the gardens. Call for seasonal hours.

You really can't kiss here—it's just too crowded. But if you want to get a glimpse of what heaven looks like, tour these elysian, astonishing gardens. Each flower seems to have been hand-stroked to full bloom, the hedges could have been trimmed with a scalpel, and the sinuous pathways were carved from the earth by artisans who knew how to create a model Eden. It is really that sublime. And Christmastime at the gardens will make you believe in Santa Claus again. Ignore the crowds, concentrate on the flowers, and hold hands tightly.

◆ **Romantic Suggestion: THE DINING ROOM,** (604) 652-4422, (Moderate to Expensive), at the gardens is an elegant, regal place for lunch or high tea, and the food and presentation are quite excellent. No mere tourist attraction here; the interior is perfectly designed to merge harmoniously with the outside. Stunning!

MOUNT DOUGLAS PARK, Victoria

From Highway 17, five miles north of downtown Victoria, exit to the east on Cordova Bay Road. Follow this road south to the park.

Minutes away from the center of Victoria is a 500-acre rain forest on the ocean's edge, light-years away from the tourists and the city. A walk down one of the many beach trails will bring you out to a winding stretch of shoreline. From here you can look across to island-dotted Haro Strait. This area is surprisingly quiet and serene. Don't forget to bring a blanket and picnic provisions so you can spend a leisurely afternoon out here without interruption.

Sidney

Restaurant Kissing

DEEP COVE CHALET, Sidney
11190 Chalet Road
(604) 656-3541
Expensive to Very Expensive

Call for directions.

Quintessentially French and enticingly romantic through and through is this secluded restaurant 20 minutes north of Victoria. Overlooking stunning Saanich Inlet, the enchanting stucco-and-wood building is set on forested manicured lawns. Inside, everything is gracious and elegant with a congenial, homey feeling—that is, if you can forget the prices. Every dish is prepared with the greatest skill, and the presentations are beautiful. The choices include savory crêpes with mushrooms and a smooth beurre blanc sauce, an airy yet rich cheese soufflé, a flavorful lobster bisque, and perhaps the best escargots in puffed pastry to be found anywhere. Meats and fish are always perfectly prepared, and the sauces are light but distinctive.

Metchosin

Hotel/Bed and Breakfast Kissing

SEASIDE BED AND BREAKFAST, Metchosin
3807 Duke Road
(604) 478-1446
Moderate

Call for directions.

A potential deterrent to staying at this contemporary seaside mansion is that you might not want to leave. The setting is simply spectacular, and it is only 25 minutes west of Victoria in the pastoral town of Metchosin. A rocky shore with lapping waves frames the front of the peach-colored stucco home. In the distance are the snowcapped Olympic Mountains, visible across the flowing blue waters of the strait. The one suite here adjoins the main house and has its own private entrance. A separate bedroom, a living room surrounded by windows, heaven-framing skylights, and a sliding glass door that opens to a private tiled patio create a prime atmosphere for relaxation. The furnishings are comfortable though simple, and all the proper amenities are seen to with great care, but the real attraction of this bed and breakfast is the 50-foot seaside swimming pool (heated to 85 degrees) edged by a delightful natural-rock-and-carved-cement perimeter. A full breakfast is served in the dining room in the main house by the amiable innkeeper.

Sooke

Twenty-five miles west of Victoria lies the undeveloped and reason-ably undiscovered town of Sooke. Starting in Sooke, and continuing for another 40 miles north to the town of Port Renfrew, civilization has not yet claimed this area for its own purposes, which translates to plenty of wide open spaces for you and yours. For miles around, the rugged forested terrain, outstanding views of the Olympics across the Strait of Juan de Fuca, rocky isolated beaches, and notable accommodations present many options for enamored travelers seeking solitude and Canadian Southwest beauty. After you've wrapped up all the necessary tourist requirements in Victoria, be sure to include extra time for this remark-able stretch of countryside.

Hotel/Bed and Breakfast Kissing

RAVEN TREE IRIS GARDENS, Sooke   ❂❂❰
1853 Connie Road
(604) 642-5248
Inexpensive to Moderate

Twenty-three miles west of Victoria, just off Highway 14, on the west side of the road.

Without question, this is a horticulturist's dream come true. Ten acres of impeccable, idyllic gardens, second-growth forest, and botanical treasures surround the inviting modern Tudor home. The three com-fortable and attractive guest rooms on the top floor offer soothing views of the surroundings, but the real enticement is the prodigal flower garden. The bed and breakfast derives its name from its owners' first love, the cultivation of iris rhizomes. Starting in April, thousands of irises blanket the landscape with a rainbow of glorious colors. From all over the island, flower lovers come to purchase these rhizomes for their own gardens. If you've ever had a passion for floral splendor, you can spend time leisurely indulging your fantasy with the amiable, informative hosts. They also specialize in dried floral arrangements—and tending to their guests' needs.

MALAHAT FARM, Sooke
Anderson Road
(604) 642-6868
Inexpensive to Moderate

Directly off Highway 14, a short drive west of the town of Sooke.

Set back from the road, with little else around but 45 acres of forested meadows, thriving farmland, soaring hawks overhead, and abundant serenity, Malahat Farm offers gracious hospitality and comfort to its guests. This country farm home is a rustic hideaway where hours float by as you renew your relationship with each other and the earth. Suffolk sheep, cows, barred rock chickens, peacocks, and a formidable black bull dot the landscape. You can wander freely through the pastures (except for the bull pen) with boots provided by the innkeeper (a necessary amenity) and get to know the animals on a more personal basis. The sheep here are loving creatures who long to be petted and will devotedly follow along during your walk, snuggling close to get their ears scratched.

A separate building next to the owners' residence is where the four guest rooms are located. They are large and cozy, with fireplaces and views of the surrounding peaceful landscape. To firmly establish the English farm ambience, each room has a hot water bottle to warm the sheets, and afternoon treats of cookies and crumpets are left in the common rooms. Breakfast is a hearty undertaking with homemade breads and jams, farm-fresh eggs, and fresh honey served next to the fireplace in the kitchen. This place doesn't offer luxurious accommodations—just pure and simple relaxation and beauty.

OCEAN WILDERNESS, Sooke
109 West Coast Road
(604) 646-2116
Moderate to Very Expensive

Just off Highway 14, eight and a half miles west of the town center.

The interesting blend of homey comforts with touches of elegance makes this an intriguing getaway. To the small original log cabin was added a new wood-framed wing featuring seven surprisingly spacious rooms. Surrounded by old-growth forest, the home has a narrow but incredible view of the water and mountains. A steep trail adjacent to the property leads down to a rocky, thoroughly secluded beach. Inside, an eclectic mix of handsome antiques, plush furnishings, and handmade canopied beds fills each room. Two of the rooms on the top floor have Jacuzzi tubs and large, private, glass-enclosed sun decks that share in the scenery. A full breakfast is served next to a crackling fireplace in the log cabin section of the home.

POINT NO POINT RESORT, Sooke
West Coast Road
(604) 646-2020
Inexpensive to Moderate

Forty miles northwest of Victoria, on Highway 14, watch the west side of the road for a small sign for Point No Point.

Despite the name, there is nothing resort-like about Point No Point. The rustic cabins (which actually leave much to be desired) are set amidst pure rugged beauty and seem eons away from civilization. Regardless of the weather or time of year, the isolation of this place can spell romance and is the main reason to visit. In addition to the spartan, overly simple cabins (some with fireplaces), there are rooms in an adjacent building that rests on the edge of a cliff overlooking a crashing granite shoreline. Trails with foliage-covered stone archways lead down to a nearby inlet and small beach. The 15 units have ample windows revealing an unobstructed view of the ocean and the Olympic Mountains. Three newly built cabins designed for two are the best, and five more are being built. Sadly, smoking is allowed and can be evident when you enter.

A light lunch and high tea are served every day in a small dining room with an immense view. The simple menu includes soup, sandwiches, and dessert, and they are quite good, particularly the fresh soups. High tea is authentic and the fresh-baked treats excellent.

RICHVIEW HOUSE, Sooke
7031 Richview Drive
(604) 642-5520
Expensive

Go west of Victoria on the Trans-Canada Highway until it intersects with Highway 14. Take Highway 14 to the town of Sooke, about 25 miles northwest of Victoria. North of town you will see signs for Sooke Harbour House. At Whiffen Spit Road, turn left and continue till the dead end.

Well off the main road, poised atop an 80-foot cliff with an expansive view of the Strait of Juan de Fuca and the Olympic Mountains, this is one of the most tasteful, sophisticated bed and breakfasts to be found anywhere on the island. Immaculate lawns border the two-level home, which has a separate wing dedicated to the two guest suites. Expansive windows, lofty ceilings, and light wood paneling make the luscious outside an integral part of the inside.

The modern designer rooms are incredibly comfortable. Each one has a private deck with an outdoor Jacuzzi tub, plus king-size bed, wet bar, beach-stone-and-slate wood-burning fireplace, and radiant-heat floors that give the rooms a rare seductive warmth. The elegantly served breakfast is equal to the accommodations. Pad down to the glass-enclosed dining room and you may find sweet lemon-yogurt muffins, strawberry-glazed papaya, and fresh fruit crêpes laced with a light maple sauce. The restaurant at Sooke Harbour House is only moments away, and the beach just a short hike from your front door.

SOOKE HARBOUR HOUSE, Sooke
1528 Whiffen Spit Road
(604) 642-3421
Very Expensive to Unbelievably Expensive

Go west of Victoria on the Trans-Canada Highway until it intersects with Highway 14. Take Highway 14 to the town of Sooke, about 25 miles northwest of Victoria. North of town you will see signs for Sooke Harbour House. At Whiffen Spit Road, turn left and continue till the dead end.

Sooke Harbour House is a smashing lovers' getaway. A building next door has exquisite guest rooms, and the rooms in the main house have been completely refurbished. All are simply sensational. No detail has been overlooked in any of the rooms, and the views are captivating. Regardless of which you choose, you'll find yourselves in the lap of luxury. Each suite has a private spa tub or outdoor hot tub, a fireplace, separate sitting area, vaulted ceiling, view of the water, wet bar, balcony or patio, king-size bed, and beautiful furnishings. This *must* be what heaven is like. These suites are hard to leave, even for the delectable breakfast and lunch (both are included in the price of the room) that are served daily.

The restaurant has a stellar reputation, and the menu reads like an exotic novel. Recent reports have been disappointing, and although the presentation is impeccable the preparations can be bland. The ingredients are still the freshest around; the herb garden supplies the seasonings and an outdoor tank keeps the shellfish. The dining room is located in a charming two-story country house where windows facing the harbor let in warm, soothing sunlight.

◆ **Romantic Suggestion:** For either a short morning hike or a rugged all-day jaunt, **EAST SOOKE REGIONAL PARK** provides 3,500 acres of wilderness with phenomenal views and trails winding through beautiful beaches and pristine forest.

Restaurant Kissing

MARGISON TEA HOUSE, Sooke
6605 Sooke Road
(604) 642-3620
Inexpensive

In the town of Sooke, off Highway 14. As you enter Sooke on Highway 14, watch for a sign indicating the driveway to the house.

A table draped with linen and set with fine china; steaming aromatic tea in silver service; finger sandwiches and cakes on a silver caddy—all are essential to the English tradition of afternoon tea. While passing through this ravishing countryside, take the time to do what the natives do and sip some tea, have a bite of cake, and nibble a finger sandwich or two.

There is no better place to do all this than the Margison Tea House. This enchanting, delightfully arrayed home-turned-restaurant is just off

the main road in the seaside town of Sooke. The garden supplies all of
the fare, including the floral arrangements. The emphasis here is on
superior quality, service, and cozy surroundings. Everything is meticulously displayed and proudly served. Succumb to the romance of it all as
you hold hands in this engaging atmosphere. Dinner is also available on
weekends.

◆   **Romantic Note:** A self-contained cottage set in the expansive
garden here is available for a devoted twosome. This adorable bungalow
is a comfortable private haven where you'll have everything you need,
including a great breakfast.

Outdoor Kissing

BOTANICAL BEACH,

Thirty miles north of Sooke, just outside of Port Renfrew.

Tide pools full of sea urchins, crabs, starfish, chitons, coralline sea algae,
and other saltwater animals thrive along this rock-clad beach. At low tide
the world of the ocean opens up for your viewing and entertainment. It is an
adventure worth sharing, but please leave the creatures alone; this wonderland is an integral part of nature and should stay that way.

CHINA BEACH and FRENCH BEACH

*Follow Highway 14 past Sooke. You will see a sign 10 miles down the road for
French Beach. Reach French Beach via a short tree-lined path down to the shore.
Farther along Highway 14, one mile past the Jordan River, look for the China Beach
sign. China Beach is accessible by a 15-minute walk through rain forest.*

These two beaches are separated by a few miles but share similar
settings and a rugged character. You can ramble through young, re-
planted forests or formidable groves of ancient trees or along white
sandy beaches that stretch forever in either direction. Surefootedness is
a prerequisite, though, for you will occasionally have to make your way
over projecting headlands of rocky coast and woods. At either location,
you can bask in solitary freedom while being lulled by the water's music
on the shore. Beautiful views are abundant along this relatively undiscovered coastline, just a short jaunt from the bustling town of Victoria.

◆   **Romantic Note:** French Beach has a spotless, well-maintained

69-unit campground set in old-growth forest. It is one of the most picturesque sites for setting up a tent for two on the entire island.

WHALE WATCHING

Anywhere along this coast from Sooke to Port Renfrew.

Sighting a whale is an exhilarating experience. The grace and agility of these aquatic giants is amazing to witness. Resident and transient whales circle the island and are clearly visible from most shores when they are in season. Boat excursions are also available to take you out to greet them where they are known to feed. No matter how you encounter these creatures, it is a singular moment in your life that you will always treasure.

GULF ISLANDS

Saturna, Mayne, Pender, Galiano, Saltspring, Gabriola, Hornby, Denman, Quadra, and Cortez islands are accessible via ferryboat from Tsawwassen (just south of Vancouver), from several locations on Vancouver Island, and between the individual islands as well. For ferry information in Vancouver, call (604) 669-1211; in Seattle, (206) 624-6663; in Victoria, (604) 386-3431. Depending on the season and during most weekends, reservations and advance payment may be necessary to assure your place on the ferry. Departure times are limited, so be sure to make your travel plans with this in mind.

The Gulf Islands lie nestled between Vancouver Island and mainland British Columbia, scattered like a heavenly constellation up and down the coast. There are more than 300 forested isles, whose populations vary from zero to several thousand. The Gulf Islands resemble the San Juan Islands of Washington state, and they are all places of transcendent splendor and solitude.

A handful of the Gulf Islands are accessible by ferryboat, and each of these has what's required to give you a hassle-free, all-absorbing time away from everything except nature and each other. Whichever island you choose, you will be certain to find oceanfront parks with sweeping views of the other islands, bed and breakfasts set on hilltops or hidden in the woods, intimate restaurants where "leisurely" is a way of life, and miles of meandering paved roads that lead to island privacy. Nothing will be able to distract your attention from the out-of-this-world scenery and the eyes of the person you love.

Saturna Island

Hotel/Bed and Breakfast Kissing

STONE HOUSE FARM RESORT, Saturna Island
207 Narvaez Bay Road
(604) 539-2683
Inexpensive to Moderate

Call for directions.

Saturna Island is one of the more remote destinations of the Gulf Islands. Ferryboat schedules are tricky but worth the effort to find yourselves as close to the middle of nowhere as you can get. For the sake of romance, solitude, and relaxation, you would be wise to find your-selves sojourning at this traditional 17th-century-style English country home surrounded by 25 acres of farmland and forest, banked by a half mile of waterfront and sandy beach. As the name implies, a formidable stone exterior and ceramic-tiled roof form a picturesque visage as you approach from the long winding dirt road. Inside, the massive Tudor-style wood beams and paneling create an equally impressive appearance.

Three comfortable, although modest and unadorned, guest rooms have private balconies, stunning views, vaulted ceilings, private baths, and plush down comforters. An exceptionally hearty, bountiful English breakfast is served in the dining room at your own personal table.

Mayne Island

Hotel/Bed and Breakfast Kissing

FERNHILL LODGE, Mayne Island
610 Fernhill Road
(604) 539-2544
Moderate

Call for reservations and directions.

This place is a food-lover's must. Besides being a comfortable and meticulously maintained bed and breakfast, Fernhill Lodge also offers totally exotic dining experiences. It's hard to imagine that feasts like this could possibly be found in the countryside of a remote island—or anywhere else, for that matter. Even Julia Child would be envious of the chef's skill. The meals are served in the lodge's somewhat austere, rustic dining room.

On any given night between May and October, you will find three different four-course theme dinners based on a particular time in history. The Renaissance is evoked with slivers of smoked eel in fruit sauces, a garden-picked salad with quail eggs, barbecued lamb in sweet-and-sour citrus sauce, and sweet and spicy pear pie. The Roman motif is high-lighted with dates fried in honey and olive oil and sprinkled with pepper, barbecued pigeon with mustard and nut sauce, lentil-and-chestnut potage, and cheese and honey balls. Fabulous!

When dinner is over you can retire to your room, which overlooks the extensive garden and hillside and is decorated in one of four period themes. An overnight adventure at Fernhill Lodge will be a rapturous time for your hearts and your taste buds.

OCEANWOOD COUNTRY INN, Mayne Island
22 Dinner Bay Road
(604) 539-5074
Expensive

Call for reservations and very detailed directions on how to get here. This island can be tricky, and the map is almost impossible to follow.

Oceanwood is a renovated Tudor home with an assortment of outstanding rooms, cozy sitting areas, and a 30-seat country-gourmet restaurant. Our spacious suite was flawless, exquisitely designed for cherished time together. French doors opened onto our own patio overlooking a forested inlet of the island, the spa tub was positioned next to a glowing marble-hearthed fireplace, a flower-patterned sofa was placed in front of the crackling embers, and the firm, ultra-cushy bed and down comforter were splendid for snuggling. It was sheer bliss. All the rooms we saw at Oceanwood were just as beautifully done as ours, but the rooms with fireplaces, private terraces and patios, views of the water, and en suite spa tubs are, without question, the best.

Breakfast and dinner are served in the idyllic dining room, framed on one side by a brick fireplace and on the other by a glass-enclosed solarium. The continental dinner menu is impressive. Potato-leek soup, stuffed leg of lamb, fresh halibut in parchment, and strawberry cheese-cake with hazelnut crust are some of the selections you might find on the menu. Breakfast is served to guests only and is a scrumptious presenta-tion of fresh-baked muffins and breads, pancakes with fresh berries, and freshly squeezed juices.

My recommendation is that you pack your bags right now, because there's no better time to take advantage of what Oceanwood has to offer.

Galiano Island

Hotel/Bed and Breakfast Kissing

GALIANO LODGE, Galiano Island
134 Madrona Drive
(604) 539-3388
Moderate to Very Expensive

From the ferry dock, turn left and look immediately on your left for the signs to the lodge.

For many years, Hastings House on Saltspring Island has been the only elite, ultra-deluxe place to stay in the Gulf Islands. Wildly successful, often full to overflowing, it showed that there was a call for upscale hideaways that blended magnificent surroundings with kid-glove service. A handful of properties dotted among the islands now offer a similar, although nowhere near as gilt-edged, style of accommodation. Galiano Lodge is one of those sparkling new additions; well, almost.

The recently opened lodge has 10 splendid suites with all the appropriate furnishings and details for a luxurious sojourn. White-and-yellow tiled baths with Jacuzzis or large soaking tubs, sumptuous down comforters, floral fabrics, wood-burning fireplaces, private decks, and floor-to-ceiling windows that look out to the view all add to the elegance of the rooms. Regrettably, the location could be better; it is just too close to the ferry terminal for comfort. The view from all the rooms features that centerpiece, and when the ferry comes and goes, the car lineup is too reminiscent of city life and the feeling of seclusion is temporarily lost.

One strong point is the stylish new dining room with an impressive menu. Divided in half by a stunning marble fireplace, one side offers fine dining while the other is a more casual and reasonably priced bistro. It's too early to tell what you can expect consistently, but you can be assured of expert service and exciting combinations of fresh ingredients. Penne noodles with chorizo and sun-dried tomatoes, filet mignon finished with port wine demi-glace, and venison burgers are some of the early selections. High tea here is a wonderful midday pick-me-up.

LAIDLAW'S BED AND BREAKFAST, Galiano Island
150 Alder Way
(604) 539-5341
Inexpensive to Moderate

Call for directions.

Those who appreciate rustic island simplicity along with superlative views of the forest-outlined waters of the Strait of Georgia, can't do better than this remote bed and breakfast. The affectionate, attentive innkeepers will welcome you with open arms, offering the shared enjoyment of a home with spectacular towering windows that make the scenery a part of the decor. Multilevel stone terraces set on a cliff at water's edge provide plenty of vantage points for watching eagles soaring overhead or resident whales passing by in the distance.

Two exceptionally basic, bordering on pioneer, cabins are situated a short distance from the house and command the same view. Efficient but small kitchens, firm beds, soft quilts, and private decks are the more gracious assets. Other than that, they are almost what some would call roughing it. Inside the house is perhaps the best room of all, a wonderful bedroom with expansive floor-to-ceiling windows that open to a stone deck, a well-stocked large brick fireplace, ample space, and a huge tiled shower. There may be cat hairs on the cushy reading chair, but that's part of the ambience. A more than generous breakfast is served to all guests. Laidlaw's isn't for everyone, but it is a true Northwest lovers' experience.

TALL TREES, Galiano Island
Montague Harbour Road
(604) 539-5365
Moderate

Call for reservations and directions.

There is only one room in this bed and breakfast, so you know that it will be a remarkably tranquil spot in which to spend time with your beloved. The room has floor-to-ceiling windows that overlook stunning views of the harbor, forested cliffs, and sparkling water. A madrona-embraced deck— with your own private entrance—has the same scintillating view. Floral fabrics, a spacious bathroom with a large soaking tub, Japanese kimonos, and a fire-warmed living room (part of the main house that is practically all yours) make Tall Trees deliciously cozy and enchanting.

In the morning, the innkeeper, who trained as a chef in the south of France, prepares a gourmet feast that is brought to your room on an antique wooden tea trolley. In the afternoon, tea service comes complete with cookies and chocolates. A four-course dinner created by this culinary virtuoso can be arranged. Leg of lamb, scallops caught that morning, a salad bouquet, and creative presentations of seasonal vegetables are examples of what you can expect, and add to the indulgence of your stay.

WOODSTONE COUNTRY INN, Galiano Island
743 Georgeson Bay Road
(604) 539-2022
Inexpensive to Moderate

From the ferry landing, turn left and follow Sturdies Bay Road to Georgeson Bay Road. Turn left to the inn.

Set amidst forested farmland, Woodstone Country Inn is a newly built hideaway nestled in the hills of Galiano Island. My only hesitation about this beautifully constructed inn is the location. Generally, when it comes to islands, I prefer shimmering water views. On the other hand, a rural setting hardly inhibits kissing. Of the 12 lovely rooms here, most have views of the forest or rolling valley, 10 have fireplaces, and a handful have soaking tubs. Each unit is attractively furnished, though a bit plain, and each radiates a great deal of warmth. In only a few hours here, you will achieve maximum relaxation and peace of mind.

A charming country-style restaurant occupies the ground floor of the Woodstone Country Inn. This charming room, scattered with wood tables covered in lace tablecloths, is immaculate and gracious; floor-to-ceiling windows provide a serene view of the valley. A complimentary breakfast is served here to guests every morning, and at night an excellent four-course dinner is presented by candlelight to the accompaniment of soft classical music. Broccoli-apple soup served with homemade herb bread, oysters gratin, sole stuffed with salmon mousse in a grape cream sauce, and espresso cheesecake are some of the menu's delectable surprises. If you are on Galiano, don't miss this epicurean country dining spot.

Restaurant Kissing

LA BERENGERIE RESTAURANT, Galiano Island
Montague Harbour Road
(604) 539-5392
Inexpensive to Moderate

From the ferry landing, turn left and follow the signs to Montague Harbour along Sturdies Bay Road, merging left onto Georgeson Bay Road and then Montague Harbour Road, where you will see a sign for the restaurant.

Tucked away in the woods is this authentic French country restaurant that doesn't quite know it isn't 1968 anymore. Rumpled tablecloths, a deteriorating interior, and a very laid-back staff add to the Woodstock/island ambience. Still, the French influence is unmistakable and the food can be quite good. There are only 10 tables (a little too close together for comfort during the summer weekends) and a very limited prix fixe menu. The fresh tomato soup, stuffed chicken breast, and blueberry cheesecake were delicious the night we were there, and other reports have been favorable. If nothing else, it is a unique experience and, depending on your generation, well worth the encounter.

North Pender Island

Hotel/Bed and Breakfast Kissing

CLIFFSIDE INN, North Pender Island
Armadale Road
(604) 629-6691
Moderate

From the Otter Bay ferry terminal, follow all highway signs indicating Hope Bay. At the Hope Bay dock, take Clam Bay Road for half a mile east to Armadale Road. Turn north and proceed 800 feet to the Cliffside.

A requirement for any romantic holiday is to travel to an awe-inspiring place and, once you arrive, not go anywhere else for anything. This enables you to spend precious, uninterrupted time relaxing and cuddling. Ferrying to Pender Island will grant you awesome scenery and seclusion, and the Cliffside Inn provides all the cozy romantic amenities.

This bed and breakfast inn straddles a rocky hillside above three acres of isolated oceanfront with wondrous panoramas that take in Mount Baker and Navy Channel. All the rooms have sun-welcoming windows, private patios, fireplaces, and titillating glimpses of the gardens or the ocean. An outside deck also has a hot tub that you can reserve for steamy private interludes. The cozy restaurant is housed in an enchanting glass-enclosed solarium that opens onto a deck with more of the same entrancing vistas. If weather permits, your meals will be served out here. The inn's kitchen consistently prepares supremely fresh, delicious meals. Morning may bring fresh-made muffins, a smoked salmon omelet seasoned with herbs from the garden, and homemade rhubarb-raspberry compote topped with yogurt. In the evening, your epicurean repast might consist of mushrooms stuffed with cream cheese and crab, rack of lamb or smoked salmon pasta, lettuce and herbs from the garden tossed with a dill-honey dressing, and desserts that are a taste of chocolate heaven. The presentations are beautiful and the service attentive. All of this is lovingly served in the candlelit dining room as you watch a stunning sunset.

Saltspring Island

Hotel/Bed and Breakfast Kissing

BEACHHOUSE BED AND BREAKFAST,
Saltspring Island
930 Sunset Drive, Ganges
(604) 537-2879
Expensive

Call for directions.

Located on the northwest shore of Saltspring Island, far removed from the bustling villages of Ganges and Vesuvius, this enticing bed and breakfast is an idyllic retreat. Perhaps the most romantic of your choices here is the self-contained cedar cabin resting on an incline above its own private cove. Wraparound decks and bay windows allow for dramatic views of sensationally gorgeous sunsets over the mountains of Vancouver Island. There are bathrobes to snuggle in as you rest on your deck, watching the otters and seals frolic in the waves.

Two delightfully plush rooms have been added in a new wing of the main house. Private decks with the same view make these almost as wonderful as the cabin. Both rooms have down comforters, feather pillows, lovely floral fabrics, and separate sitting areas. Breakfast is a culinary event at the Beachhouse; one of the innkeepers was schooled at the Cordon Bleu in Paris. Delicacies such as blueberry coffee cake, salmon quiche, fresh brioche, homemade sausages, and unusual fruit drinks may be served to you in the morning.

CRANBERRY RIDGE BED AND BREAKFAST, Saltspring Island
269 Don Ore Road, Ganges
(604) 537-4854
Moderate

Call for directions.

Located near the town of Ganges, on a ridge with a mesmerizing view of the islands, inlets, and the imperial snowcapped mountains of the mainland, this home has one of the most magnificent panoramas imaginable. The three ample guest rooms are located in the bottom section of the house; all are charming and immaculate. Wicker and willow furniture, sitting areas, terrycloth robes, and handmade patchwork quilts enhance each room. Two rooms have single Jacuzzi tubs, and one has a wood-burning fireplace; all have floor-to-ceiling sliding glass doors that look out on the stunning scenery. There's an expansive deck with a great hot tub for stargazing during late-night soaks.

In spite of all this praise, I should mention one drawback: when the shades are drawn open to let in the view through the beautiful glass doors, you'll feel rather exposed to the rooms next to you. The gourmet breakfast more than makes up for any of these considerations. The homemade lamb sausage and the smoked salmon Benedict are incredible—and there's that endless vista to admire.

HASTINGS HOUSE, Saltspring Island
160 Upper Ganges Road, Ganges
(604) 537-2362
Expensive to Unbelievably Expensive

Call for directions.

Hastings House is a sparkling gem of a country inn, poised over Ganges Harbour and the rolling hills of Saltspring Island. Everything about this place will tug at your heartstrings, imploring you to stay longer and luxuriate in the distinguished renovated buildings of this 30-acre seaside estate. Unfortunately, Hastings House will also pull at your pursestrings, even if you select one of the smaller rooms. And the strings may break altogether if you want a two-story suite with a classic stone fireplace, two bathrooms, and personalized afternoon tea service.

Every morning before your full-course breakfast is served in the fireplace-warmed cottage dining room, a basket of fresh pastries and hot coffee are delivered to your door. The Hastings House brochure aptly states: "Meticulous attention is given to character, courtesy, comfort, calm, and cuisine." One couple who stayed here told me, "Every time we kissed, someone wanted to come in and straighten up the room."

Hastings House is one of the most expensive, exclusive places to stay on the west coast of Canada. If the cost exceeds your holiday budget but you want a taste of this regal style of living, have dinner at the country restaurant, which serves sumptuous, tantalizing gourmet fare. Almost everything is harvested from the estate's meticulous herb and vegetable garden. The inn is devoted to its patrons, so this sublime ($52 per person—plus $30 to $40 for a bottle of wine) five-course dinner is available to the public only if the guests don't take the limited reservations first. Regrettably, there's a dress code; men *must* wear jackets, which is fine if you remembered to pack one. The management hasn't yet adapted to West Coast ways. They must think they're in Toronto or Montreal.

OLD FARMHOUSE BED AND BREAKFAST, Saltspring Island
1077 Northend Road, Ganges
(604) 537-4113
Inexpensive to Moderate

Call for reservations and directions.

The number of bed and breakfasts on Saltspring Island has grown from 31 to 85 in little more than a year. This explosion means a lot of work for a travel writer and a lot of confusion for travelers about the quality of the accommodations. Sometimes having only a few choices is better than having too many. After exhaustive lip research, I found the best this wonderful island oasis has to offer, and The Old Farmhouse is one of those discoveries.

Nestled among billowing trees, bountiful orchards, and lush meadows, this revitalized turn-of-the-century farmhouse has everything you'll need for an outstanding getaway. The four guest rooms are located in a separate building that is attached to the main house but has its own private entrance. Each room has a private bath, a separate balcony or patio overlooking the peaceful landscape, high dormers, down comforters, cheerful decor, and lots of space. Outside, you'll find a gazebo with a picnic table in the orchard and plenty of sweet, fresh air and serene quiet. In the main dining room, a gourmet country breakfast is meticulously served each day, with selections like crème fraîche over kiwis and blueberries, delicious homemade cinnamon buns and croissants, and eggs Florentine in a light pastry shell. The responsive, kind-hearted hosts will help make your stay a rich and rewarding experience.

◆ **Romantic Alternative:** One of the long-standing, professionally run bed and breakfasts on the island, and one of the more reasonably priced ones, is **WESTON LAKE INN,** 813 Beaver Point Road, Fulford Harbour, Saltspring Island, (604) 653-4311, (Inexpensive). The contemporary country farmhouse, overlooking the tranquil forest-lined expanse of Weston Lake, is set on 10 idyllic acres. The smallish rooms don't have an accessible view, but they are very comfortable and have private baths. Private outside decks, a noteworthy rock garden, sumptuous morning meals, an attentive hostess, and acres of quiet make this island getaway ripe for romance.

SKY VALLEY PLACE BED AND BREAKFAST,
Saltspring Island
421 Sky Valley Road, Ganges
(604) 537-4210
Moderate

Call for directions.

Hand-crafted pine furniture, ultra-plush down comforters, wicker accents, skylights, pretty tiled baths (one with a two-person Jacuzzi tub), thick white cotton robes, and sliding glass doors that open to a heated swimming pool surrounded by an aggregate patio are the components of this immaculate bed and breakfast. Sounds good? Well, that is only the beginning of what makes this a dazzling place to stay. Ensconced on a forested mountaintop, the contemporary home has a scintillating view of the islands, snowcapped mountains, and the sparkling waters of the Strait of Georgia. The rooms are a bit on the smallish side and privacy drops to a minimum when the shades are opened, but the other details help smooth out these rough edges. The tantalizingly fresh breakfasts include an array of fruits such as kiwis, figs, marionberries, pears, and raspberries—all straight out of the garden—soufflés, and tidbits such as Black Forest ham wrapped around banana slices and sautéed in butter.

Restaurant Kissing

BAY WINDOW RESTAURANT, Saltspring Island
375 Baker Road, Ganges
(604) 537-5651
Moderate to Expensive

Call for information about seasonal hours, reservations, and directions.

Through the lace-covered windows of the rustic, tasteful Bay Window Restaurant, located in the time-worn lodge of Booth Bay Resort, you can observe the changing contours of Vancouver Island as the sun moves effortlessly through the sky. Dinner here is a perfect accompaniment to the scintillating panorama. The menu is traditionally French, with such dishes as coq au vin, rack of lamb béarnaise, and fillet of sole meuniere. Everything here is cooked to perfection, and even the baked Alaska is a delight. After dinner, if the tide is low, you can walk along the shore and dig for clams and oysters. If high tide brings the crystal-clear blue water closer in, you can take off your shoes and walk along the warm surf.

◆ **Romantic Note:** There are a handful of rustic cabins on the property with small kitchens, decks, and views of the water and, sadly, the pulp mill across the strait at Crofton.

TIDES INN, Saltspring Island
132 Lower Ganges Road, Ganges
(604) 537-2777
Inexpensive to Moderate

Call for directions.

Simple country elegance accompanied by precisely prepared meals is a rare combination, but that's what you'll find inside this unassuming heritage building overlooking Ganges Harbour. The softly lit dining room, its tables draped with white linens, presents a warm backdrop. The tantalizing menu provides culinary heaven. The perfectly moist salmon Wellington and a robust lamb and black bean chili were excellent. Desserts are scandalously rich; I defy anyone to resist the dark chocolate-walnut torte or the caramelized pear cheesecake. Lunch and weekend brunch are also delightful here.

Outdoor Kissing

MOUNT MAXWELL PARK, Saltspring Island

From the town of Ganges, take Lower Ganges Road south out of town and follow the signs to the park.

"On a clear day you can see forever" is just the beginning of what you will experience at the end of the dusty gravel road that takes you to the top of Mount Maxwell. If you do nothing else on this island, you must see the view from up here and kiss passionately for at least a moment or two while you do. I can't begin to describe how magnificent and inspiring the scenery is from this vantage point. To the north are the snow-crowned mountains of the Canadian Rockies; to the south stands the glacial peak of Mount Baker; all around, for 360 degrees, are the forested islands and the sparkling, crystalline waters of the Strait of Georgia. Ahh, the sheer beauty of it all. Kissing isn't really mandatory, but you'll find it very hard not to indulge, the sensory stimulation is that potent.

ARTISAN SUNDAYS, Saltspring Island

Get a map with the addresses and information at the travel information center in Ganges or Vesuvius.

Loosely organized but exceptionally interesting are Sundays on the island, when the craftspeople open their studios to the public for browsing and shopping. Every imaginable artistic mastery and innovation is to be found in all kinds of hideaways dotted along forested hillsides and down long winding roads. Candle making, glass blowing, knitting, paper art, ironwork, painting, pottery, weaving, sculpting, basket making, quilting, and dried flowers are just some of the specialties you can discover during your journey. It might not sound romantic on the surface, but once you ferret out a place that can create something you will share forever, it will become an affectionate memory for a long time to come.

Hornby Island

Outdoor Kissing

TRIBUNE BAY, Hornby Island

From Vancouver Island, take the ferryboat from Buckley Bay to Denman Island. Cross Denman, following the signs to the Hornby ferry. From the Hornby ferry dock follow Central Road to the small Co-op Center and follow the signs a short distance to the bay.

A visit to Hornby Island is like a visit to Woodstock, New York, circa 1968. The dress, manner, and conversations in the Co-op Center, where most of the island activity takes place, will make you feel as if you've entered a time warp. (I'm young enough to remember this life-style and old enough to be startled when I see it still operating in full swing.) Two rather good food stands here serve the most delicious vegetarian fare I've had in a long time, and darn good espresso to boot. But none of that is a romantic reason to come to Hornby Island; the gorgeous sandy beaches, crystal-clear blue water, and gentle coves and bays are what make this island a desirable destination.

Summertime doesn't feel this good anywhere else in southwestern Canada. The soft sand under your feet, the surf warmed by the sun, and the forested backdrop of Tribune Bay are absolutely transporting.

Quadra Island

Hotel/Bed and Breakfast Kissing

APRIL POINT LODGE, Quadra Island
April Point Road
(604) 285-2222
Moderate to Unbelievably Expensive

Take the ferryboat from Campbell River to Quadra Island; after exiting follow the signs to the lodge.

Starting at 4 A.M., fishing boats in all shapes and sizes race across the narrow channel between Quadra Island and Vancouver Island, leaving a high-pitched buzz in their wake. The early-morning activity is fueled by a passionate, single-minded intent to go for, at the very least, a respectable-size king salmon or, at the very most, the record catch of the season. With tariffs like these, you'd think people would prefer shopping for fresh fish, but they don't, because fishing like this is utterly civilized.

Painter's (reviewed in the "Vancouver Island" section), Tsa Kwa Luten (reviewed elsewhere in this section), and April Point lodges all offer anglers a stylish, extremely elegant getaway where they can chase, and often catch, the elusive king. If either of you loves fishing, these are the places to do it in style. But if part of your goal is to get some good snuggling in at the same time, your choice has to be April Point Lodge.

The suites, rustic cabins, and guest houses here provide an eclectic assortment of accommodations. What they all share are scintillating views of the water and mountains, extremely comfortable furnishings with touches of elegance, down comforters, and separate seating areas. Some of the units are remarkably spacious, with large decks, Jacuzzi tubs, TV/VCR, small kitchens, and wood-burning fireplaces.

Dining at the lodge's restaurant is a culinary treat. Log pillars, handsome cedar paneling, and wraparound windows that showcase the scenery set a pleasing yet casual mood. The hearty and delectable meals offer amazing variety. French toast stuffed with Brie and strawberries for breakfast, authentic Texas-style chili for lunch, and sushi for dinner: extraordinary!

◆ **Romantic Note:** During summer the emphasis is on fishing groups, the lodge is packed to overflowing, and the water buzzes loudly with the flurry of boat traffic. From mid-September all the way till May, the crowds are gone, the restaurant is usually closed, the room rates are 50 percent off, the comfort is the same, and your privacy is increased considerably.

TSA KWA LUTEN LODGE, Quadra Island
Quathiaski Cove
(604) 285-2042
Expensive to Very Expensive

Take the ferry from Campbell River to Quadra Island; after exiting follow the signs to the lodge.

This is the new kid on the block of upscale fishing lodges. Set on a Native Canadian reservation, it is a handsome, uniquely constructed lodge. Most impressive are the soaring entry and the almost cavernous interior supported by massive log beams and pillars. Striking floor-to-ceiling windows look out to a stunning view of the water and the mountains on the mainland. The rooms are simple and hotel stylish, with high ceilings, tall windows, plain bathrooms (some with single-person Jacuzzi tub), gas fireplaces, and comfortable, although sparse, furnishings.

Dinner is a beautiful presentation of gourmet treats. The thin, tender crêpes wrapped around layers of smoked salmon, caviar, and Japanese seaweed were delicious; chanterelle and other exotic mushrooms flavored a hearty soup; and the fresh salmon and halibut combination was perfectly prepared.

Outdoor Kissing

WE-WAI-KAI CAMPGROUND, Quadra Island
Rebecca Spit
(604) 285-3111
Very Inexpensive

From the ferry landing follow the signs to the ferry for Cortes Island or Heriot Bay. When you see the water, start looking for signs to Rebecca Spit. The campground is located on the spit.

I don't usually think of camping as being particularly romantic. It's not that I don't enjoy it, but I don't think it's the best environment for intimate, tender moments. Kids running about, other campers too nearby, mosquitoes, hard ground, somewhat inaccessible showers, and my personal nemesis—outhouses—tend to keep the mood neighborly but not private. So when I tell you that We-Wai-Kai campground is one of the most beautiful and well laid out of any I've seen in the islands, you can be certain this is one spectacular setting.

One group of campsites is located on the beach facing the calm inner bay; another group is just above the shore, surrounded by trees lining the upper bank; and yet another lies in the forested hills overlooking the water. Each one is beautifully maintained and spacious. Even the common facilities are decent. I wouldn't go so far as to say that your privacy is guaranteed, but your relationship with each other and nature will be greatly enhanced.

◆ **Romantic Note:** Just a few feet from the campground is **REBECCA SPIT PROVINCIAL PARK**. This rare parkland has remarkable vistas, short but wonderful trails, the shoreline of tranquil Heriot Bay on one side, and the open waters of the Strait of Georgia on the other. The contrast between the two, only a stone's throw apart, is stupendous. There are picnic tables here and a convenient parking area as well.

VANCOUVER AND ENVIRONS

Vancouver

Vancouver has so much to offer and its geography is so beautiful. I know this sounds like an exaggeration, but once you visit, your idea of city life will never be the same. It's a phenomenal example of a big city done right. From Stanley Park and the sea wall to the historic-preservation district of Gastown, from the skyline encircling English Bay to the formal gardens and magnificent conservatories, from the sophisticated architecture of downtown to the three mountains that border the city on the north and the island-flecked Strait of Georgia—all is romantic and all is fastidiously maintained.

Here the excitement of city life is manifested in miles of lights, steel-girded bridges, and skyscrapers, yet the urban landscape also embraces snowcapped mountains, forested parks, and saltwater beaches. The vibrant, varied surroundings will entice you to seek out the inexhaustible daytime sights and the hot nightlife action. Prepare yourselves for the time of your lives.

◆ **Romantic Note:** For more detailed travel guidance while in British Columbia, consult the Visitor Information Centres scattered generously along most major roads and in most towns. The people here are lovely; you should stop in just to say hello and get your first taste of Canadian hospitality. For Vancouver information, write to the **VANCOUVER TRAVEL INFORMATION CENTRE,** 1055 Dunsmuir, Vancouver, B.C. V7X 1L3, or telephone (604) 683-2000.

◆ **Romantic Warning:** Be aware that the border crossings into and out of Canada are exceptionally tricky. Peak travel times during the summer and weekends are the worst, but it can be very fickle. Sometimes there is no telling when to expect a backup or clear sailing. And the Canadian side is no more predictable than the U.S. one.

Hotel/Bed and Breakfast Kissing

BEACHSIDE BED AND BREAKFAST, West Vancouver ❖
4208 Evergreen Avenue
(604) 922-7773
Inexpensive to Moderate

Call for reservations and directions.

Although this bed and breakfast is in need of renovation and the innkeepers are rather informal about their business, the waterfront setting of this home—in a very exclusive, very wealthy section of West Vancouver—and the large suite make up for some of the less-than-romantic details. Most of the rooms here are just OK, with average comfort and style. They're located on the lower floors of the main home, without, sad to say, a share in the spectacular view. That's the downside. The upside (which is extremely up) is that the largest room has a private entrance down to the beach, which is a stone's throw away, a view of the water, and a private en suite bathroom with a tiled Jacuzzi tub the size of a swimming pool (you have to see this one to believe it). All the guests have access to the living and dining rooms (which have floor-to-ceiling windows overlooking the water), the beachside hot tub, and an outdoor barbecue area that is perfect for nighttime bonfires (check with the innkeepers about time—they are not always clear about usage). In the morning a full breakfast is enriched by the sound of the waves lapping against the shore.

BESSBOROUGH COTTAGE, West Vancouver ❖❖❖
2587 Lawson Avenue
(604) 925-3085
Inexpensive

From the Lions Gate Bridge follow the signs for Marine Drive and West Vancouver. Take Marine Drive to 25th Street, turn right, go to Lawson, and turn left.

Nestled in a tranquil, posh neighborhood in West Vancouver, this charming cottage remains an affectionate place for a not-so-out-of-town sojourn. A beach-stone entry, bordered by a slightly overgrown garden bursting with an array of colorful blooms, frames this modest white home. There is a view of the bay in the distance. Attached to the house is an exceptionally cozy cottage (ample enough for two), with its own private entrance. The room is appointed with white wicker and white linens, the bay window is covered in lace, and the cathedral ceiling has a sizable skylight that makes the suite bright and cheerful. A generous breakfast can be served either in the comfort of your room, on your personal patio, or in the family dining room, where the view is best. There is only one unit here, so if you're lucky enough to get a reservation you'll have a delightful place to stay.

BRAMBLEWYCK, West Vancouver   ◆◆◆◆
4713 Piccadilly South
(604) 926-3827
Moderate

OUT OF BUSINESS

From the Lions Gate Bridge follow the signs for Marine Drive and West Vancouver. Take Marine Drive to Piccadilly South and turn left.

Most bed and breakfasts have one room that is their most sensuous and romantic—the hideaway you can escape to and never emerge from until your stay is over. Here at Bramblewyck there are two such suites, and they are luxurious, shining places for special time together. The entire home is a showcase. A garden pathway leads you past an aggregate patio and a blue-tiled Jacuzzi into the refined English-style living room. The larger suite is upstairs, with a private balcony overlooking the nearby bay, a king-size bed, floral fabrics and wallpaper, and a big bathroom with a large faux marble soaking tub. The main-floor suite has a private entry that opens to a terra-cotta spiral staircase leading to the sunken bedroom, which is framed by bay windows with a view of the water. This handsome room is filled with serenity and calm. Breakfast is a sumptuous procession of fresh fruit, scones, and unique egg dishes.

ENGLISH BAY INN, Vancouver   ◆◆◆
1968 Comox Street
(604) 683-8002
Moderate to Expensive

On Comox between Chilco and Gilford.

A welcome addition to a city short on amorous bed and breakfasts, this relatively new entry offers an enchanting experience for those who want to snuggle close to Vancouver and each other. Located in the heart of the West End, only half a block from the sea wall, is where you'll find this eye-catching, newly renovated home. Of particular romantic interest is the suite on the top floor, with skylights, a separate sitting area, and a soaking tub. Some of the other rooms are a bit snug, but they are all handsomely outfitted and extremely comfortable. The breakfast is excellent, although separate tables would be preferable.

ENGLISH ROSE BED AND BREAKFAST, West Vancouver
2367 Lawson Avenue
(604) 926-2615
Moderate

From the Lions Gate Bridge follow the signs for Marine Drive and West Vancouver. Take Marine Drive to 23rd Street and turn right, drive to Lawson, and turn left.

This unassuming, pocket-size, white frame country home is surrounded by laurels, cedars, and more than 50 English rosebushes. The fetching interior exudes relaxation and charm. The entire front half of the home is yours, with a living room warmed by a glowing red-tiled fireplace, a dining room with bay windows lined by a pillow-filled banquette, and a cozy bedroom. A more attractive bathroom would be nice, and you can hear the innkeepers working in the adjoining (though separate) kitchen, but everything else is so appealing it is easy to ignore. The furnishings are decidedly English and comfy; a noteworthy art collection lines the walls. Full breakfast is served in the privacy of your own breakfast nook or out in the verdant, picturesque garden.

HOTEL VANCOUVER, Vancouver
900 West Georgia Street
(604) 684-3131, (800) 828-7447
Very Expensive

On Georgia Street at Hornby.

Of all the major downtown hotels in Vancouver, and there are several, this one is as venerable a hotel as you will find, and is probably the best. This is nothing like the average high-rise hotel. The formidable stone exterior, replete with gargoyles and Old English style, contrasts with the bright, crystal-chandeliered, red-carpeted, lush interior. The rooms have been nicely redone in a formal, business-executive style, slick and professional, with all the amenities in place. Guests are welcome to use the large, outdoor glass-enclosed pool. Optimum service is part of the glamour and it comes in three class categories, of which Entrée Gold is the best. The lobby lounge is a great spot for tea or cocktails. For your own exclusive celebration in an august setting in downtown Vancouver, this is the place.

◆ **Romantic Note: GRIFFINS RESTAURANT** in the hotel isn't romantic, but its 25-foot-tall yellow ceilings, black-and-white tile floors, and remarkable, reasonably priced meals distinguish it from most hotel restaurants. It is very popular at lunch, due to the outstanding buffet ($12 per person) serving honest-to-goodness gourmet delights.

JOHNSON HOUSE BED AND BREAKFAST, Vancouver ◗◆❮
2278 West 34th Avenue
(604) 266-4175
Inexpensive to Moderate

From Granville Street turn west onto 33rd and proceed to Vine Street, turn left to 34th, and turn left.

Of the three guest rooms here, two share a bath. Although they are quite nice, sharing a bath isn't romantic. Luckily, the largest room is simply irresistible, and that makes the Johnson House a truly desirable place to stay. The Craftsman-style home has been exhaustively renovated and every detail is sensational. The outside veranda has a clear view of the mountains, antique carousel animals decorate the living and dining rooms, and both areas are warmed by a sizable brick fireplace. Upstairs the choice suite has a cathedral ceiling, wood-framed windows that look out to the mountains, a cozy sitting area, and a very sexy bathroom that contains a large wood-framed tile shower, two pedestal sinks, a soaking tub, a bidet, and all the room you need to spend *spotless* time together. A full traditional breakfast is served in the dining room.

LABURNUM COTTAGE, North Vancouver ◗◆❮
1388 Terrace Avenue
(604) 988-4877
Moderate

Call for directions.

Double ~~Queen~~ 135 C

Many improvements over the past two years have made Laburnum Cottage by far one of the finest and most professionally run bed and breakfasts in the Vancouver area. The name refers to a rustic, cozy cabin set amidst a lush English garden, and haloed by forested parkland in back of the main house. The cabin is a very private, very attractive, though somewhat compact, place to spend quiet moments. (Of course, where intimacy is concerned, small is not necessarily a problem.)

115
Queen

Inside the main house, on the second floor, are three bright, extremely comfortable, nice-size rooms, each with its own newly renovated bath, ultra-thick carpeting, luxuriant down comforter, and views of the garden. Attached to the main house is another cottage with a fireplace, kitchenette, and comfortable sitting area. The formal English-style living room is now available for high tea and sherry. A quality full breakfast in the morning is served in the newly renovated kitchen or terra-cotta-tiled sun room.

LE MERIDIEN HOTEL, Vancouver
845 Burrard Street
(604) 682-5511, (800) 543-4300
Expensive to Unbelievably Expensive

On Burrard Street between Smythe and Robson.

In some regards this is just another one of the many elite high-rise hotels in the heart of downtown Vancouver that specialize in flawless attentive service, posh restaurants, and efficient but attractive rooms. But where other hotels stop, Le Meridien begins. The three restaurants here—**GERARD RESTAURANT** (reviewed elsewhere in this section), **CAFÉ FLEURI,** and **LE CLUB**—are superb and, believe it or not, less expensive than many of the other first-class restaurants in the area. All the rooms are attractive and bright, with marble-tiled bathrooms and all the amenities. Service is the hotel's specialty and it is evident from the moment you step inside. Everyone here is concerned with your comfort and offers to help. It's more business-oriented than anything else, but it is still one of the most sexy distinguished hotels in Vancouver.

◆ **Romantic Note:** Meridien Hotel features a truly lavish Sunday brunch—considered one of the finest in town—at their attractive **CAFÉ FLEURI.** It is also worth a visit for their daily Chocoholic Buffet: decadent and wantonly sinful, but worth every mouth-watering caloric bite and the weeks of repentance that follow.

PAN PACIFIC VANCOUVER, Vancouver
999 Canada Place
(604) 662-8111
Expensive to Unbelievably Expensive

On the waterfront at the north end of the city, between Burrard and Howe streets.

Achieving romance at the huge Pan Pacific Hotel in downtown Vancouver may at first seem impossible. The entire complex is like a small city, complete with a large shopping mall on the lower floors and cruise ships that dock nearby. The gargantuan exterior and interior have an air of sterile impersonality. Nevertheless, this landmark building is an exceptionally stunning, professionally run, and exciting place to stay, with nicely designed rooms. All the units have interesting to stupendous views, firm beds, soft colors, and chic marble bathrooms. Of course, the less expensive rooms (which are still fairly expensive) are rather small, while the rooms in the Unbelievably Expensive category are more spacious and luxurious. The health club is as up-to-date as they get, and the immense outdoor pool and sun deck are impressive. The Pan Pacific is still just a hotel, but one with enough style to make it a rare experience.

PARK ROYAL HOTEL, West Vancouver
540 Clyde Avenue
(604) 926-5511
Expensive to Very Expensive

Call for directions.

Covered in ivy, surrounded by gardens, and backed by the stone-clustered Capilano River, this small, highly regarded hotel conveys a distinct country elegance. The feeling continues inside with the regal, captivating **TUDOR RESTAURANT**, where stately continental meals are beautifully served in a handsome fireside dining room or on a glass-enclosed deck overlooking the gardens and river. If all this elegance were also present in the suites upstairs, this would easily be a premier in-city getaway. Alas, only five of the rooms have been beautifully refurbished; the others are in pressing need. The rooms to request are 206, 207, 208, 211, or the grand suite 215, with its Jacuzzi tub and superb detailing. If you can reserve one of these, there is much to appreciate at the Park Royal.

◆   **Romantic Note:** Be sure to ask about the hotel's V.I.P. Package for Two, a first-class romantic deal. A night's stay, bottle of champagne, a five-course gourmet dinner for two, and continental breakfast for $150: not bad for a kissing celebration.

THE WEDGEWOOD HOTEL, Vancouver
845 Hornby Street
(604) 689-7777
Expensive to Unbelievably Expensive

On Hornby Street in downtown Vancouver, between Burrard and Howe.

Many hotels want you to believe they specialize in European-style elegance and service. Most don't, but the relatively petite Wedgewood does with exceptional grace and finesse, blending both romance and five-star hotel efficiency. Its white French doors open onto an elegant lobby and an attractive, exceedingly comfortable lounge that has not been taken over by the serious business-suit crowd. Many of the guest rooms have separate sitting areas, which helps you feel that you're staying in an uptown apartment rather than a downtown hotel. There are fireplaces in some of the suites, and all of the beautiful rooms have foliage-draped decks with sliding glass doors to help alleviate the claustrophobia high-rise hotels tend to induce.

◆   **Romantic Note:** I know you will want to dine at one of the many notable restaurants in the area (after all, you're already here and you'll want to get out into the city life), but don't neglect the Wedgewood's **BACCHUS RISTORANTE**. It is a robust, rich place for dining and dancing (after 9 P.M.) to live music with a Latin flair. The menu is simple but superb, with fresh fish being the kitchen's forte. The fresh halibut breaded with pistachio nuts and nestled on a peppercorn sauce was perfect and magnificently served.

WEST END GUEST HOUSE, Vancouver
1362 Haro Street
(604) 681-2889
Inexpensive to Expensive

Located on Haro Street one block south of Robson Street, between Jervis and Broughton.

Except for its overly bright exterior, everything about the West End Guest House is wonderful, including its six-block proximity to Stanley Park. This electric pink turn-of-the-century house is dwarfed by two large, modern apartment buildings on either side, in a neighborhood that is almost exclusively high-rises; it is a bit startling when you first see it. The inside, which has a much gentler persona, has been beautifully restored and decorated in an imaginative blend of country and Victorian touches. You'll love the blond wood trim, high ceilings, crystal chandeliers, bay windows, soft down quilts, quaint private bathrooms, and breakfast area with individual tables. Breakfasts are quite gourmet, and there is an outside deck for enjoying summer teatime or sherry. The rooms are a bit snug, but this is a practical place without the usual sterility, and a romantic change from ritzy, skyscraper hotels.

Restaurant Kissing

BEACHSIDE CAFÉ, West Vancouver
1362 Marine Drive
(604) 925-1945
Expensive

On Marine Drive between 13th and 14th.

Combine fabulous, fresh ingredients with a creative kitchen, a lovely soft contemporary interior, and a spacious heated deck overlooking the bay, and you'll have a lovely evening of conversation and excellent cuisine. A rough tile entry, a glass wall, one long banquette tossed with pillows, and blond wood trim define the dining room. Sit outside and sunset becomes an occasion worth celebrating. Exotic fresh fish (one night we had escolar from Egypt) and hearty appetizers such as Brie wrapped in phyllo are part of the restaurant's repertoire.

CAFFE DE MEDICI, Vancouver
1025 Robson Street
(604) 669-9322
Moderate to Expensive

On Robson Street between Burrard and Thurlow.

Robson Street is like a river of specialty shops, bakeries, cafés, bistros, superb restaurants, and designer boutiques, traveling a half-mile course through downtown. Located in one of the swankier clusters of shops, tucked away from the bustle of the street, is Caffé de Medici. This Northern Italian restaurant is artistically designed with high arched ceilings and plush drapery. The restaurant has grown over the past year and the service has become a bit haughty, but the polished, unmistakably romantic interior is still lovely. The entrées are delicious and nicely presented, although the appetizers are a bit lackluster. Desserts are exquisite.

CAFÉ IL NIDO, Vancouver
780 Thurlow
(604) 685-6436
Moderate

On Thurlow Robson between Robson Burrard and Alberni, in the back of a small arcade off the main street.

Richly colored peach walls, hunter green accents, and a handful of tables make up this small Italian hideaway. Set back from the bustle of Robson Street, you can enjoy delectable Northern Italian cuisine in an intimate atmosphere. There is also outdoor seating on warm summer afternoons.

CAPERS, West Vancouver
2496 Marine Drive
(604) 925-3316
Inexpensive to Moderate

At 25th and Marine Drive.

There is no way anyone could have convinced me that a restaurant located at the back of a health-food-oriented grocery store could be a suitable or desirable setting for a gourmet meal at almost any time of day. Well, seeing (and eating, with a kiss or two thrown in for good measure) is believing, though early morning, before the grocery opens, and dinnertime, after the grocery has closed for the evening, are definitely the most suitable times for intimate dining here. The casual interior—wood paneling, white tablecloths, forest green accents, large glass-enclosed deck with a view of the shore and English Bay, and soft classical music playing in the background—is appealing. The menu (almost entirely vegetarian except for seafood) is a whole-wheat, organic, al dente dream come true. Everything we sampled was excellent; even the faux New York steak was perfectly cooked and the service was professional and friendly. I know this kind of cuisine is not for everyone, and a grocery store backdrop is not the best, but it is definitely for you if you admire wholesome cooking served with an elegant flair.

CHESA RESTAURANT, West Vancouver
1734 Marine Drive
(604) 922-2411
Moderate to Expensive

On Marine Drive between 17th and 18th.

Previously located down the block, Chesa has returned to its original, smaller storefront location on well-traveled Marine Drive. The outside still isn't romantic, but the casual, cozy interior is inviting and so is the food. Open for lunch and dinner, Chesa offers appetizers and entrées that are brilliantly prepared. The duck parfait with port wine and Amaretto, the linguine with a rich basil cream, and the incredibly fresh seafood were excellent. The desserts are tantalizing and entirely too good to exclude; kiss until you have room for more.

DELILAH'S, Vancouver
1906 Haro Street
(604) 687-3424
Moderate
On Haro Street near Gilford Street.

Everything here is an exuberant blend of fantasy, elegance, and eccentricity. For some tastes, this restaurant's personality may be a bit too exuberant; it is not the most subtle of dining spots. Delilah's is located in the basement of the old Buchanan Hotel, in the heart of the West End, just a few blocks from Stanley Park. A small pink-and-yellow neon sign marks the entrance. Inside you'll find a dramatic mural-painted ceiling, plush red-velvet scalloped banquettes, floral carpeting, and chandelier lighting. There is also outdoor seating in the garden. The menu is a fill-in-the-blank prix fixe affair that you hand over to the waitperson when you have made your selections. You can check off herb-roasted pork tenderloin with a bourbon demi-glace; spinach tortellini with grilled scallops in an orange, sesame, and soy cream sauce;

or grilled smoked black cod with a sauté of fresh mangos, peppers, and shiitake mushrooms, topped with a mango sauce. The service is friendly and the food is smashing. With its ornate setting and cuisine, dinner at Delilah's makes for a flamboyant evening.

IMPERIAL CHINESE SEAFOOD RESTAURANT,
Vancouver
355 Burrard Street
(604) 688-8191
Expensive to Very Expensive

On Burrard Street between Hastings and the waterfront.

Grandiose 25-foot ceilings, crystal chandeliers, and floor-to-ceiling windows with a stellar view of the mountains and inlet enhance this ultra-elegant Chinese restaurant. This isn't your ordinary scene for Peking duck or fresh crab dim sum; it is opulent and unusually romantic. Almost all the dishes are superior (there's an occasional glitch with some of the fried dishes), so order with confidence. Now if they would only turn down the lights a little at night and let the soft luxury and magnificent view quietly fill the room, I'd give it another lip.

◆   **Romantic Note:** Ask about the Imperial's private rooms, located on the upper floor and accessed by a baronial winding staircase. Now you're talking romantic.

GERARD RESTAURANT, Vancouver
845 Burrard Street, in Le Meridien Hotel
(604) 682-5511
Expensive to Very Expensive

Located in Le Meridien Hotel in downtown Vancouver, on Burrard Street between Smythe and Robson.

Gerard Restaurant is more popularly known as Gerard's, but that is as abbreviated as it gets—you would never think of calling it Gerry's. This very posh and very dignified dining room is located in the very extravagant **LE MERIDIEN HOTEL**, and dinner here is not in any way, shape, or form a laid-back dining event. Quite the contrary; it is one of those stately, glamorous affairs where dressing to the nines is a must. (I have since been informed by management that the dress requirements have been relaxed. It seems they have come to terms with their Northwest location; men no longer have to wear jackets. Still, I wouldn't call this place casual.) The renowned dishes can be ordered à la carte or prix fixe. If a bit of posh continental dining is your way of celebrating together, Gerard's is *de rigueur*. The lounge at Gerard Restaurant, a handsome mahogany-paneled room with a glowing fireplace, features intimate corners where privacy is almost always guaranteed.

IL GIARDINO DI UMBERTO, Vancouver
1382 Hornby Street
(604) 669-2422
Expensive

On Hornby Street near Pacific.

Umberto has five restaurants in the Vancouver area, one in Whistler, and one on Vancouver Island. With all these Umberto's competing for attention, one would imagine that the quality suffers as it can with most other chain restaurants. That isn't a problem with this series of Italian restaurants. Most people argue about which Umberto's is the best, but assuredly the most romantic one is this location. A beautifully restored Victorian home with a lavish decor of terra-cotta-tiled floors, plush fabrics, and tall ceilings is the backdrop for excellent cuisine. The emphasis is on fresh veal and pheasant with rich, delectable sauces. A garden terrace is open for summer dining.

LA BROCHETTE, Vancouver
52 Alexander Street
(604) 684-0631
Moderate

On Alexander near Columbia.

The interior is all dark wood paneling and dim lighting, and the intimate lounge on the lower level features cozy seating around a stone fireplace that is well stoked all evening long. Freshly roasted quail, duck, and lamb are standard items on the hearty French menu.

LA TOQUE BLANC, West Vancouver
4368 Marine Drive
(604) 926-1006
Moderate to Expensive

On Marine Drive, past the town center in back of a gas station. Look for it on the left side of the road.

You can't imagine a less suitable spot for a restaurant: stuck behind a gas station and a convenience store, sans view and signage (save a plastic one spread across the back). However, inside the romantic atmosphere is totally French, and the dinners are excellent. La Toque Blanc refers to the "hat" awarded to chefs depending on their talent. I can't award hats, but I can award raves and kisses. Both are deserved.

LE GAVROCHE, Vancouver
1616 Alberni Street
(604) 685-3924
Expensive to Very Expensive

On Alberni Street between Cardero and Bidwell.

Perhaps one of the most traditionally romantic dining atmospheres in the entire Vancouver area is to be found at Le Gavroche. The restaurant is lodged in a renovated Victorian home with a view of the bay from cozy nooks and alcoves that used to be the dining and living rooms. You enter on the ground level and walk up a carpeted staircase to the dining area, which has all the appropriate polished detailing. In style, everything here is essentially French. The service is nearly regal, yet really quite friendly. Though ultra-formal dining is not usually my idea of an affectionate undertaking, there is something very romantic about this place. After all, formal doesn't have to be stuffy. It's all in the management's disposition and your frame of mind. Of course, the food here is a gastronomic triumph, with every dish a complete masterpiece. *Bon appetit et bon amour.*

PICCOLO MONDO RESTAURANT, Vancouver
850 Thurlow Street
(604) 688-1633
Moderate to Expensive

On Thurlow Street one block south of Robson Street, in the heart of downtown.

The interior is a handsome blend of taupe and brown, with white pillars and well-spaced tables. Northern Italian is the specialty here, and the pasta combinations are a blend of the freshest herbs and cheeses with rich silky sauces. The salmon can be a bit dry and the appetizers lack luster, but the pasta is worth a visit.

PROW RESTAURANT, Vancouver
999 Canada Place
(604) 684-1339
Moderate to Expensive

Canada Place is at the intersection of Howe and Cordova streets, on the eastern coastline of downtown, where the cruise ships dock beside the Pan Pacific Hotel.

Dinner at this establishment will be an indelible romantic episode in your lives. How can it fail? The dining room overlooks Burrard Inlet, set off by mountains, glittering city lights, and imperious ships forging their way through the water. The interior is dressed in pastel peaches and greens, and the tables have room to spare between them. Add to all this a menu as outstanding as the view, and you have a restaurant that transcends its touristy location. The fish seem to have jumped from the water to the kitchen, where they are carefully cooked, then adorned with oyster mushrooms and light cream sauces that have been lovingly prepared. The desserts are bountiful—and, well, there's that view again.

◆   **Romantic Note:** If the Prow is crowded, you can always relax a while next door in the **CASCADES LOUNGE** in the **PAN PACIFIC HOTEL**, (800) 663-1515. This immense, airy, echoing bar shares the same astonishing view as the restaurant, through arresting floor-to-ceiling windows. Not the prettiest of interiors, nor even vaguely intimate, but with each other and what's outside you'll do just fine until your table at the Prow opens up.

THE RAINTREE RESTAURANT, Vancouver
1630 Alberni
(604) 688-5570
Moderate

On Alberni between Bidwell and Cardero.

For three years running this pretty restaurant has topped *Vancouver* magazine's Best Restaurant list in several different categories, including setting, quality of food, and wine list. We can vouch for all these: the setting is pretty (and the view is equally lovely); the food quality is without question superior and generous; the wine list is both varied and ample (and the waitstaff is knowledgeable about their recommendations). The readers' poll doesn't have a category for Most Romantic, but if it did, Raintree would probably top that list as well.

ROOF RESTAURANT and LOUNGE, Vancouver
900 West Georgia Street, in the Hotel Vancouver
(604) 684-3131
Very Expensive

On Georgia Street at Hornby.

This is not the most beautiful restaurant in Vancouver nor is it the place to come for renowned French cuisine, but I still think it's a distinctive setting for celebrating a special occasion. This is obvious from the moment you enter the room. The Roof is located on top of the Hotel Vancouver, with a sweeping view of the city from the glass-enclosed dining room. Up here on cloud nine, with the city lights twinkling below, you can enjoy some cheek-to-cheek, arm-in-arm dancing while the band plays on and on. The melodious tones of a three-piece band, with a somewhat Latin flavor, are heard five nights a week. If you ever wanted to trip the lights fantastic, this is the place to do it in style, with supreme atmosphere and service.

◆ **Romantic Note:** If the price of dinner seems a bit steep or if you prefer to dine somewhere else, The Roof's lounge area is separated from the dining room and band by only a rise in elevation, and is totally accessible to the dance floor. They also have special discounts that offer 50% off your dinner tab; ask if these deals are available when you call. Closed Sunday and Monday.

SALMON HOUSE ON THE HILL, West Vancouver
2229 Folkestone Way
(604) 926-3212
Moderate to Expensive

From Marine Drive in West Vancouver turn right on Taylor Way (which is also Highway 1 West). Take Exit 10 for Folkestone Way and head up the hill to the restaurant.

Sometimes the view alone is enough to establish a place's romantic dining credentials. When the sunset casts vibrant color over the sky as the two of you share your deepest thoughts, authentically intimate moments can occur. In such places, more often than not, the view is all there is, and the food is given only a superficial amount of attention from the management. Believe it or not, the Salmon House has both a stupendous view and good food. Reserve a table near the window, order the savory alderwood-broiled salmon, then sit back and let the evening drift by your ringside seat on the world.

SYLVIA RESTAURANT, Vancouver
1154 Gilford Street
(604) 681-9321
Inexpensive to Moderate

On Gilford Street just off Denman.

Enjoying the view is definitely a major romantic pastime in Vancouver, and there are phenomenal views from many vantage points. One of the prettier spots for any meal is the Sylvia Restaurant, attached to the Sylvia Hotel. The elegant glass-enclosed dining room and outside balcony look out to English Bay and the mountains.

THE TEAHOUSE RESTAURANT, Vancouver
Stanley Park at Ferguson Point
(604) 669-3281
Moderate

From the north end of the park, turn west off Highway 99 and follow Stanley Park Drive along the park's western side. Follow the signs to the teahouse.

This restaurant is a truly extraordinary kissing place. It's hard to believe that such a major tourist attraction can also be one of the more beautiful places to dine in British Columbia. A large part of the sparkle comes from the location: the teahouse rests in the middle of a sloping lawn overlooking English Bay and, on the horizon, Vancouver Island. The building itself is dazzling—half of it is a pastel-colored country home, the other half a glass-enclosed atrium. Here you can watch the sun gently tuck itself into the ocean for a peaceful night's rest—that is, if you have reservations. Everyone, including the busloads of tourists, knows about the Teahouse Restaurant. The restaurant serves fairly standard Canadian and French cuisine that is a tad too standard and generally oversauced, but not all the time. The seafood, baked egg dishes, and meats, when prepared au natural, can be tasty, so order carefully. But that view! Sigh. Your hearts and eyes will be thankful for a long time to come.

Outdoor Kissing

BOTANICAL GARDENS, Vancouver

There are many acclaimed, exquisite, lush gardens in the Vancouver area, but the most beautiful are the **VANDUSEN BOTANICAL GARDENS**, 37th and Oak Street, (604) 266-7194; the **UNIVERSITY OF BRITISH COLUMBIA BOTANICAL GARDEN**, 6804 Southwest Marine Drive, (604) 822-4208; the **BLOEDEL FLORAL CONSERVATORY**, 33rd Avenue and Cambie, (604) 872-5513; and the **DR. SUN YAT-SEN CLASSICAL CHINESE GARDEN**, 578 Carrall, (604) 689-7133. Each one has its own captivating beauty. Coaxed from the earth by skilled artisans, the verdant presentations are creative and dramatic. Sculpted shrubbery crowned by specially pruned trees, tranquil ponds, and exotic arrangements are all here for your pleasure. Of course, there are the occasional tour buses to look past, but depending on the season you could be the only ones walking through these elysian paradises.

GROUSE MOUNTAIN, West Vancouver ◆◆◆◆
CYPRESS PROVINCIAL PARK, West Vancouver
MOUNT SEYMOUR PROVINCIAL PARK, North Vancouver

These three mountain areas are accessible from Highway 1 and Highway 1A/ 99. Capilano Road in West Vancouver leads to Grouse Mountain. Cypress Bowl Road in West Vancouver takes you to Cypress Provincial Park. To get to Mount Seymour Provincial Park, follow the signs from Highway 1 heading east from the Lions Gate Bridge.

One extraordinary aspect of Vancouver is that in its very own backyard there are three separate mountains high enough above sea level to be active ski areas, and they are only about 30 minutes from the city (45 minutes if you take your time or get lost). It is quite feasible to spend an invigorating day on any of these mountains hiking, lake swimming (depending on the season), gazing out over the stupendous

views, or skiing, and still have more than enough time to get back to the
city and dress up for a candlelit dinner in Gastown.

On a moonlit winter's eve, more adventurous couples may consider
doing the above scenario in reverse. After an early dinner in the city,
gather your cross-country ski equipment, toss it in the car, and drive up
to Cypress Provincial Park. Stride over the sparkling white snow until
the park lights shut off at 11:00 P.M..

◆   **Romantic Warning:** These park areas are well known. Grouse
Mountain tends to be the most touristy of the group, but it also has
dining on top of the world overlooking the city lights. For general
information for Grouse Mountain, call (604) 984-0661; for dinner
reservations, call (604) 986-6378; for ski information, call (604) 980-
9311. The crowds are worst during the summer and on sunny weekends.

LIGHTHOUSE PARK, West Vancouver

*From Highway 1/99 in West Vancouver, take the 21st Street exit to Marine
Drive. Follow the signs on Marine Drive to Lighthouse Park.*

At the southwestern tip of West Vancouver is a peninsula called
Lighthouse Park. It is a small, water-bound fragment of granite hanging
on to the mainland. From the parking area, the shores of the Strait of
Georgia and the cliff tops of the parkland are both only a brisk 15-
minute walk over trails through rocky forest. Along any of the trails you
can inhale the freshness of sea air mingled with the scent of sturdy fir and
spruce trees. At trail's end, you'll get a far-reaching view on a clear day.
On a cloudy day, Lighthouse Park obligingly resembles the kind of dense
forest that exists deep in the distant Canadian Rockies, enabling you to
feel far away from city life. The two of you will scarcely remember how
close civilization really is.

LYNN CANYON SUSPENSION BRIDGE,
North Vancouver

*Take Highway 1 east from the Lions Gate Bridge and follow the signs to Lynn
Canyon Park.*

While everyone and their aunt from White Rock are lining up at the
well-touristed **CAPILANO SUSPENSION BRIDGE,** you can discover the bridge less traveled. There are no entrance fees and no tourist
shops, and when school is in session you may even have a certain

amount of privacy. The suspension bridge across Lynn Canyon hovers and sways (as suspension bridges are inclined to do) over a rocky, forested gorge where a waterfall and river etch their way through the canyon floor below. On the other side of the bridge are trails that lead to a boulder-strewn brook with freshwater soaking pools. You can cross over the rocks and find a refreshing niche all to yourselves.

◆ **Romantic Warning:** Trails here are periodically washed out, and crystal-clear pools that look inviting can be dangerous and not as inviting as they look. Be cautious, stay on the trails, wade in the shallows, and the solitude will be invigorating.

MARINE DRIVE, West Vancouver

Marine Drive follows the southern shoreline of West Vancouver. Heading north over Lions Gate Bridge, turn west onto Marine Drive.

Marine Drive follows, at water's edge, a stellar residential and commercial neighborhood in the Vancouver area. Summertime graces this road with perfect views of the city and Vancouver Island. During the fall, overcast rainy days make this sinuous road more reclusive, emphasizing its dark, rocky cliffs and the thick, moist foliage that veils the houses along the way. Stores and restaurants along the way have a quaint, congenial style. There's the occasional major bank and gas station, but for the most part this area is a quieter alternative for a stroll or drive than Vancouver.

Besides being scenic and conducive to sitting close (if you don't have bucket seats), Marine Drive has an added attraction: several satellite roads lead northward and connect with two alternative routes to Whistler—Cypress Access Road through Cypress Provincial Park, and Capilano Road over Grouse Mountain. Let the beauty of the drive lead you wherever your hearts desire.

◆ **Romantic Alternative:** Adjacent to Marine Drive, just west of Lions Gate Bridge, look for a waterfront park called **AMBLESIDE**. The long, winding sidewalk that outlines the park is bordered on one side by a stone sea wall with marvelous views of the water and city, and on the other by grass and playgrounds. This is a much smaller, less crowded version of the sea wall in Stanley Park, and a definite romantic option if crowds are something you like to avoid.

HYAC WILDERNESS ADVENTURES, Vancouver
(604) 734-8622
Expensive

One hour outside of Vancouver is the Chilliwack River, churning with white water and, if you'll excuse the phrase, a thrill a minute. Running a passage through rugged canyons, unanticipated gorges, and momentary still water along riverbanks crowned with cedars and pinery makes for a trip that is nothing less than sensational. Depending on the season, the impact of your excursion can vary from awesome to electrifying. Packages are available for one- or two-day adventures. It is all an immense amount of fun, even if you've never been in a wet suit before or are afraid of how you'll look in one. Let go and jump in; the surging water is terrific.

STANLEY PARK

In the West End, just off Georgia Street.

Stanley Park is a spectacular oasis of thick forest, green hilly lawns, and jewel-like lakes, with paved trails weaving through its 1,000 acres of cloistered parkland. The park is almost like an island, projecting as it does into the water, with English Bay on one side and Burrard Inlet on the other. From the **SEA WALL PROMENADE** that wraps around the park, to the zoo, aquarium, and abundant picnic areas, from the lengthy shoreline at Sunset Beach to vistas and more vistas, restaurants, and lakes, Stanley Park is a refuge from the cityscape only moments away. The only problem is that because it's so extraordinary, everyone loves it, and that doesn't leave much room for privacy. But the surroundings are so welcoming that you can forgive the busloads of camera-clicking tourists and find yourselves a corner to call your own—at least for a while.

WHISTLER AND ENVIRONS

From Vancouver, heading north over the Lions Gate Bridge, follow the signs for Highway 1 west, which will split off to Highway 99 north to Whistler.

When the first serious snowfall of the year blankets the slopes of Whistler and Blackcomb mountains, it beckons skiers the world over to spectacular downhill skiing. The world-class resort facilities of Whistler Village and the surrounding area are unsurpassed anywhere in the Pacific Northwest and Canadian Southwest.

Whistler's other raison d'être is the enjoyment of every outdoor recreational activity you can imagine: cross-country skiing, kayaking, canoeing, windsurfing, white-water rafting, hiking, mountain biking, and golfing. If you like fast-paced fun and an easygoing party atmosphere amid purple mountains' majesty, Whistler delivers in the slickest, most impressive way possible.

Perhaps the only drawback to this mountain holiday mecca is that the town of Whistler is growing so fast the area has some elements of urban sprawl—functional for skiers and highly social, but not necessarily intriguing or charming. Designer homes, mountainside condominium complexes, chateau-style hotels, and an assortment of inns, bed and breakfasts, and lodges can accommodate more than 1.5 million visitors to these slopes a year. However, you needn't be too concerned with any of this, since the suggestions that follow will help you find the romantic sparkle and secret solitude that still abound in this part of Canada.

◆ **Romantic Note:** During the summer, glacier skiing is available at the very top of Blackcomb Mountain. It's not the mile-long runs of the winter season, but then again, in winter you can't wear your bathing suit on the slopes. Also, be sure to ask about discount packages or special seasonal rates. Most places have several different price categories.

Whistler

Hotel/Bed and Breakfast Kissing

CHATEAU WHISTLER RESORT, Whistler   ◆
4599 Chateau Boulevard
(604) 938-8000
Expensive to Unbelievably Expensive and Beyond

At the foot of the Blackcomb Mountain ski run.

I know: you've heard so much about Chateau Whistler that you're shocked at my one-lip rating. After all, isn't this the hotel that all the celebrities want to stay in? The one that's the talk of Whistler? Well, it is, at least for the moment, until the elite Pan Pacific hotel chain finishes construction in a couple of years. Chateau Whistler is really just a hotel with very nice, but fairly standard, upscale hotel rooms, some of which have exceptional views. The location is great, right at the foot of the mountain, and the lobby lounge, with its soaring glass windows, is one of the most exquisite in the area, but you can't sleep there. You should know about Chateau Whistler if you want a reliable hotel stay with an attentive staff. But pretty soon everyone will be talking about the new kid on the block, and the celebrities will move there.

CHALET LUISE PENSION, Whistler   ◆◆
7461 Ambassador Crescent
(604) 932-4187
Inexpensive to Moderate

About one mile north of Whistler Village, turn right on Nancy Greene Drive, and then right again on Ambassador Crescent. Go two blocks to the pension.

Whistler has several pensions that cater to visitors who want a more reclusive, less hectic residence than those in the heart of the Village or in a condominium complex. Almost all of these Swiss- or German-style, professionally run bed and breakfasts provide a homey environment with a hearty meal served first thing in the morning just before the lifts open. Chalet Luise is just such a place, with a little bit of everything for couples who want to be close to the mile-long mountain runs: quaint, exceptionally neat rooms (some a bit on the snug side), one with a fireplace, some with views and balconies; an outdoor whirlpool; and all the extra comforts and crisp clean detailing you would expect from a European-style bed and breakfast. Breakfast is served in a fireside lounge; individual tables are placed around the room, allowing for a private morning repast of creative juice combinations, waffles, cereals, breads, and jams. Chalet Luise is only moments away (ski in, ski out) from the slopes and cross-country ski runs, so once you arrive you may not need to use the car again during your winter stay.

DURLACHER HOF, Whistler
7055 Nesters Road
(604) 932-1924
Moderate to Expensive

Just north of Whistler Village, turn left on Nesters Road.

Top to bottom, the Swiss influence is strong at the Durlacher Hof. Elaborate breakfasts and cozy rooms are standard amenities, but where some bed and breakfasts stop, Durlacher Hof starts. The innkeeper here serves a most bountiful morning meal of freshly baked breads and Danishes, homemade jams, cheese soufflé, blueberry and apple pancakes, and fresh fruit—and that was just one morning. Afternoon tea with fresh-from-the-oven cakes is also a delicacy. The rooms are pretty, immaculate, and cheerful; some have spa tubs and are quite spacious. Unfortunately, the inn is a bit too close to the highway for comfort, but once the quiet of night embraces the area, it really doesn't matter.

◆ **Romantic Note:** During the winter, the Durlacher Hof offers five-course gourmet dinners. Chefs from all over the world come to take part in these culinary productions. It makes for an incredible, exclusive evening without crowds or pretense.

THE GABLES, Whistler Village
Sea-To-Sky Accommodations
(604) 932-4184
Moderate to Unbelievably Expensive

Call for directions.

Besides excellent ski runs and the latest in express chair lifts, Whistler is filled with condos of every size, shape, and price. From the heart of the Village to the base of the gondola that ascends Whistler Mountain to even farther out on the back roads, there are more than enough accommodations to suit the tastes and budgets of the hordes of winter-sports enthusiasts. The one thing you may find lacking is a place to soothe the muscles and the heart after a day of tackling the slopes.

The Gables is a small, elegant development just a two-minute walk from the Village and right across the street from the Wizard Express. In spite of this easy access, the units are surprisingly sedate and beautifully appointed, a far cry from most units in the area. Each apartment has a small entry hall that nicely handles wet clothing and snow-laden boots. The living room is then entered through glass-paned French doors. All of the units have fireplaces and fully equipped kitchens, and the bathrooms have spa tubs. A cozy loft bedroom overlooks the capacious living room. You can even choose whether your apartment will have a staggering view of the mountain or a soothing view of the rushing creek at the back of the property. All in all, The Gables' proximity to everything and the inviting quality of the rooms make it a fetching place to escape after a day's mountainous pursuits.

INGLESIDE BED AND BREAKFAST, Whistler   ◆◆◆◆
6425 St. Andrews Way
(604) 932-4588
Moderate

Call for directions.

Cozy and elegant can be a luxurious combination when they are in the right balance, which they are at this rare Whistler bed and breakfast. The one suite here has a private entrance, and is attached to a contemporary country home up in the exclusive Whistler Cay Heights neighborhood. Inside you'll find knotty pine paneling, a slate fireplace, white wicker chairs, pine furnishings, a cushy featherbed, an ample Jacuzzi tub, a wet bar with sherry, and tea or coffee service. The private deck with a view of the mountains (facing the driveway) is a nice extra. A continental or full breakfast, depending on the length of your stay, is served in your room on an antique silver service. Fresh-squeezed juice and perfect lattes are accompanied by croissants, muffins, parsley eggs, tomato-and-mushroom sauté, hash browns, and fruit.

One potential drawback: the warmhearted innkeepers have children, but you won't hear them. If that detail doesn't bother you, this is a superlative romantic find.

LE CHAMOIS, Whistler
4557 Blackcomb Way
(604) 932-2882, (800) 777-0185
Expensive to Unbelievably Expensive

At the foot of Blackcomb Mountain, in front of the Chateau Whistler Resort.

Claustrophobia is a new problem in Whistler and it's getting worse. Everyone wants to be a stride or two away from the slopes, which means so do the developers. New high-rise accommodations are going up everywhere, right on top of each other. In the middle of all these exploding steel girders is Le Chamois, a comparatively petite (62 units), elegant five-star hotel with tasteful furnishings, some rooms with views, all the amenities, and impressive restaurants, located directly at the foot of the Blackcomb ski run. Surprisingly, Le Chamois offers six stunning (and I mean stunning) designer studios, each with ample space, wonderful views, cozy alcoves, high ceilings, a kitchenette, and a two-person marble Jacuzzi tub in the living area. And these are the least expensive rooms in the hotel! During the summer they are an incredible kissing bargain.

◆ **Romantic Note:** At the time of this review the new restaurant at Le Chamois, **LA RUA**, hadn't opened yet. The possibilities and view of the mountain are exciting. The chef has an outstanding reputation and the cuisine will be California/Spanish with a European flair.

POWDERHORN, Whistler
Sea-To-Sky Accommodations
(604) 932-4184
Moderate to Unbelievably Expensive

Call for directions.

From the outside, given the highly stylized developments we passed on the way through town and the Village to get here, we found Powderhorn disappointing. Its exterior is an uninviting mix of black steel and rose-colored cement that makes it look like a rather average apartment high-rise. The single elevator and sterile hallways confirmed our impression. But once we turned the key on our unit, we were shocked: could this be the same building? Everything was picture perfect. The interior was bright and sunny, with expansive windows, comfortable furnishings, a large kitchen, and a huge amount of space. Actually, our unit was designed for a group of six or more, but we didn't miss those other bodies. If we had come with a group, though, we could still have accommodated our need for privacy. The master bedroom is in a separate wing just off the living room. Its huge bathroom features a large spa tub and lofty windows. Outside on the roof, another spa tub is available for everyone. The moral is: Don't judge a book by its cover. (Except this book, of course.)

TIMBERLINE LODGE, Whistler
4122 Village Green
(800) 663-5474
Expensive

Turn into Whistler Village and follow the signs to Timberline Lodge.

For those who want to stay in the heart of the Village and be a part of this hub of mountain activity, Timberline Lodge is a good choice. The comfortable rooms are equipped with fireplaces, four-poster beds, terraces, wet bars, and spa tubs. Each room is unique, so request a detailed list to figure out which one will exactly meet your needs. All can satisfy the wishes of two skiers' hearts.

◆ **Romantic Option:** If the two of you would like to dine in the Village, consider an evening at **MYRTLE'S RESTAURANT**, 4122 Village Green, (604) 932-5211, (Expensive), in Timberline Lodge. The elegant French Colonial atmosphere, superior service, and exceptional cuisine make every meal a formal romantic treat.

WOODRUN, Whistler
4910 Spearhead Place
(604) 932-3317
Expensive to Unbelievably Expensive

Call for directions.

Certain celebrations require a splurge. Mountain buffs and ski lovers who also love each other will find luxurious space in a select number of Woodrun's foremost romantic apartments. The most extravagant rooms, and the ones you'd be interested in knowing about, have cathedral ceilings, floor-to-ceiling windows, wonderful views of the mountains and ski area, a full designer kitchen, marble and hardwood floors, a gas fireplace, and a huge Jacuzzi tub in the master bedroom. The furnishings are casual but plush, and the space is considerable. The outdoor swimming pool and hot tub have a view (for those in the rooms without the sexy private baths). Woodrun is not a hotel, but it is a sizable lodge set up in the impressive Benchlands (above the base of Blackcomb) with ski-in, ski-out ability and a front desk (limited hours) for check-in. You can't splurge all the time, but when you do, this should be a strong consideration.

Restaurant Kissing

CHRISTINE'S, Whistler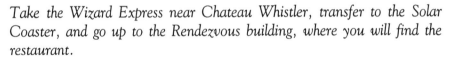
On Blackcomb Mountain
(604) 932-3141
Moderate to Expensive

Take the Wizard Express near Chateau Whistler, transfer to the Solar Coaster, and go up to the Rendezvous building, where you will find the restaurant.

At the top of Blackcomb Mountain, Christine's awaits you with an impressive five-course, prix fixe dinner (summer only). As good as the food is, it is only a minor part of your transcendent evening up here. It will take a while for your eyes to adjust to the magnitude of the view from this dining location. This must be what dining in heaven is like. Whistler's early winter sunsets (about 4:00 P.M.) make this dining and viewing event a summer fling (when sunset waits till 9:00 P.M.). Summer months up here are filled with visual ecstasy. When the snow has melted (except for the perennial glacier patch at Blackcomb's summit), sunsets seem to linger forever across the countenance of the endless rugged mountain peaks.

The restaurant is open for lunch during the winter and summer (the patio barbecue is also a visually thrilling experience), but there is something about dinner and sunset that is wildly romantic. Unfortunately, the summer dinners take place sporadically; there is no set schedule. Call to find out if they are available the weekend you are in town.

LES DEUX GROS, Whistler
1200 Alta Lake Road
(604) 932-4611
Moderate to Expensive

As you enter the town of Whistler, look on the east side of the road for Alta Lake Road. The restaurant is immediately up the hill on your left.

Management has undergone some changes and dinners of late have been hit or miss, but things are smoothing out and well worth a romantic investigation. Located two miles south of Whistler Village, this elegant country restaurant sits on a forested bluff overlooking the woods and mountain. The timbered exterior blends fittingly with the area. Inside, the casual elegance of wood-beamed cathedral ceilings, floor-to-ceiling windows, and cascading floral draperies complement the sumptuous courses the kitchen composes. There is also an outdoor patio for sultry summer dining. Your classically French meal will be fantastic, particularly if you order the fresh fish or veal.

RIM ROCK CAFÉ AND OYSTER BAR, Whistler
2101 Whistler Road
(604) 932-5565
Moderate

After you enter the town limits of Whistler go past the first stop light and take the next right onto Whistler Road. Look for the Highland Lodge; the restaurant is on the second story.

Ask any innkeeper what is the best seafood restaurant in Whistler and you are likely to be directed to the Rim Rock Café. Two stone fireplaces fill the wood-paneled room with a blushing glow in the winter, and there is outdoor seating on the umbrella-covered patio during warm summer days. The food is spectacularly good: the freshest of fish, napped nicely with light sauces and served with tender vegetables, all flawlessly prepared and served. After a madcap day of skiing or hiking, or a lazy afternoon communing with nature, this is a handsome place to have dinner. Unfortunately, it is very popular and usually full (reservations are a must, sometimes a week in advance). The nearby lounge has a live band playing first-rate rock'n' roll. The music can be a bit loud and the volume of conversation increases to compete with the tunes, but between the food, the setting, and the music, you will have a delightful evening.

VAL D'ISERE, Whistler
Whistler Village
(604) 932-4666
Expensive

In the heart of Whistler Village, on the top floor of St. Andrew's House.

The most exquisite French food in Whistler can be sampled here at Val D'Isere. An elegant pale pink dining room with white tablecloths and gleaming china and crystal sets the mood for an unhurried evening. The food is traditional French with rich sauces, succulent fresh fish, and veal. The lentil soup with smoked sausage was savory and the boneless duck breast with black currant sauce was excellent.

Outdoor Kissing

BRANDYWINE FALLS

Take Highway 99 north to Whistler. A few miles before Whistler, you will see signs directing you to the falls.

A brisk 10-minute walk through lush forest will bring you to a feat of natural construction that deserves a standing ovation. At the end of your jaunt, pine trees open out onto a cliff from which you look across to the top of Brandywine Falls. The water drops down a tube-like canyon into the river, which cuts through a valley of interlacing mountains and meadows. During the summer you can climb down to the rocky ledges under the falls and, side by side, sit under the surging waters and feel the spray cool your faces.

HELI-SPORTS, Whistler
(604) 932-2070, (604) 932-3512
Expensive

Free shuttle service to the departure pad from anywhere in Whistler.

I cannot begin to describe to you the literally awesome landscapes you will witness during a helicopter flight over this magnificent realm. The experience will engulf your souls with images that will last a lifetime. Heli-Sports offers various ways to partake in the spectacle of true mountain alpine wilderness. You can sightsee for 20-, 30-, or 45-minute flights. There are also heli-hiking excursions accompanied by a guide that take you deep into the heart of this glacier-crowned rugged terrain. Another option is a heli-picnic that sets you down in the midst of pristine, untouched mountain streams or ridges where you can enjoy a respectable gourmet lunch. But it's really the scenery that will awaken taste buds you never before knew you had.

HIGHWAY 99

From Vancouver, cross into West Vancouver via Highway 1 north over the Second Narrows Bridge, or via Highway 1/99 over the Lions Gate Bridge. Follow the signs to Squamish and Whistler. Depending on the road conditions, this is about a one-and-a-half-hour drive. Winter driving conditions can be hazardous.

The combination of perilously dropping cliffs, cerulean glacial flow, dramatic waterfalls, and uninterrupted, fragrant pinery forms the best of all outdoor worlds. The drive along Highway 99, nicknamed the Sea-to-Sky Highway, is so gorgeous that you'll actually be relieved when a curve takes you away from the view and lets you get your mind back on driving. That doesn't happen very often during the first half of your trip, so be sure to agree beforehand about who's going to drive, or else take turns. Both of you should get a chance to gawk at the wonders that line the 90 miles of curvaceous highway from Vancouver to Whistler.

SHANNON FALLS

North of Vancouver on Highway 99, about halfway to Whistler on the east side of the road. Look for signs that identify Shannon Falls.

Highway turnoff sites are practical places to stop for momentary respites from the road and to review where you've just been or where you're heading. You don't have to hike anywhere, and the big-screen viewing begins the instant you stop. The turnoff to Shannon Falls is a turnoff-lover's view extravaganza.

Immediately after you pull off the main road into the parking area and silence the engine, you'll hear the thunder of a huge waterfall plummeting straight down the face of the mountain. One would expect to find such a spectacle at the end of a long, arduous trail and not in the middle of a rest area, but here it is nevertheless.

Before you leave Vancouver to start your trek up the mountain, be sure to pack a picnic to enjoy at the base of this lofty cataract. Then you can take full advantage of this very accessible scenic paradise.

WHISTLER RIVER ADVENTURES, Whistler
(604) 932-3532
Moderate

Call for directions and river conditions.

There's river rafting, and then there's river rafting through the majestic snowcapped peaks of Whistler's rugged, supernatural terrain. You will find that the memory of the journey lingers for months and perhaps even years. It is truly that awesome. Several different water excursions are available depending on your temperament and budget. Don't miss the excitement.

Gold Bridge

Hotel/Bed and Breakfast Kissing

TYAX MOUNTAIN LAKE RESORT, Gold Bridge
Tyaughton Lake Road
(604) 238-2221
Moderate

Call for directions; the trip up here is a long one and the road conditions can be arduous. There are alternatives to getting here that are less painful than driving directly.

An alpine meadow in the heart of the Canadian Rockies, a crystal-clear lake, mountain goats roaming the hillside, and eagles soaring overhead: this is the stuff of a country escape. Include in that picture an imposing log building enclosing 28 attractive rooms, rustic private cabins, an outdoor hot tub, and all the outdoor and indoor adventures you can imagine, and you have described Tyax Resort. It's all there, along with three meals graciously served in the main lodge every day.

Depending on the package you choose and the time of year you visit, the following are available to assure your outdoor entertainment:

snowshoes, skates, toboggans, mountain bikes, ice-fishing equipment, snowmobiles, horseback riding, windsurfing, river rafting, heli-hiking, fishing tours, floatplane fishing, sleigh rides, canoeing, cross-country skiing, tennis, and hayrides. You can even pan for gold, and if you don't find any the excursion is free. This unique lodge 110 miles north of Vancouver is a popular destination for conferences and, during the summer, family vacations.

SUNSHINE COAST

The Sunshine Coast is accessible only by ferryboat from the Horseshoe Bay ferry terminal, just past West Vancouver on Highway 99. The 40-minute ferry ride takes you through the mountain-ringed waters and islands of Howe Sound to Langdale. Here is where the Sunshine Coast starts.

It may seem odd that a part of the gray, rainy Canadian Southwest is referred to as "sunshine," yet once you travel this section of the world you'll find no more applicable term. The Sunshine Coast provides all the wonderful rugged sights and sounds you could want, and some other getaway opportunities you probably didn't think existed. Regardless of weather conditions, even on a misty foggy morning, the Sunshine Coast is beautiful.

The Sunshine Coast is geographically unique. You'll feel as though you've stumbled accidentally onto a remote, lengthy peninsula or a long skinny island, yet it is neither. This section of Canada, beginning at Langdale's ferry dock and ending at Powell River, is indeed part of the mainland, but because it's bordered on the north, south, and west by water and on the east by mountains, it is accessible only by ferry. And even though the ferry from Horseshoe Bay may seem packed, particularly on a summer day, and you may have to wait awhile to board it, the other cars will seem to disappear as you head north along the coast. It is unlikely you will encounter crowds again until you return to the mainland. The ferryboat ride is also one of the most visually glorious excursions you can experience. Don't hesitate to see the world from this vantage point; it is absolutely beautiful.

◆ **Romantic Warning:** The Sunshine Coast, for all its spectacular scenery, falls short in the area of accommodations and restaurants. There are plenty of places to stay and eat, but they are not of the same caliber as those found on the Canadian islands or in Whistler. Come here to enjoy the isolation and the incredible scenery available to the two of you at every turn.

Gibsons

Hotel/Bed and Breakfast Kissing

CASSIDY'S, Gibsons   💋
Cassidy Road
(604) 886-7222
Inexpensive

From Highway 101 heading north, look for the Lower Road sign and turn left and then immediately veer to the right. A mile down the road, turn left at Gulf Road and then right onto Cassidy.

I would love to give this place a four-lips rating. We were pampered and comfortable during our entire stay here. Breakfast was an outstanding array of freshly picked berries, a luscious cheese soufflé, homemade huckleberry muffins, carrot-coconut bread, and jams, all presented on English bone china. We were attentively served in the glass-enclosed solarium, where a wicker table and high-backed wicker chairs were framed by lush plants. On the sun deck there was a huge spa tub that overlooked a diverse, well-tended garden, tall fir trees, and the sparkling waters of the Strait of Georgia in the distance. Upon our departure we were even given a jar of the innkeeper's own blackberry jam.

It was all marvelous—except for the room, which was very small, and the bathroom, which was down the hall. Cassidy's is an authentic bed and breakfast where you literally share the home with the owners. It can feel a bit awkward if you're not accustomed to this style of accommodation. However, on the Sunshine Coast you will be hard put to do much better.

Restaurant Kissing

CHEZ PHILIPPE RESTAURANT, Gibsons   💋💋
Gower Point Road
(604) 886-2887
Moderate

From the ferry landing in Langdale, drive the short distance to Gibsons. Follow School Road north and turn left on South Fletcher Road, which becomes Gower Point Road. Follow the signs to Bonniebrook Bed and

Breakfast Lodge. Chez Philippe Restaurant is located in the lower half of this bed and breakfast.

Celebrate the rugged beauty of the Sunshine Coast (where it rains more often than it shines) from the shelter of a window table in the quiet country elegance of Chez Philippe's dining room. The hardwood floors, subdued floral fabrics, and Victorian decor are time-worn but commodious, and reminiscent of the lodge's former years.

Rouse your appetites with a view of a blazing sunset over the ocean's turbulent surf just across the street, and relish the flavors and aromas of ambrosial French cuisine. The grilled salmon served in a savory tarragon sauce or choice rack of lamb roasted with a mustard and seven-grain crust are two of many excellent entrées to enjoy next to the warm glow of a crackling fire.

◆ **Romantic Note:** The lodge offers six upstairs guest rooms, all sorely in need of renovation and not even remotely worth the money. Fortunately, plans for refurbishment are in the making. You might consider taking a peek, but you won't want to stay unless they've made some significant improvements.

Roberts Creek

Hotel/Bed and Breakfast Kissing

COUNTRY COTTAGE BED AND BREAKFAST,
Roberts Creek
Roberts Creek Road
(604) 885-7448
Inexpensive

From the Langdale ferry dock, drive north for 10 miles on Highway 101 to the turnoff for Roberts Creek. Turn left on Roberts Creek Road; the Country Cottage is on the right, before you come into the small town of Roberts Creek. Call for reservations.

Just up the street from Creek House (reviewed elsewhere in this section), this perfect country retreat is one of the few professionally run bed and breakfasts around here, and it is assuredly a place that is concerned with the needs of its guests. Only two rooms are available (although they have begun preparations for a third in a separate house in the backyard). The first is a snug, upstairs room in the main house, decorated in pink floral linens, where you can cozy up in a wicker chair in the connecting glass-enclosed, sunlit bathroom that doubles as a sitting room. The second, a rustic cabin adjacent to the main house, is even more conducive to romance. It is comfortable and secluded, geared for couples who like to be away from everything and everyone.

Breakfast is served in the kitchen to the sound of the wood-burning stove crackling in the background. Visit the sheep, hen house, and rambling rose gardens on your morning stroll as you sip coffee and wait for your farm-fresh breakfast to be served. After a hearty morning meal, the rest of the day can be spent lounging or searching out the area's adventures.

WILLOWS INN, Roberts Creek
3440 Beach Avenue
(604) 885-2452
Moderate

From the Langdale ferry dock, drive north for 10 miles on Highway 101 to the turnoff for Roberts Creek. Turn left on Roberts Creek Road, left again on Cedar Grove Road, then right on Beach Avenue. The Willows Inn is on the right just after Marlene Road.

Luxuriate in the sweet-smelling breeze of this Canadian Southwest paradise in the cozy warmth of a newly constructed wood cabin located two blocks from a private beach. Myriad colorful hanging plants and a surrounding, well-tended yard seclude the picturesque cabin from the owner's nearby log home, enhancing its intimate potential.

The cabin's fresh and simple country decor features sparkling hardwood floors, scattered throw rugs, green floral fabrics, comfy rocking chairs, and a wood stove set against a brick hearth. Wake to sunlight streaming through the skylights overhead and enjoy a healthy and abundant country breakfast of fresh-squeezed orange juice, seasonal fruit mixtures, granola, and fresh-baked muffins served directly to your cottage.

Once you've tasted the solitude and quiet splendor of this pastoral respite, you're likely to feel it's the Sunshine Coast's truest romantic option.

Restaurant Kissing

CREEK HOUSE, Roberts Creek
1041 Roberts Creek Road
(604) 885-9321
Expensive

From the Langdale ferry dock, drive north for 10 miles on Highway 101 to the turnoff for Roberts Creek. Turn left on Roberts Creek Road; Creek House is in the tiny town, across from the general store and post office.

French country dining has a romantic flair all its own, due in part to the blend of elegance and rural comforts. At Creek House, the supreme French cuisine and the relaxed, cordial ambience of a simply adorned dining room heated by a stone fireplace are more than any two hearts can endure without succumbing to romantic urges.

◆ **Romantic Suggestion:** After dinner, take a walk or drive to **ROBERTS CREEK PARK** and behold a sunset that will complete a gratify-ing day.

Sechelt

Hotel/Bed and Breakfast Kissing

BELLA BEACH MOTEL, Sechelt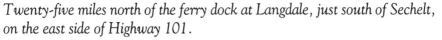
Highway 101
(604) 885-7191
Inexpensive to Moderate

Twenty-five miles north of the ferry dock at Langdale, just south of Sechelt, on the east side of Highway 101.

As I've mentioned, there isn't much in the way of romantic accommodations on the Sunshine Coast, unless you bring your own tent and stay in one of the many forested campgrounds lining the beaches and bays. But if roughing it isn't your idea of romance, Bella Beach Motel is one of your better options. Its large, comfortable, plain rooms face the vast ocean, with Vancouver Island looming in the distance. One drawback is that the main road lies between the motel and the water. Still, the view will engage you for hours and the traffic is never all that heavy, so the highway doesn't get in the way as much as you'd think.

The beach across the road and the accessibility to the entire coast make this a worthwhile place to use as a base while you explore the area. You'll also be pleased that right next to Bella Beach is **THE WHARF RESTAURANT**. Breakfast and lunch are reasonably priced, the food is well prepared, and the ambience cozy and attractive.

Outdoor Kissing

SMUGGLER COVE   ❤

Follow Highway 101 north for 10 miles past Sechelt to Smuggler Cove. The highway turns into an unpaved road, which ends at a parking area. From the parking lot, a short hike takes you out to the cove.

This is one of the coast's dozens of spectacular and isolated watery enclaves. After meandering a short distance through rain forest, you will be exposed to a view that is provocative in any weather. A sunny day reveals an entirely private inlet, etched from a fine assortment of rocky, jagged coastal formations. In the overcast opaqueness of a fall or winter day, you may imagine an English seaside underneath the clouds. Why not bring along some scones and a thermos filled with tea to snack on while you enjoy this haven. If by chance you hear some sounds emanating from the water or islands, don't be surprised. You've probably just happened upon a group of playful sea lions or otters frolicking in the afternoon sun or the evening tides.

◆ **Romantic Note:** There are really only two dining options in this section of the Sunshine Coast and both of these restaurants are attached to relatively time-worn accommodations. The first is **the JOLLY ROGER INN**, Secret Cove, (206) 885-7184, (Moderate). Jolly Roger's restaurant definitely isn't romantic, though the view of the cove is beautiful; the food is bland but fresh. Privately owned one- and two-bedroom condominiums are available for rent here. Although some of them have lovely water views, the decor throughout is dated and tasteless.

The second dining option is **LORD JIM'S**, Ole's Cove Road, Halfmoon Bay, (604) 885-7038, (Moderate to Expensive). Lord Jim's country-elegant dining room attains high scores in the "trying" cat-egory: candle-lit tables covered in neatly matching linens, natural wood paneling, and large bay windows that offer intimate views of the rocky crevasses lining Sechelt Inlet below. It is all exceedingly pretty. The food is good but not great. I think the kitchen is straining to do what it does. Perhaps a breakfast or lunch here is the best idea, when everything—including the menu—is a bit more relaxed.

Egmont

Outdoor Kissing

FERRYBOAT RIDE FROM EARL'S COVE
TO SALTERY BAY

From the ferry dock at Langdale, follow the signs on Highway 101 to Earl's Cove at the northern end of the highway. Be sure to check the schedule for ferry crossings from Earl's Cove.

If you don't have a chance to become acquainted with the Sunshine Coast from your own or a chartered boat, then the ferry crossing from Earl's Cove to Saltery Bay is a must. The passage affords a rare opportunity to partake of the marine enchantment this area is famous for. An array of snowcapped mountains frames your tour through the Jervis Inlet. The forested, rocky promontories jutting into the water are magnificent. Depending on the season, you may see whales as the ferry makes its way around and through this watery highway: stay here during the late winter and early spring, and they can perform at the most unexpected times of day.

SKOOKUMCHUCK NARROWS, Egmont

Drive north from Gibsons on Highway 101 for about 60 miles, following the signs to the ferryboat at Earl's Cove. Just before reaching the dock, you will see signs for Egmont and the narrows. Turn east and follow the road to the parking area. A quarter-mile hike will take you out to the narrows.

The Canadian Southwest and the Pacific Northwest are filled with more than enough natural wonders to impress the most jaded world traveler. Skookumchuck Narrows is one of the more intriguing phenomena. The enormous energy that passes through this place is so moving (figuratively and literally) that indescribable feelings are triggered. The trail to the narrows has abundant foliage; the ground is often carpeted in autumn-colored leaves and trees are wrapped in leis of moss. As you make your way out to the tip of the peninsula, you'll approach Sechelt Inlet on the east side. You can stand almost at the edge of the rock-bordered gateway to this body of water. Through this tiny portal, at high or low tide, the rush of water is so intense that the land actually shakes beneath your feet. This is the time and place when, without even kissing or touching, you can really feel the earth move.

> *"Love does not consist of gazing at each other but in looking together in the same direction."*
>
> Antoine du Saint Exupery

Washington State

OLYMPIC PENINSULA

Poulsbo

Hotel/Bed and Breakfast Kissing

THE MANOR FARM INN, Poulsbo   ◆◆◀
26069 Big Valley Road Northeast
(206) 779-4628
Expensive to Very Expensive

Call for directions.

A country outing can revive city-tired spirits to renewed ardor and ease, and the drive to Manor Farm Inn, through miles of idyllic landscape, will start the process. The inn deftly provides the rest of your amorous needs.

The French country farmhouse, encircled by a white picket fence and friendly farm animals, blends lovingly into the inn's 25 acres of pastoral scenery. Six cozy rooms fronting a long open veranda, plus an intimate loft hideaway, are located within the inn. Those who prefer more privacy can stay in an exclusive farm cottage with French country furnishings and vaulted ceilings, located directly across the street, or in a luxurious beach house (Unbelievably Expensive) with multilevel decks, a private hot tub, and stupendous views of Hood Canal. These two accommodations are the most romantic spots here. Throughout, hand-crafted pine furnishings and high, open-beamed ceilings enhance the authentic country atmosphere. The plush decor in neutral tones adds a certain elegance.

Mornings begin with a friendly knock and a wake-up call of "Scones!"—meaning that hot scones, homemade raspberry jam, and fresh orange juice are waiting just outside your door. Don't forget to save room for a hearty, all-American, three-course breakfast consisting of more scones, jam, porridge, eggs, bacon, sausage, new potatoes, and sautéed mushrooms. Unfortunately, this generous presentation is the same every day, which may disappoint guests who stay more than one or two nights.

The Manor Farm Inn's restaurant (Expensive) is open to all for dinner and is considered by many to be *the* place to eat on the Kitsap Peninsula. Its popularity can make the small dining room busy and loud. The four- and six-course (depending on the night) prix fixe meal has some great moments, plus the irresistible possibility of romance in a stark but elegant setting. Grilled game hen with brandied apple filling and seared scallops crusted with hazelnuts and wine are wonderful. The locals may keep things less than sedate, but dining like this is worth the chance.

◆ **Romantic Warning:** One of the guest rooms is too close to the hustle and bustle of the reception area and dining room. The sounds of clanking dishes and loud voices could certainly put a damper on an otherwise amorous mood.

Seabeck

Hotel/Bed and Breakfast Kissing

WILCOX HOUSE, Seabeck
2390 Tekiu Road
(206) 830-4492
Moderate

Call for directions.

The Wilcox House is one of the premier places to kiss on the Kitsap Peninsula. What we found here exceeded our wildest imaginings. After we got off the ferry and passed Bremerton, we drove through 14 miles of towering evergreens and rolling countryside. As we reached the turnoff for the house, the road took a steep turn down to the water and we passed under a dramatic log-and-stone archway. In front of us appeared an enormous, copper-roofed mansion with terra-cotta tiles, resting on a forested bluff with views of Hood Canal and the Olympics.

The 10,000-square-foot interior is a masterpiece (a bit on the eclectic side) that cost more than $300,000 to restore. Each room has been diligently brought back to life, from the copper-framed fireplaces, walnut paneling, and scarlet wool carpeting to the wood parquet floors and the 600 new window panes. This place has to be seen to be believed! The two comfortable guest suites have views of the sweeping lawn, the gardens, mountain peaks, and water; one has a spa tub, the other a private deck. There is also a built-in swimming pool in the backyard. Breakfast is a remarkable presentation of fresh fruits and waffles with homemade apple and blueberry syrups and apple and blueberry butters, served in a glass-enclosed dining room with the same impressive views.

◆ **Romantic Must:** The innkeepers at Wilcox House serve a formal four-course dinner on weekends that is available to guests as well as those not staying overnight. This is a meal you will thoroughly appreciate. Your salad will include 20 different greens and edible flowers, and you'll enjoy freshly baked herb bread and creatively prepared vegetables, among other savory delights.

Port Ludlow

Hotel/Bed and Breakfast Kissing

WEATHERFORD INN, Port Ludlow
941 Shine Road
(206) 437-0332
Moderate

Call for reservations and directions.

This immense, newly built Nantucket-style house is situated directly on the Hood Canal, with an amazing six acres of private sandy waterfront. Depending on the time of year, great blue herons, bald eagles, orca whales, and sea lions pass through this area; like you they are enjoying a true Northwest habitat. What is not so purely Northwest is that during the heat of summer, you can actually take a dip in the shallow inlet, it gets that warm—well, almost.

Inside, the main living room has floor-to-ceiling French doors that fill the country-dignified room with light. Guests can gaze at the spectacular scenery and glimpse Mount Rainier in the distance, or warm themselves in front of the wood-burning fireplace. Five rooms are available, three of which have views of the water. The innkeeper's attention to detail can be seen everywhere: canopied beds decorated in floral linens, perfectly matched hand-painted lamps, fabrics and linens imported from Europe, private bathrooms with hardwood floors covered by ultra-soft throw rugs, plush sitting areas, and wide windows lined with colorful flower boxes. The two rooms that don't have views are compensated with large soaking tubs that can accommodate two (but one room has double beds; *not* romantic). The view rooms have simple, smaller bathrooms.

In the morning, enjoy more of the view as you relish a full breakfast that may include fresh fruit, fresh-squeezed juice, and a cheese omelet.

◆   **Romantic Note:** At present, the yard is unkempt, but plans for a traditional English garden are in the making.

Port Townsend

From Seattle take the Winslow ferry to Bainbridge Island and follow the signs north to the Hood Canal Bridge. Take Highway 104 north to Highway 20, which leads directly into Port Townsend.

Port Townsend, a small town at the extreme northeast corner of the Olympic Peninsula, was originally settled in the 1800s. Authentic and loving restoration of period architecture is this town's trademark. Its beautifully restored, vintage Victorian homes perch on a bluff overlooking the waterfront, and the nearby parks, shops, and restaurants project an aura of charm and tranquillity. A favorite weekend getaway for Seattleites escaping hectic urban life, especially in the summer, Port Townsend is cozy and slow-paced all year long. A walk around the waterfront district and the bluffs above it will give you outstanding views of the Olympics and island-dotted Puget Sound.

Hotel/Bed and Breakfast Kissing

THE CABIN, Port Townsend
839 North Jacob Miller Road
(206) 385-5571
Inexpensive

Call for directions.

The Cabin is a very small, rustic cedar home that doesn't look like much from the outside, but the ultra-secluded location and the pioneer motif of the interior design make it really quite cozy (except for the rustic bathroom, which is not the best). The place is stocked with all the necessities of romance, including a tiny kitchen where fresh-baked delectables are delivered daily. You are invited to use the innkeepers' designer deck, which has an expansive view over the Strait of Juan de Fuca to Vancouver Island, and there is a fire pit outside for late-night bonfires. The real reason to come to The Cabin is for the peace and quiet, because the only sounds you'll hear during your stay are the breezes rustling in the trees, the waves lapping the shore, and the occasional horn of a tug or ship as it passes by on a cloudy morning.

JAMES HOUSE BED AND BREAKFAST, Port Townsend ◆◆◆
1238 Washington Street
(206) 385-1238
Inexpensive to Moderate

Take Highway 20 into Port Townsend, where Highway 20 becomes Sims Way. Before you enter the main part of town, look on your left for Washington Street, which branches off and heads up a hill overlooking the waterfront.

James House has undergone some much-needed refurbishment by the new innkeepers, who are infatuated with this venerable structure and are turning it back into the showplace it used to be. This handsome building—filled with recovered and refinished period pieces, intricate handcrafted wood moldings, and capacious, unique rooms—is as Victorian as they get in Port Townsend, and that's saying quite a bit. The 12 guest rooms are scattered along a labyrinth of hallways. There are lots of bay windows, fireplaces, white linens, views of the bay and mountains, and cozy alcoves designed for snuggling. A private cottage set in the well-tended garden is also available.

OLD CONSULATE INN, Port Townsend
313 Walker Street
(206) 385-6753
Inexpensive to Moderate

Take Highway 20 into Port Townsend, where it becomes Sims Way. Before you enter the main part of town, look on your left for Washington Street, which branches off and heads up a hill overlooking the waterfront. Follow Washington Street for about three blocks to Walker Street and turn left.

If you're smitten with the idea of pampering yourselves in an atmosphere of days gone by, with the modern addition of pleasing creature comforts, then the Old Consulate Inn is exactly right for you. This gracious inn has a music room with an antique organ and grand piano, a fireplace-warmed study, a reading nook in the front parlor, a billiards/games room in the newly finished basement, and a handsome wood-framed breakfast area. Elegant period antiques abound, but never to excess. At the top of the grand oak staircase you'll find eight spacious private rooms, each with its own bath. There are sitting alcoves, turret lookouts, canopied king-size beds, and expansive views of the waterfront. They are all such wonderful retreats that you'll want to leave only for breakfast.

The morning meal is a gastronomic fantasy come true. The inn proudly serves its own blend of designer coffee along with five full courses—fresh fruits, liqueur cakes, pastries, egg bakes, homemade granolas, and sherry or an appropriate liqueur.

RAVENSCROFT INN, Port Townsend
533 Quincy Street
(206) 385-2784
Inexpensive to Moderate

On Quincy Street between Clay and Franklin.

I've often heard that the best way to judge the overall quality of a hotel, inn, or bed and breakfast is to look at the least expensive rooms in the house. If these units are nearly as splendid and comfortable as the more expensive ones, then you are assured of a sensational place with a management that really cares about its guests. Such is the case at Ravenscroft Inn.

Every guest room in this newly constructed redwood inn is supreme. Many of the suites have French doors that open onto a balcony with views of the bay and mountains, some have spacious sitting areas and fireplaces, and every room has immaculate, attractive baths, plush comfort, unlimited privacy, and room to spare. The open kitchen borders the dining area, where a stone fireplace warms the room as your breakfast is served. Classical music accompanies such creations as a frappé of frozen berries, bananas, and yogurt; a layered egg dish of tomatoes, onions, and spinach; Cointreau-drenched French toast; and fresh-baked breads. Sheer perfection!

A ROOM WITH A VIEW, Port Townsend
319 Tyler, at Jefferson
(206) 385-4504
Moderate

Call for directions.

True to its name, this romantic respite, sheltered beneath old honey locust trees in the backyard of an 1887 Victorian home, offers serene water views from its perch on a bluff with the utmost privacy. The singular wood-shingled cabin exudes a rural country charm unique to the area, and is surrounded by an overgrown garden and enclosed by a white picket fence.

You are sure to feel at home in the cabin, which is graced with high ceilings and a skylight, ample sunlight, well-polished wood floors, and an inviting queen-size four-poster bed. Luxuriate in the plush red sofa next to the wood stove or cook dinner for two in the full adjoining modern kitchen. Conclude your interlude with a cup of steaming coffee on the deck in the morning, and bask in the sunshine filtering across views of distant but shimmering Puget Sound. Although breakfast is not included with your room, you can run to the nearby bakery for desired sweets.

ANN STARRETT MANSION, Port Townsend
744 Clay Street
(206) 385-3205
Inexpensive to Expensive

Follow Highway 20 into Port Townsend, where it turns into Sims Way and then into Water Street. From Water Street, turn left on Quincy and follow it up the hill. Turn right on Adams and right again on Franklin.

Port Townsend's luxurious past has been beautifully and authentically reclaimed in this sprawling green-gabled Victorian mansion, settled on a bluff in a quiet residential district overlooking Puget Sound and the mountains beyond.

Be forewarned that this estate is popular with tourists and is open daily for self-guided tours before guests are allowed to check in. Fortunately, the tourists should have cleared out by the time you arrive, and you can delight in the private opulence of this magnificent Victorian home.

The authentic turn-of-the-century architecture, frescoed ceilings, and circular staircase that spirals toward the eight-sided dome ceiling above embrace you in stunning splendor. The rooms, needless to say, are no less extravagant. The downstairs garden suites are the least expensive, but are still extremely pleasant, with brick walls, a burbling fountain in the garden just outside, and snuggly floral down comforters; most have private baths with antique claw-foot tubs. All of the rooms are plush yet comfortable, complete with rich color schemes, original period furnishings, antique brass and canopied beds, and lace curtains. The upstairs Gable Suite, located in the top of the mansion, is especially grand and private, with skylights, views of the water, and a private soaking tub. Despite the enticement of a full gourmet breakfast served in the elegant dining room, honeymooners have been known to disappear for entire weekends up here.

SECRET GARDEN GUEST HOUSE, Port Townsend
3333 Eddy Street
(206) 385-6983
Moderate

Call for directions.

This garden cottage is the best-kept secret in Port Townsend. Obscure, very private, and nestled in the trees amidst miles of rural country, it is a nature lover's dream. Although the grounds are rundown and could use some tending, they provide a unique and tranquil alternative to the commercialized luxury of the sprawling Victorian-style bed-and-breakfast mansions found elsewhere in Port Townsend.

The cabin is spacious but cozy, replete with a queen-size bed, snug floral down comforter, a homey assortment of pillows, a wood stove, an eclectic assortment of antiques, and convenient kitchen amenities, including a refrigerator, microwave, wok, and hot plate. Breakfast is not served in the morning, but granola, popcorn, wine, cheese, fruit, and scones are provided beforehand for your leisurely enjoyment. Sip some wine, nibble on a strawberry, and relish the breezy country privacy as you run to and from the nearby private outdoor hot tub ensconced in the woods.

Restaurant Kissing

BELMONT RESTAURANT AND SALOON,
Port Townsend
925 Water Street
(206) 385-3007
Inexpensive

Follow Highway 20 into Port Townsend, where it turns into Sims Way, and then into Water Street. The restaurant is located three blocks past the ferry landing.

The brick-and-wood interior, lofty ceilings, and unhindered water views of the Belmont Restaurant and Saloon will lure you to stay for lunch or dinner, despite its vinyl peach-colored tablecloths and paper napkins. The wood booths nestled along the entrance offer the most privacy, but you'll want to request window or patio seating to partake in the heavenly waterfront views.

An adjoining saloon might project more noise than you care for and the seafood is mediocre, if not bland and boring. However, the magnificent views and phenomenally low prices will assure you that you've made the right romantic choice.

MANRESA CASTLE RESTAURANT
AND LOUNGE, Port Townsend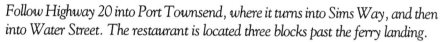
Seventh Street and Sheridan Street
(206) 385-5750
Moderate to Expensive

From Highway 20 heading north, turn left onto Sheridan, just before you enter the town of Port Townsend. The castle is ahead of you on the right.

Manresa Castle was closed for a while to undergo renovations that were supposed to return this esteemed mansion to its former brilliance and glory. Unfortunately, the only brilliance and glory to be found here is on the main floor, where the restaurant and lounge are located. Both of these spots are thoroughly captivating. But the 36 rooms upstairs appear to have been left untouched except for some new bedspreads, televisions, and Queen Anne-style dressers.

Even though I don't recommend an overnight stay, you will be enchanted by a lunch, dinner, or a drink in the lounge. The stately cocktail lounge is a most irresistible setting for a romantic interlude, and next to it there's an unpretentious dining room where tall lace-covered windows, soft lighting, and handsome wood furniture create an intimate, inviting atmosphere. The service is attentive and considerate, and the innovative continental menu is wonderful.

RANDAL'S RESTAURANT, Port Townsend
1004 Water Street, lobby of the Palace Hotel
(206) 379-9659
Moderate

Follow Highway 20 into Port Townsend, where it turns into Sims Way and then into Water Street. Randal's is located two blocks past the ferry landing, in the lobby of the Palace Hotel.

The brick-faced Palace Hotel is nestled among the storefronts in Port Townsend's charming downtown. Although it's delightfully reminiscent of a turn-of-the-century Victorian seaport hotel, you'll find more pleasing and restful accommodations elsewhere, away from the city's bustle.

The Palace Hotel's finest space is its cozy restaurant, nestled in the upper floor of the Victorian-style lobby. A handful of tables draped in white linen and accented with fresh flowers brighten up the otherwise unadorned room, making it a favorable location for a quiet dinner for two. Savor grilled salmon with fresh ginger and sesame sauce, or fresh prawns stuffed with herbed cream cheese, shrimp, salmon, and halibut. Your meal will be a delectable and affordable appetizer to an evening stroll along the picturesque waterfront streets of Port Townsend.

Outdoor Kissing

CHETZEMOKA PARK, Port Townsend

Follow Water Street east through downtown Port Townsend until it dead-ends just before the marina. Go north on Monroe Street for seven short blocks and then east on Blaine for one block to the park.

I told a group of people I was off to explore romantic locations on the Olympic Peninsula. Within moments one of them slipped me a note that read: "There are parks and then there are parks, but there is only one Chetzemoka." I agree. This ocean-flanked park makes picnicking a treasured outing for two people, particularly a couple who love surroundings that enhance the aesthetic appeal of cheese, fruit, and wine.

Here you can wander through scattered pinery along a cliff with an eagle's-eye view of Admiralty Inlet and Whidbey Island. Thick grass, a footbridge over a babbling brook, a few well-spaced picnic tables, and swings make this traditional, picturesque park a standout. Whether your penchant is for a playful or a peaceful diversion, you will be pleased by Chetzemoka Park.

Port Angeles

Hotel/Bed and Breakfast Kissing

DOMAINE MADELEINE, Port Angeles
146 Wildflower Lane, on Finn Hall Road
(206) 457-4174
Moderate

Call for directions.

Olympic National Park serves as a backdrop to the town of Port Angeles, filling the area with natural wonder. Wonderful accommodations, however, are not so easy to come by. Most of the local bed and breakfasts are geared toward comfort but lack style. Domaine Madeleine is a definite exception to this rule. Nestled behind tall Douglas firs, this contemporary home perched on a bluff above the Strait of Juan de Fuca offers incredible views of Vancouver Island and the San Juans, the Canadian Coast Range, and Mount Baker. As if the view weren't enough, the grounds are covered with rhododendrons, flowering perennials, maples, cedars, pines, and an intriguing replica of Monet's garden, specially designed by the resident botanist/innkeeper. While exploring here, you might catch a glimpse of browsing deer, a bald eagle overhead, or gray whales just off the shore.

Expansive windows throughout the house allow you to enjoy the captivating view. Hardwood floors, high ceilings, and an impressive basalt fireplace in the living room give Domaine Madeleine a comfortable Northwest feel, while Asian and European antiques add an international flair. All three guest suites come with fresh flowers, a fruit basket, chocolates, and an array of French perfumes. The Impressionist Suite has a great view facing the water, as well as a tiled shower built for two. The Renoir Suite is rather small and is usually used as an extension of the Impressionist Suite, but this room does have adjoining doors that open into the living room area. Guests who stay in this room are invited to close off all other doors to have that area to themselves in the evenings—a nice bonus for a less expensive room.

The Ming Suite surpasses the other rooms in comfort, style, and overall kissability. This room occupies the entire upper floor and includes a 30-foot balcony where you can watch the sun both rise and set, a free-standing fireplace, and a king-size bed. A spacious bathroom contains a two-person tiled Jacuzzi tub complete with scented candles and a stunning view of the Olympic Mountains through a diagonal window; the view is also reflected in the mirror around the tub. If the smell of fresh French bread and remarkable French cuisine weren't so tempting every morning, it would be nearly impossible to leave this room. But force yourselves! You don't want to miss seafood omelets, crêpes Suzette flamed in cognac and Grand Marnier, or Vesuvial bananas flamed in rum sauce. The innkeepers here are eager to please and will make you feel right at home—only much more pampered.

LAKE CRESCENT and LAKE CRESCENT LODGE,
Port Angeles
Highway 101
(206) 928-3211
Moderate to Expensive

On the northern edge of Olympic National Park, accessible just off Highway 101. When you approach Lake Crescent, look for signs indicating the way to the lodge. (The lodge is closed October 29 through April 29.)

A sunny day here may wreak havoc with your senses and emotions. Lake Crescent Lodge rests on the bank of its enormous namesake, and from your white-shingled cabin—heated by a wood stove or a stone fireplace—you can view this glassy stretch of water as it curves around forested mountains that ascend magnificently in the distance. Inhale deeply the fragrant air that permeates this epic landscape. The bond you and your loved one forge amid all this beauty will be strong and everlasting.

If you're just passing through, stop at the lodge's attractive restaurant and savor a traditional mountain breakfast with robust fresh coffee (a rare find outside of a major city or town), a wholesome lunch, or a selection of dinner entrées ranging from king salmon to Hood Canal oysters in a smooth remoulade.

◆ **Romantic Note:** The most romantic accommodations at the lodge are the Roosevelt Fireplace Cottages.

◆ **Second Romantic Note:** The drive around the perimeter of the lake is a monumental treat. (Be sure to check seasonal accessibility.) Take the time to see the whole thing and refresh yourselves with a swim in summer or an energetic hike at other times of the year.

Outdoor Kissing

DEER PARK

Deer Park is southeast of Port Angeles, in Olympic National Park. From Highway 101 turn south at the sign for Deer Park. The park is at the end of this 17-mile drive. For more information about Olympic National Park, call (206) 452-0330.

My recommendation to make the drive to Deer Park comes with a warning. The countless switchbacks and sharp turns you'll encounter on this predominantly unpaved road will be hair-raising. With conditions like this, you need to be guaranteed that at the end there's a payoff. Rest assured there is, and suffer this road's indignities. The reward on a clear day is an enthralling view deep into the heart of the Olympics. And because of the road conditions, you are likely to find yourselves quite alone. Most everyone else will drive the paved road to Hurricane Ridge (which has an absolutely astounding view of the Olympics), due south of Port Angeles just off Highway 101. The purple mountain majesty of Deer Park is all yours.

◆ **Romantic Note:** Ask at the ranger station (open in summer only) about the arduous hike up Blue Mountain. Even your sore thighs will thank you for the view at the summit.

◆ **Romantic Suggestion:** Before heading out on this excursion, consider brunching at the **FIRST STREET HAVEN**, 107 East First Street, Port Angeles, (206) 457-0352, (Very Inexpensive). Their hearty, health-conscious breakfasts and lunches are flavorful and creative. The Sunlight Omelet, overflowing with herbs, peppers, spinach, Parmesan, and provolone, is sure to keep you trekking while on the mountain. Most likely you'll be too stuffed for a fresh-baked pastry or muffin, but take an

apricot scone for the road—it will taste even better after your hike.
Make that two; you don't want to fight over who gets the bigger piece.

OLYMPIC HOT SPRINGS

*Just southwest of Port Angeles on Highway 101, follow the signs to the Elwha
campgrounds. Stay on this road past the ranger station and for another four miles
around Lake Mills. There the road dead-ends. Park your car along the side of
the road, where you are likely to see a handful of other parked vehicles. The old
road ahead, now in disuse, continues for 2.4 miles uphill to the hot springs.*

I don't understand why people in the Northwest seem to be infatuated
with soaking in outdoor hot tubs fashioned by nature. Even when these
bubbling springs of earth-heated water are located in the midst of
piercingly beautiful scenery, the piercing smell of sulfur is enough to
make you sick. And then there's the problem of running into people
you'd never want to share your bathtub with. I'll take a chlorinated
Jacuzzi hot tub any day.

Well, in spite of all this, my aquatic husband and my nonaquatic self
ventured up to Olympic Hot Springs on his insistence that I didn't know
what I was missing and that I would be doing a disservice to my readers
if I didn't tell them about the wonders of simmering in a mud-bottomed,
smelly pool of geothermally heated water.

The uphill walk passed through forest, and that was wonderful. And
because we started late in the day, we saw a number of drip-drying people
heading back who gave us words of encouragement: "Not much farther."
"It's great, keep going." As we crossed a log bridge over the effervescent
waters of the Elwha River, the aroma of the nearby springs hit me like
a lead balloon. The stone-and-log pools were terraced along a hillside.
When my husband saw this he joyfully ran ahead, stripped down to his
swimsuit, and enthusiastically plunged in.

When I finally took the plunge I was surprised at how clean the water
looked. The water that surges up from the earth's center constantly
replaces the "used" water, which spills over the rim. The bottom wasn't
all that muddy, though, yes, the odor was omnipresent and offensive.
But to my amazement, my skin did feel silky smooth and we didn't see
another person the entire time we were there.

Neah Bay

Outdoor Kissing

CAPE FLATTERY

Highway 101 intersects Highway 112 a few miles west of Port Angeles. Take Highway 112 west along the coast to the town of Sekiu. Twenty miles west of Sekiu is Neah Bay, and Cape Flattery is 8.5 miles northwest of there.

Sekiu is a small, unassuming fishing village with a handful of motels lining the dock. The town is only 28.5 miles from the northwestern tip of the continental United States, which makes it the gateway to some of the most scintillating scenery anywhere. Drive ahead to Neah Bay just so you can gaze along the Strait of Juan de Fuca, flanked on one side by Washington's shoreline and rugged inlets and on the other by Vancouver Island's striking mountainous profile. But don't stop here; the best is yet to come.

Drive farther northwest to Cape Flattery. Here you can camp or just stop long enough to embrace and behold nightfall. A 30-minute hike down a wooded trail brings you to an astounding corner of the world. Your urban temperaments will mellow as you watch the cinematic sunset over the rock-strewn beach and the fall of dusk on Tatoosh Island.

HOBUCK BEACH PARK, Neah Bay
645-2422
$10 per evening

Call for directions to this private campground (open summer only—June 15 through August 30).

Campers weary of campsites that are merely parking lots with modern amenities for motor homes can find refuge in a tiny piece of paradise stretching along the outer reaches of the Pacific Ocean. Located in the heart of a Native American reservation, this private oceanfront property attracts few tourists. Take your pick of campsites that are set back from the ocean (you can't pitch a tent on the beach) and secluded by trees and brush, with an expansive view of the empty beach. Share a solitary sunset that will surround you in hues of orange and pink. If you keep your eyes open long enough, you might catch a glimpse of the village horses running together across the beach or deer wandering near the campsites looking for tidbits.

For those who don't want to rough it, weathered cabins are also available, complete with showers and kitchenettes. The cabins, however, are not next to the water and offer less privacy.

◆ **Romantic Warning:** Keep in mind that this area does not typically cater to tourists. Consequently, the campground office, cabins, and surrounding village are in a state of disrepair. Also, don't leave any of your food loose or unattended; the crows will carry it away!

SHI SHI BEACH

Drive seven miles southwest of Neah Bay until you come to something that resembles a parking area with signs for the beach. Look over the embankment adjacent to this parking lot and you will see an expansive, empty beach on Makah Bay. Hike from the parking lot through three miles of forest and beach trail to Shi Shi.

In its magnitude and overwhelming presence, this eight-mile stretch of untainted beach rivals any along the entire west coast of the United States. There really are no adjectives equal to the task of describing its hundreds of sea stacks, cliffs, forest, sand, and waves. And because it takes a bit of stamina to get there, you might find yourselves alone at this edge of the world.

La Push

Outdoor Kissing

THIRD BEACH

Follow the signs on Highway 101 to La Push, on the northwestern coast of the Olympic Peninsula. There is only one road that goes south of La Push along the coast. Two miles down this road is a small, barely noticeable sign indicating Third Beach and an unmarked parking area at the trailhead. A three-quarter-mile walk on a forest path brings you to the beach.

A dear friend introduced me to Third Beach several summers ago. He said that when his city life gets too crazy, he reclaims his sanity in the wilderness, and Third Beach is one of his favorite places to go and do that. When I arrived there I understood why.

You can run barefoot for two miles along this surf-pounded beach of firm sand, and there are hidden caves and rock formations to explore along the way. At low tide you can climb onto what at high tide are islands and marvel at tide pools full of trapped sealife. As is true with any angel-sent outing, day's end will come too soon; be sure to take a seashell or some weather-aged pebbles back home with you as a keepsake of your beautiful time together.

HOH RAIN FOREST

On Highway 101 south of Forks, on the northwest side of the Olympic National Forest, look for signs directing you to the Hoh Visitor Center, (206) 374-6925, which is 19 miles east of the highway. Inquire there about the hikes available at your skill level.

The Hoh Rain Forest shows what Mother Nature can do when she has an abundance of moisture (150 inches of rain annually) to thrive on. Every inch of ground, including decaying trees, is covered with moss, lichens, mushrooms, ferns, and sorrel. As you pass under this forest canopy, you will also see some of the largest spruce, fir, and cedar trees in the world. Some of the moss-laden evergreens here are 300 feet tall and 23 feet around. On a rare sunny day, streams of light penetrate the thick foliage in a golden misty haze. Don't even try to restrain the joy and excitement you'll feel with every step. And since you can't restrain the moisture that oozes from the ground, be certain to wear waterproof shoes.

Forks

Hotel/Bed and Breakfast Kissing

KALALOCH LODGE, Forks
Highway 101
(206) 962-2271
Inexpensive to Moderate

The village of Kalaloch lies northwest of Quinault and south of the Hoh River Valley. The lodge is on the west side of the road, directly off Highway 101.

The Pacific Ocean is Kalaloch's front-yard entertainment and the primary reason to be here. During low tide, take a long, sandy hike along the shore accompanied by sea gulls drifting overhead. At high tide, the ocean surf resounds in the air. If you would like enough time to enjoy all tidal phases, stay overnight in the eclectic assortment of accommodations here. The main lodge has nine adequate, airy rooms and a mediocre oceanside restaurant. Farther down, on a bluff overlooking the ocean, are 16 newer cedar cabins and six older rustic log cabins. Several of these have fireplaces, all are very comfortable and roomy, and most have views of the sovereign sunsets and ethereal seascape. Close by, there's a fairly new motel-style building with another 10 units, most of which have wonderful views, fireplaces, sliding glass doors, and lots of room. In the evening after dinner, light a fire, turn the lights down low, and launch into a night of ghost stories, giggling, and cuddling.

Quinault

Hotel/Bed and Breakfast Kissing

LAKE QUINAULT LODGE, Quinault   💋
South Shore Road
(206) 288-2571
Inexpensive to Moderate

Thirty-one miles south of Kalaloch on Highway 101, turn east on South Shore Road. Proceed two miles to the lodge.

This isn't the fanciest lodge you will ever visit, unless you think video games in the bar and faux fireplaces in the guest rooms are fancy, and you may want to call first to be sure a convention group isn't booked at the same time you are. You'll also want to reserve a place in the older section of the lodge, where the rooms are quaint but small, and think twice about the newer units, which are comfortable but have an ultra-tacky decor.

Still, there are details that make Lake Quinault Lodge fairly enticing. What more could someone with tender intentions require than a grand, cedar-shingled rustic lodge with a massive stone fireplace in the lobby or a view of a mountain lake cradled by the evolutionary masterpiece that is the Olympic Rain Forest? Not enough? Add to that numerous eerily intriguing hikes to take after a relaxed breakfast or lunch. (Be sure to order the standard items from the menu; this restaurant doesn't do well if it has to mix more than three ingredients at a time.) And on a clear day, include a lake cruise just before sunset. Still something missing? Just nuzzle together to quickly forget which way lies civilization and realize that sometimes a location like this and your certain someone are all you really need.

SAN JUAN ISLANDS

Several of the islands are accessible by ferryboat from Anacortes, one and a half hours north of Seattle. For information on departure times, call the Washington State Ferries at (206) 464-6400, or toll-free (800) 542-7052.

There are 172 islands in the San Juan archipelago, each with stunning terrain, a distinctive character, and some with bustling villages. As you circumnavigate the most popular island grouping by ferryboat—Orcas Island, San Juan Island, and Lopez Island—you may be reminded of the island-dotted Caribbean, a notable difference being that the San Juans are much more spectacular in their topography. Of course, you won't see any palm trees here, and because you're about as far north as you can go in the continental United States, the blush on your cheeks will be from the cold and not the equatorial heat. But so much the better: cool cheeks give you a snuggling advantage.

Deciding on the one ideal destination won't be an easy task. You can opt for the comfort of the more populated islands or, if you own or have chartered a boat, you can homestead on one of the lesser-known islands, setting up camp for a more back-to-basics holiday. Wherever you put down roots, you'll be happy.

◆ **Romantic Note:** To save a lot of time and frustration, check with the **VISITOR INFORMATION CENTER,** (206) 468-3663. They can lead you in the right direction for outdoor activities and campgrounds. Always check seasonal hours and rates whenever you choose a restaurant or island accommodations.

San Juan Island

Hotel/Bed and Breakfast Kissing

FRIDAY'S, San Juan Island
35 First Street, Friday Harbor
(206) 378-5848
Expensive

From the ferry landing, take the first right onto First Street. Friday's is one block down on the left-hand corner.

The gray clapboard house, built in 1891, was a youth hostel before its attractive reincarnation as an island bed-and-breakfast/restaurant in the heart of Friday Harbor. The noise from the bar and bistro downstairs can be a big problem for guests, yet you may be able to forgive this distraction once you see the luxurious top-floor Eagle Cove Suite. It will be hard not to feel pampered here, as you melt in the large Jacuzzi tub set in a beautiful green-and-maroon tiled bathroom with brass and wood furnishings. The high ceiling, floral down comforter, king-size bed, and views of the harbor take your mind off the busy town life below. Interesting note: This suite is the most expensive on the island.

The other seven small guest rooms at Friday's on the main floor share three baths, as well as a plain but comfortable common room where continental breakfast is served, but almost feel part of the bar. These are assuredly not the reason to stay here. If you can handle the steep tab for the Eagle Cove Suite, you will be elated with this island getaway.

HILLSIDE HOUSE, San Juan Island
365 Carter Avenue, Friday Harbor
(206) 378-4730
Moderate

From the ferry landing, take the second right onto Second Street. Follow Second until you reach Carter Avenue and turn right. Hillside House is on the left, half a block down.

Don't let the dilapidated farm in the backyard deter you from appreciating the finer points of Hillside House. Perched high in the newly renovated section of this contemporary island home is the irresistible Eagles' Nest Suite, a sparkling upstairs loft awash in sunlight from the expansive windows. Cathedral ceilings give a feeling of generous space, and a Jacuzzi tub, king-size bed, and small private deck overlooking the harbor in the distance are additional welcome luxuries.

The remaining six guest rooms are pleasant but rather plain (and appropriately less expensive), and feel more like somebody's extra bedroom, especially in comparison to the upstairs suite. However, the hosts are warm and amiable, and will encourage you to relax in their plush living room or wander through their private aviary filled with pheasant and ducks. In the morning you are guaranteed to enjoy the full breakfast of orange French toast, egg dishes, and island jams.

LONESOME COVE RESORT, San Juan Island
5810-A Lonesome Cove Road, Friday Harbor
(206) 378-4477
Moderate to Expensive

From the ferry dock at Friday Harbor, follow the signs to Roche Harbor. Just before you enter Roche Harbor, turn right on Rouleau Road. Two miles east of Roche Harbor turn right at Limestone Point Road and then left on Lonesome Cove Road.

Lonesome Cove Resort combines rustic living and secluded island comfort. The cabins are located on a sandy beach, 20 feet beyond the high-tide mark, and are backed by several acres of dense forest. Manicured lawns extend down to the water, and deer leisurely eat apples on the grass. This is a desirable place for an arm-in-arm walk, with trees, beach, and rocks to explore.

The cabins are assembled like village hideaways, and they are all genuinely homespun. Their prime assets are fireplaces and big glass windows that overlook Speiden Channel, Speiden Island, and, off in the distance, Vancouver Island. By the way, the name of this resort is misleading; with the right someone, lonesomeness here is unthinkable.

OLYMPIC LIGHTS BED AND BREAKFAST,
San Juan Island
4531-A Cattle Point Road, Friday Harbor
(206) 378-3186
Inexpensive to Moderate

From the ferry landing at Friday Harbor, follow Spring Street and turn left on Argyle Avenue. Turn left again on Argyle Road, which eventually becomes Cattle Point Road. Just before you come to American Camp you'll see a little sign for Olympic Lights. Turn right to the house.

Generally, I hesitate to recommend a bed and breakfast where the rooms share baths, for all the obvious unromantic reasons. But Olympic Lights is worth making an exception for, and once you experience it you'll know why. In what seems to be the middle of nowhere, you'll find this house sitting in a pristine meadow overlooking the nearby water and mountains. Serenity here is practically guaranteed.

The interior of this sparkling clean Victorian home is whimsically appointed with soft-sculptured rabbits entwined in gold stars, along with some very unusual artwork. There is a lovely room on the ground level right off the kitchen with its own bath, but the rooms that share two baths upstairs are really wonderful. The Ra Room (named after the Egyptian sun god) is eminently comfortable, and the morning sun pours through its windows onto your well-rested faces. You won't have to leave the downy white bed to see dawn break over the waving fields and the bay. But do get up in time to indulge in the lavish farm-fresh breakfast.

◆ **Romantic Note:** When you arrive at Olympic Lights, you will be asked to remove your shoes before going upstairs to your room—and the reason is crystal clear. The upper level is completely covered with snow-white carpeting.

TRUMPETER INN, San Juan Island
420 Trumpeter Way, Friday Harbor
(206) 378-3884
Inexpensive to Moderate

Call for directions.

This contemporary bed and breakfast rests in a pastoral valley just outside the town of Friday Harbor. The name honors the beautiful trumpeter swans that glide across the nearby ponds. This is a genuinely private getaway with views in the distance of False Bay and the Olympic Mountains beyond the strait. Every room is brightly decorated and exceptionally comfortable, with private baths, down comforters, and the sounds of the countryside's own natural music. In the morning a lavish breakfast is served on the deck or in the dining room.

WESTWINDS BED AND BREAKFAST, San Juan Island
4909-H Hannah Highlands Road, Friday Harbor
(206) 378-5283
Moderate

Call for directions.

After I describe this perfect island retreat to you, please don't be angry that it can accommodate only one couple at a time. Westwinds is a wood-and-glass home that rests high atop a hill in the middle of the island. From up here you'll feel as if you can see to eternity, and the view is a significant part of the house's interior design.

As you drive up to the house, which you have to yourselves, be sure to notice the three Shetland ponies playing in the field just below. The large bedroom, living room, dining room, kitchen, and bathroom with large soaking tub are all tastefully appointed. French doors open to a private deck where you can loll away the morning over breakfast, which is artistically presented and lovingly served. This is a truly exemplary, one-of-a-kind island getaway.

Restaurant Kissing

DUCK SOUP INN, San Juan Island   ❖❖❧
3090 Roche Harbor Road, Friday Harbor
(206) 378-4878
Moderate

From the ferry, exit onto Spring Street. Turn right onto Second, and follow the signs to Roche Harbor Road. Heading north on Roche Harbor Road, continue for five miles to the restaurant.

If your taste buds and hearts long for a rustic Northwest motif and savory fresh entrées that change daily, Duck Soup Inn is your answer. The restaurant is in a wood-frame country home totally removed from the tourist trail. The country decor and relaxed service make for an easy, pleasant evening.

ROCHE HARBOR RESORT RESTAURANT,
San Juan Island   ❖
4950 Tarte Memorial Drive, Roche Harbor
(206) 378-2155
Moderate to Expensive

From the ferry, exit onto Spring Street and turn right at Second Street. At Tucker Avenue turn right again and stay to your left at the fork; this will put you on Roche Harbor Road. You will come to a T intersection eight miles down this road, where you turn right and drive to the village of Roche Harbor. Turn left at the arches to the resort.

This scenic historic harbor and marina, protected by a tiny barrier island, is a yachting playground. Every inch of the area that isn't lined with boats is covered with gazebos, rose gardens, sculpted hedges, and ivy-laden buildings. Winding brick pathways weave through this New Englandesque resort.

Roche Harbor Restaurant is San Juan Island's premier port of call, and you may be inclined to dally for a while on the deck over morning coffee or afternoon tea. When the restaurant is open, the handsome interior, gentle harbor view, and well-prepared seafood will encourage you to make an entire day of it, watching the waterborne comings and goings.

◆   **Romantic Warning:** The main hotel is old and musty, and the newer, expensive rental condos down the road are OK, but nothing to write home about. Consider staying instead at Lonesome Cove or Westwinds and enjoying a meal or two here at Roche Harbor.

SPRINGTREE EATING ESTABLISHMENT
AND FARM, San Juan Island   ◆◆◆
310 Spring Street, Friday Harbor
(206) 378-4848
Inexpensive to Moderate

At the top of Spring Street, under a very large elm tree.

The Springtree is simply adorable and unique. The white picket fence entrance is draped by a sprawling elm that covers the entire red-brick courtyard. (It took some powerful shears to cut back this mighty arbor.) Inside, everything is charming and casual, with floor-to-ceiling windows that keep the interior bright in the daytime and cozy at night. The food is country fresh; much of the produce and herbs are from the privately owned farm referred to in the restaurant's name. Every dish is flawlessly prepared, with great care given to perfecting the art of Northwest cuisine.

Outdoor Kissing

AMERICAN CAMP, San Juan Island   ◆◆◆◆

From the ferry, exit onto Spring Street and turn left on Argyle Road. Argyle jogs around to become Cattle Point Road, where you turn left again and proceed directly to American Camp.

The heavily forested terrain in the northern section of San Juan Island gives way to windswept leas carpeted with poppies, wildflowers, and waving waist-high grass at the island's southern extremity, called American Camp. Once you arrive, you can walk down to the enormous sandy beach and investigate the shoreline or meander through spacious meadows that are a mix of sand hills and sea grass. The many opportunities for ducking out of sight make this a perfect site for lovers. From your personal nook on a cliff, or as you wander along mesmerized by the glorious view of the Olympics, you can watch the sun's procession from morning to dusk as it bathes the hills in a rainbow of colors.

◆ **Romantic Alternative:** If you have the energy and a good pair of shoes, don't miss climbing the beautiful uphill trail from **ENGLISH CAMP** to **YOUNG HILL**. (To reach English Camp from American Camp, take West Valley Road, which turns into Boyce Road, to Bailer Hill Road and turn left. Then turn right on Little Road and right again onto Cattle Point Road. Follow signs to English Camp.) The view will astound you, as will the peace and solitude. You may find yourselves sharing this spectacle with the soaring eagles that make their home in this paradise. You may also come to understand why so many people say that San Juan Island is the Garden of Eden. Leave yourselves at least an hour for this round-trip jaunt.

GIANNANGELO FARMS, San Juan Island   ◗◗◖
5500 Limestone Point Road, Friday Harbor
(206) 378-4218
Free

Call for directions.

When somebody told us the best place to kiss in all of Washington is under the grape arbor at Giannangelo Farms, we decided to find out for ourselves. So, how was the kissing? Well, that part you'll have to find out for *yourselves*. But walking hand-in-hand down the white rock pathways that meander through small gardens of organic vegetables, herbs, and colorful flowers, is indeed lovely. The farm sits in the middle of 25 tranquil acres of cedar, hemlock, alder, and fir trees; the only sound you'll hear is the wind rustling in the branches and the cooing of the doves in the farm's aviaries. Every detail enhances the gentle aura of this special garden grove.

WHALE WATCH PARK, San Juan Island   ◆◆◆◆

Along West Side Road near Deadman Bay.

While you're on San Juan Island, be sure to visit Whale Watch Park on the western shore. Two pods of whales make regular trips through this area. It is from this spot that you're most likely to see these enormous creatures cavorting in play. Even if you don't have a sighting here, you'll probably witness a sensational sunset with the bay in the foreground and the white-peaked Olympic Mountains in the distance. This is a wondrous, often private section of the island.

Orcas Island

Hotel/Bed and Breakfast Kissing

BEACH HAVEN, Orcas Island
Eastsound
(206) 376-2288
Inexpensive

Call for directions.

Sometimes the hustle of ordinary life allows little to no time for romance. Imagine escaping to a waterfront island cabin where there are no interruptions—not even a telephone! A true romantic respite, Beach Haven offers 11 one-, two-, and three-bedroom log cabins, scattered along 10 acres of beautiful, private beach in the secluded shelter of an old-growth forest. The rustic cabins, complete with full kitchens and bathrooms, are about 50 years old. All enjoy magnificent views of the water and the gentle slope of mountains in the distance.

The largest unit resembles an A-frame, with floor-to-ceiling windows facing the water, an extensive front deck, four bedrooms, and a large stone fireplace to keep you cozy in the winter months. Keep in mind that the cabins are fairly close together and that many families bring their children in the summer. Even so, the views alone, and the sense that you've really left it all behind, might make this the perfect spot to rekindle any romantic flames that may be burning low.

◆   **Romantic Note:** There is a two-night minimum stay from fall through spring, and a seven-night minimum in the summer.

DEER HARBOR RESORT, Orcas Island
Deer Harbor
(206) 376-4420
Very Inexpensive

Two miles after exiting the ferry, turn left on Deer Harbor Road. Pass by West Sound Marina and continue approximately three miles until you see the marina. You are there when you reach the water!

A small grouping of A-frames, cottages, and bungalows crowds the shore and hillside of Deer Harbor Marina—at first glance clearly not the most romantic place to stay on Orcas Island. Most of the cottages are badly in need of renovation, particularly those farthest from the water.

Nevertheless, there are two weathered gray cottages here with unobstructed water views that are hard to resist, especially considering the price. Both are very private, separated from the cluster of other cabins, and are the only accommodations built directly on the beach. The decor dates back to the 1970s, leaving much to be desired, but it is still comfortable and cozy. Both cottages have full kitchens, although in the winter a continental breakfast is served, moments away, at the small **HEMINGWAY'S CAFÉ.**

Snuggle up in front of the fire or relax under the stars in the resort's outdoor spa, located farther up the hillside. Don't count on finding much privacy up here, but when you get island accommodations and water views at this price, you really can't go wrong.

DEEP MEADOW FARM, Orcas Island   ◆◆◆◆
Corner of Comorant Bay Road and
Cedar Valley Road, Deer Harbor
(206) 376-5866
Inexpensive

Call for directions.

Cricket songs swell in a mighty chorus as you step out of your car and sigh appreciatively at the serenity embracing this lovely bed and breakfast. Reached from the access road by a long, private drive, the 52-year-old farmhouse is set in 40 acres of forest and farmland. The wide, grassy meadow next door is interrupted only by an old ramshackle barn, a chicken coop, and a wooden fence. Somewhere off in the distance you can hear a stream. Ah, bliss!

Midwestern farm furniture and Kansas antiques decorate the cozy living room. The two upstairs guest rooms are spacious, replete with farm-country furnishings, private baths, and comfortable iron double beds, all of which lend a real touch of authenticity to this distinctive retreat.

A full, delightful breakfast, made from fresh fruits and vegetables grown and harvested in the farm's garden and orchard, can be enjoyed indoors or outside on the peaceful porch, where you can while away the morning in one of several lounge chairs.

NORTHSHORE COTTAGES, Orcas Island
Sunset Road
(206) 376-5131
Moderate (no credit cards)

Call for directions.

The Northshore Cottages are actually two rustically handsome cabins. The Artist's Studio, with its own outdoor deck and hot tub overlooking the Canadian Gulf Islands and the glistening waters of the Strait of Georgia, is charming and cozy. Inside, a small efficient kitchen, stone fireplace, and comfortable quilt-covered bed feel lovingly romantic, while large bay windows amply let in the majestic view. The other cottage, set back from the view, but embraced by tall pines, is much larger, nicely furnished, and exceedingly comfortable. It also has its own outdoor hot tub. Both cottages have access to a pathway to the beach, where you'll find seating and a fire pit for blazing sunset watching.

◆ **Romantic Warning:** Northshore Cottages is located in a neighborhood setting with neighbors a bit too close for comfort. The hot tub for the Artist's Studio is in plain sight of the house next door, and you might be asked not to run the jets after 10 P.M. Also, this is not a bed and breakfast, but both cabins have small, fully equipped kitchens.

ORCAS HOTEL, Orcas Island
Orcas ferry landing
(206) 376-4300
Inexpensive to Expensive

Just above the Orcas Island ferry dock.

"Hotel" is really a misnomer here, since that term often conjures up an image of a sterile building with identical rooms and basic detailing, none of which applies to this striking, three-story Victorian inn. The view from the wraparound windows in the dining room and lounge—and from many of the rooms upstairs—is striking. From this vantage point you can watch the comings and goings around Harney Channel, Wasp Passage, and Shaw Island.

Actually, this 1904 landmark has only two rooms to offer in the way of kissing-preferred accommodations. Most of the other rooms are on the small side, and only those on the third floor have their own bathrooms, which are smallish too (after all, this is an old building). But the two new suites, called "Romantic Rooms," are just that—completely romantic. French doors open onto a private deck, the bathrooms have Jacuzzis built for two, and the bedrooms are lovely and comfortable. The price tag is a bit steep for these spots—among the most expensive on the island—but after all, this is a special occasion we're talking about, isn't it? To help ease the strain on your pocketbook, a full breakfast served in the hotel's restaurant is included in the rate. Any meal in this window-lined country-perfect dining room will be a pleasure, and the food, though basic, is quite good.

◆ **Romantic Note:** Since this hotel is located at the foot of the ferry dock, there is exceptionally heavy tourist and car traffic during the summer season. The downstairs public rooms can get crowded when there is a delay in boarding the ferry.

TURTLEBACK FARM INN, Orcas Island
Crow Valley Road
(206) 376-4914
Inexpensive to Moderate

From the ferry dock follow Horseshoe Highway and turn left on McNallie Road. Turn right at Crow Valley Road and watch for the sign indicating the inn.

When the sun begins to warm the air and the colors of the countryside come alive with the glow of daybreak, Turtleback Inn is a delightful place to be. Every corner of this old farmhouse has been painstakingly renovated by people who clearly were sensitive to the landscape that surrounds it. The rooms and private baths range from charming to more charming (though the less expensive rooms are rather small). The pastoral setting—80 acres of hills, pasture, ponds, and meadow—will warm your hearts, as will the plentiful breakfast served at your own table in the window-enclosed dining room. You will be wholeheartedly pleased with your stay here.

Restaurant Kissing

CAFÉ OLGA, Orcas Island
Horseshoe Highway
(206) 376-4408
Inexpensive to Moderate

Two miles east of Moran State Park, at the bottom of Olga Hill.

A few miles south of Mount Constitution, in the Orcas Island Artworks store, is where you will find this rustic café. The atmosphere is laid-back, with strong overtones of the late '60s, but the food is anything but. Exceptional dishes such as Sicilian artichoke pie, creamy rich manicotti with walnuts, and Moroccan salad brimming with couscous, dates, almonds, and spices are just a few choices from the eclectic menu. As you leisurely dine, you'll have ample time to share your thoughts and get to know each other a little better.

BILBO'S FESTIVO, Orcas Island
Eastsound
(206) 376-4728
Inexpensive

In the town of Eastsound, at A Street and North Beach Road.

The interior of this charming Mexican restaurant features hand-tiled wooden benches, a stone fireplace, and soft lighting. Outside, in the center of a courtyard garden, is a blazing fire pit surrounded by outdoor seating. The food is authentic and light, mildly spicy, with generous portions and remarkably fresh seafood. This is a local favorite, so reservations are a good idea. Try a Mexican beer or a Northwest microbrew while you wait for your table.

CHRISTINA'S, Orcas Island

Horseshoe Highway, Eastsound
(206) 376-4904
Moderate to Expensive

At the intersection of North Beach Road and Horseshoe Highway. Call for seasonal hours.

Christina's reputation for fine Northwest dining is more impressive than ever, which is saying a lot. You can savor fresh local clams, superb moist salmon, and creamy pasta dishes that are sheer heaven. The setting is island elegance, right on the waterfront. The glass-enclosed porch has stunning views of the mountains surrounding the Eastsound inlet. On sunny summer evenings, the rooftop terrace is an alluring alternative for dinner.

ROSARIO RESORT RESTAURANT, Orcas Island
One Rosario Way, Eastsound
(206) 376-2222
Moderate to Expensive

From the ferryboat landing, go north on Horseshoe Highway to Eastsound, loop around the water, and head south. Rosario Resort is about five miles down the road.

I won't be the first or the last person to rave about Rosario's location and views. And I won't be the only person to warn you about the rundown, shabby accommodations, which are very expensive and in urgent need of renovation. I'm also not the first to comment on the restaurant, but I can't resist: sitting at a corner table, near the floor-to-ceiling windows that expose a sparkling view of the area, is enough to fill anyone's heart for the day or night. Yes, the food is American-standard and just slightly better than ordinary, but the service is adequate and they try hard. Then there's that view! All in all, Rosario is a good enough place for a morning or afternoon time-out from your day's activities; dinner is too expensive and mediocre to be worth it, and the rooms don't even remotely justify the expense.

SHIP BAY OYSTER HOUSE, Orcas Island
Horseshoe Highway, Eastsound
(206) 376-5886
Expensive

From the ferry, follow Horseshoe Highway just past Eastsound. The restaurant is on the right.

Deer grazing on the lawn in front of the white Colonial-style house set the mood for a splendid evening to remember. The building is nestled on a cliff only yards away from a shimmering bay, so request a window seat and watch the sun set behind the trees. The dining room is simple and understated, done in a tasteful white-and-gray color scheme. An excess of windows allows ample sunlight to fill the room in the afternoon.

Superior, fresh local seafood is diligently prepared and delicious. Daily specials reflect what came off the boats that morning. Charbroiled Pacific king salmon and Pacific red snapper are excellent. The seafood gumbo, a spicy Cajun dish with mussels, clams, shrimp, crab, and fresh fish, turned out to be superb. With food like this and a fiery sky in the background, the entire experience is enticingly romantic.

◆ **Romantic Note:** Ship Bay Oyster House is closed Sunday and Monday.

Outdoor Kissing

ISLAND KAYAK GUIDES, Orcas Island
Doe Bay Village, Olga
(206) 376-2291
Moderate

Call for directions and detailed information about your trip.

The brochure said "no experience necessary." It's not that I'm a wimp, it's just that I'm not much of a swimmer, and the idea of paddling the cold waters around the islands seemed not only dangerous but exhausting, and as far removed from romantic as one can get. The staff assured me that instructions in paddling and the use of the equipment would be thorough and that the trip would be geared to my skill level. Great, I said, that meant I'd be stuck paddling around the dock for an hour. They insisted that nothing of the sort had ever happened before, and I was encouraged to be open-minded and give it a try. OK, but just this once.

Wouldn't you know it? Now I can't wait to do it again! There is something quite remarkable about propelling yourselves in a two-person kayak through the open waters around the forested islands of the San Juans. It's exciting to be part of nature's aquatic playground, where eagles and seabirds swoop down across the water's surface, otters and seals dart in and out of the current, and, on occasion, a great orca effortlessly glides by. There are no words to describe the sensation of watching the world from this vantage point, and the strength of your arms (or lack of it) has little bearing on the quality of the experience. All kinds of special trips are possible, some of which include time for picnicking, sunbathing, and island exploration. Whichever one you choose, you won't regret giving it your best shot.

MOUNT CONSTITUTION, Orcas Island

From the ferryboat landing, go north on Horseshoe Highway to the town of Eastsound. Loop around the sound and head south, following signs to the mountain, which is in the center of Moran State Park.

The road into Moran State Park will lead you to Mount Constitution, the tallest elevation on the San Juans. Its easily attained summit boasts a stone lookout tower well above the treetops. From here you have a stupendous 360-degree view of this part of the Northwest. To the east are the majestic Cascades; to the north, the Gulf Islands demand your attention; to the west, looming on the horizon, are the Olympics; to the south are the San Juan Islands; and above is the endless blue sky. There is wonderful camping to be found up here. Unquestionably, Mount Constitution is one of the more spectacular spots on the islands.

◆   **Romantic Note:** Mount Constitution is a well-visited frontier. For a less-touristed experience, hike the mountaintop trails and claim a landmark of your own.

Lopez Island

Hotel/Bed and Breakfast Kissing

BLUE FJORD CABINS, Lopez Island
Elliott Avenue
(206) 468-2749
Moderate

Call for directions.

Lopez Island appears untouched, with its miles of farmland and rolling tundra. Only here can you find the ultimate seclusion of a Nordic chalet, nestled in the heart of a 16-acre forest. Both of these cabins, sequestered beneath groves of cedar and fir trees, are perfect for honeymooners, with queen-size beds, full kitchens, and privacy on all sides. The decor of the cabins is plain, almost too plain, although they do have relaxing views of the surrounding forest from the windows and deck.

Just yards away is a short nature trail (a five-minute walk) that will take you to Jasper Bay. Savor the stillness as you relax in the gazebo on the beach, with a stunning view of Mount Baker in the distance. You may also catch a glimpse of your only other neighbors (besides the owners): a bald eagle, blue herons, and a cluster of sea otters.

◆ **Romantic Note:** This is not a bed and breakfast, so you are expected to supply all of your own food. There is also a two-night minimum on weekends and a three-night minimum in July, August, and on holidays.

EDENWILD INN, Lopez Island
In Lopez Village
(206) 468-3238
Moderate to Expensive

From the ferry landing, follow the signs to Lopez Village. The inn is located on the main road in town (there is only one), Lopez Road South.

In some respects Edenwild Inn isn't really a Northwest island getaway. Every detail of this sparkling new, contemporary, totally elegant, upscale bed and breakfast feels somewhat out of place in such pristine surroundings. However, depending on your point of view, it is a beautiful, thoroughly romantic addition to the area. The seven rooms here are all simply decorated with choice furnishings; some have fireplaces, some have views, all have tiled private baths. Breakfast is a generous display of fresh baked-egg dishes, pastries, and breads. To some people, the Edenwild may seem a bit slick for this semi-remote island, but it is the perfect compromise between getting away from it all and having convenient uptown amenities.

INN AT SWIFT'S BAY, Lopez Island
Port Stanley Road
(206) 468-3636
Inexpensive to Expensive

Heading toward Lopez Village from the ferry, take the first major left onto Port Stanley Road, opposite the Odlin Park entrance. Go approximately three-quarters of a mile. The inn is on the right.

The gracious hosts have left no stone unturned in creating an enchanting, luxurious Tudor inn. Tucked behind a stand of cedar trees, just minutes from the beach, the inn fills every requirement necessary for a romantic interlude. Lounge in the plush common rooms, which are adorned with rich colors, floral draperies, and adorable hand-sewn teddy bears, or stargaze from the very private hot tub in the quiet backyard (which you can reserve to ensure privacy).

Each guest room is endowed with soothing colors, and a unique flavor of elegance. Three of the five have private baths, but even the two rooms that share a bath are beautiful. The two attic suites are particularly alluring, with skylights, queen-size beds, generous space, and private entrances.

Make a toast to your love with a bottle of chilled sparkling white wine, delivered to your bedside. If you're in a literary mood, launch your career as an author and add an entry to the inn's ongoing write-your-own mystery that guests have created. A weekend here really feels like a treat, particularly when you have tasted the exquisite gourmet breakfast (we had fresh crab cakes).

MACKAYE HARBOR HOUSE, Lopez Island
MacKaye Harbor Road
(206) 468-2253
Inexpensive to Moderate

Call for directions.

Kayakers, beachcombers, and romantics alike can find a haven for their hearts and hobbies in this gracious farmhouse overlooking MacKaye Harbor. Although the five guest rooms are comfortable and cozy, and several have views of the harbor, only one has a private bath and the common rooms are fairly bland. Nevertheless, MacKaye Harbor House is an ideal getaway for those who wish to take advantage of the beach setting. This is the only inn on Lopez that literally has a beach right out its front door. Borrow some of the assorted recreational equipment and row off to sea at sunset or kayak away after a plentiful breakfast served by your courteous hostess.

Restaurant Kissing

BAY CAFÉ, Lopez Island
Lopez Village
(206) 468-3700
Moderate to Expensive

From the ferry take Ferry Road and turn left on Fisherman Bay Road. Follow this until you see a sign for Lopez Village and take a right. The Bay Café is at the end of the main street, across from the post office.

Lopez offers few romantic options for lunch, so it's a shame the Bay Café only serves dinner—we would have gladly come here twice, or even more. The casual, eclectic atmosphere, with a green canoe hanging overhead and a piano against the wall, is enhanced by an agreeable mixture of European and American furnishings. The food, also eclectic, is excellent. The spicy prawns in couscous were done to perfection, as was the swordfish with red pepper tapenade; both are sure to tempt you into ordering dessert. (If dinner was this good, how could you go wrong?) Needless to say, the chocolate torte and raspberry cobbler proved to be exquisite. The staff is remarkably accommodating, and you'll feel comfortable lingering over a cup of hot coffee, relishing the warm glow of an evening that has just begun.

Artist's Studio Loft — hot tub water site TV VCR
~~carriage house~~ $75 nit
Cont breakfast

also

Puget Sound Area

Vashon Island   *reserv service 463-6737*

Hotel/Bed and Breakfast Kissing

GOOSIE'S BED AND BREAKFAST, Vashon Island   ❤❤
18017 Thorsen Road Southwest
(206) 463-2059
Inexpensive

From the ferry dock, take the Vashon Highway to Southwest Bank Road and turn right. Southwest Bank Road turns into Thorsen Road Southwest.

Two black-and-white llamas, three cats, an affectionate Lab, and, appropriately, a gaggle of large, white, rather militant geese appear to own this quaint bed and breakfast. Fortunately, they generously allow you to share their charming property. The small cottage nestled in a flower garden and the private suite in the main house are both desirable romantic getaways. The tiny secluded cottage is decorated in dusty blues; the rustic furnishings infuse the main room, small kitchenette, bedroom, and bath with a soft country feel. Seclusion is the strong point here, but it is almost too cramped inside and overfilled with knickknacks.

The suite has an impressive view of the Olympic Mountains to gaze at through French doors and expansive windows. Its tasteful decor closely resembles a Ralph Lauren ad. Rich tones of forest green and warm red are accented by a plaid down comforter on the king-size bed.

For both accommodations, a full breakfast that might include a fresh pesto omelet or waffles and fresh fruit is delivered right to your room. On warm days, guests in the suite can sit out on the deck to eat breakfast, breathe the fresh air, relish the view, and watch the escapades of the eccentric geese.

◆ **Romantic Alternative:** Accommodations on Vashon Island tend to be family-oriented and equipped mostly for children. The **MAURY GARDEN COTTAGE**, 22705 Deppman Road Southwest,

(206) 463-3034 or (206) 463-3556, (Inexpensive), is one such place, but if you don't have kids in tow, it does have genuine romantic potential. If you don't mind cooking your own breakfast with the ingredients provided by the host, this bright, secluded cottage with skylights in every room and simple decor is worth considering.

HARBOR INN, Vashon Island   ◆◆◆◆
9118 Harbor Drive
(206) 463-6794
Inexpensive to Moderate

Call for directions.

This immense, august English Tudor-style home seems out of place in a quiet neighborhood on Vashon Island, but the refinement found here is a desirable change of pace. Dark woodwork, towering windows, fine antiques, and rich decor fill the inn with a handsome allure. Admiring the sensational views of Quartermaster Harbor from this aesthetic vantage point is heartwarming. No matter which of the three guest rooms you stay in, it is possible to admire each morning's sunrise right from your pillow. Be sure to nudge your significant other awake to savor the magic together.

The largest room here is breathtaking. A king-size four-poster bed sits on lush deep green carpet, there is a gas log fireplace, and bay windows cover an entire wall. As if this bedroom weren't seductive enough, the all-white bathroom with accents of pink continues in the same spirit. Bay windows and mirrors surround a deep, two-person Jacuzzi tub where you and yours can bathe by moonlight.

After you leisurely allow the full, skillfully prepared full breakfast to settle, use the mountain bikes supplied by the innkeeper to explore the many trails in **BURTON ACRES PARK**. It is seemingly undiscovered, so you may have the whole area to yourselves.

◆ **Romantic Alternative:** The same discriminating owners are in the process of remodeling an early-20th-century home into the **TRAMP HARBOR INN**, 8518 Southwest Ellis Port Road, (206) 463-5794, (Inexpensive), which appears to possess an elegance akin to the Harbor Inn, as well as a trout-stocked pond and a sprawling lawn. The only drawback is that it is located on a fairly busy street.

Restaurant Kissing

BACK BAY INN, Vashon Island
24007 Vashon Highway Southwest
(206) 463-5355
Moderate to Expensive

From the Vashon ferry dock take the Vashon Highway to the restaurant.

To start a sunny summer evening off right, take the 6 P.M. ferry from West Seattle (at the Fauntleroy ferry dock) across to Vashon Island. This is only a 15-minute trip, so hurry to the bow of the boat and stand watch on the deck to fully enjoy the scenic crossing.

Locals eagerly recommend the newly opened Back Bay Inn as a romantic dinner spot. The intimate atmosphere of this Victorian-style inn certainly deserves romantic praise. Subtle lighting, bay windows facing the water, and pleasant music playing softly while you eat creates a lovely dining environment. Sad to say, it would be several lips better if a busy intersection didn't interrupt the view, service wasn't so slow, and the food tasted as good as the menu makes it sound. The small menu does offer inventive dishes such as polenta served on chanterelle mushrooms and crab ravioli with shiitake mushrooms and curry broth, but the sauces on both of these dishes can be more like heavy gravy, drowning the flavor of the original ingredients. Inventiveness is usually commendable, but perhaps these ambitious, romantically disposed owners should have started out with more basic items.

SOUND FOOD, Vashon Island
20312 99th Avenue Southwest
(206) 463-3565
Inexpensive to Moderate

From the Vashon ferry dock, drive eight miles on the main island road to the restaurant.

At nearly the center of the island is Sound Food, where you'll find the country atmosphere, freshly baked pastries, and health-aware gourmet cuisine a genuine change of pace. Unfortunately, the service can be abrupt and indifferent, but still take time to savor the subtleties of your meal, indulge in a second helping of fresh-baked bread, and treat yourselves to dessert. The blueberry bear claws, lightly glazed and covered with walnuts, are fantastic!

Bainbridge Island

Restaurant Kissing

PLEASANT BEACH GRILL AND OYSTER BAR,
Bainbridge Island
4738 Lynwood Center Road
(206) 842-4347
Expensive

From the Winslow ferry dock, go to the first light and turn left. Head through the town of Winslow and turn right on Madison Street. At the next stoplight turn left on Wyatt. Follow this road as it curves around, then follow the signs to Lynwood. Watch for the sign indicating the restaurant.

The ferryboat ride from Seattle to Bainbridge Island in and of itself provides a romantic excursion across the sound, with the majestic Olympic Mountains on the western horizon and the city skyline to the east. Once you dock at this nearby island, a short drive will complete the experience. Pleasant Beach Grill is in an English Tudor-style building, skillfully renovated from what was once an old, secluded mansion, yet the atmosphere and food are totally Northwest. You are served in what was formerly the living room. Beautifully arranged about the room are linen-draped tables accented with china and crystal. As formal as this may sound, the mood and pace are relaxed and comfortable; nothing stuffy is to be found here. Attentive hospitality and imaginative fresh food are the pride of this establishment. Their half-dozen or so exotic oyster concoctions will convince you that what they say about these mollusks is true.

After dinner you can step down into the restaurant's petite fireside lounge and sink into one of the leather sofas that surround the stone hearth. Snuggling close together, relax as the crackling fire casts its light on the mahogany-paneled room. For an extra treat, when you're both toasty warm, drive down to the water and watch the twinkling lights of the marine traffic as it passes through the channel.

Outdoor Kissing

THE BLOEDEL RESERVE, Bainbridge Island
7571 Northeast Dolphin Drive
(206) 842-7631
$4 entrance fee

From Seattle take the Winslow ferry to Bainbridge Island and follow Highway 305 to the north end of the island. Turn right on Dolphin Drive, which leads to the estate. Call for reservations; access is limited to a specific number of people each day.

There are more than 150 acres of meticulously maintained gardens here at Bloedel Reserve, so you're sure to find a peaceful haven for an afternoon interlude. The reserve is a place where the artistic splendor of sculpted plant life brings pleasure to the senses. Wander through the bird sanctuary, verdant woods, and Japanese gardens; pause at a reflecting pool and admire the dense moss garden. All of it is divine. As the brochure for the Bloedel Reserve plainly states: "Man's first recorded home was a garden, no sooner known than lost... and we've been trying to return ever since." This might not be Eden, but it is the next best thing.

Whidbey Island

Aside from being one of the most charming, easily accessible islands from the Seattle area, Whidbey Island is also the longest island in the United States. "Longest" is just one more superlative statistic in this realm that irresistibly attracts romantic travelers. There is an unusually large selection of engaging restaurants, wonderful bed and breakfasts, spectacular vistas, and idyllic forested parks here. If you're looking for a quick escape from city life, this island is an exemplary destination.

◆ **Romantic Note:** Whidbey Island is accessible by ferryboat from Mukilteo, 20 minutes north of Seattle, and from Port Townsend, on the Olympic Peninsula; and by car from Anacortes via the Deception Pass Bridge, 90 minutes north of Seattle.

Hotel/Bed and Breakfast Kissing

CLIFF HOUSE, Whidbey Island
5440 Windmill Road, Freeland
(206) 321-1566
Unbelievably Expensive

From the ferry dock, follow Highway 525 for 10.6 miles to Bush Point Road. Turn left and drive 1.5 miles to Windmill Road, where you turn left again. Cliff House is on the right.

Bed and breakfasts, more often than not, are preferable to the run-of-the-mill hotels and motels that line tourist areas all over the Northwest. Cliff House not only triumphs over standard hotels, it alters the entire concept of bed-and-breakfast establishments. This is a sensuous, architecturally distinguished, Northwest contemporary home, whose owner turns the keys over to you for 13 acres of island exclusivity.

The wood-timbered home rests on a towering bluff overlooking Admiralty Inlet. Awesome island sunsets seem to be part of the interior floor plan; an outdoor hot tub gives you a steamy perspective on this nightly performance. A glass-enclosed atrium stands in the center of the house, allowing the elements safely inside the home for your observation. There are stone floors and soft pastel colors throughout, international antiques, a featherbed covered by the softest down comforter, and floor-to-ceiling panoramic windows (we're talking the width and height of the house). There are no interior doors (except on the bathrooms), yet every room has an abundance of privacy; the house simply flows effortlessly from one level to the next. The kitchen is a gourmet's heaven. Cliff House is an island utopia built for two.

◆ **Romantic Alternative:** SEA CLIFF, 5440 Windmill Road, (206) 321-1566, (Moderate), once again proves that the owners of Cliff House have a rare talent for creating remarkable places where you and your special someone can retreat from the world. This gingerbread cottage sits a short distance from Cliff House, on the same bluff with the same premium view. Its private deck is the ideal lounging spot from which to watch the boat traffic navigate its way through Puget Sound. Inside, everything is warmed by a striking stone fireplace, and there is a petite kitchen where continental breakfast delicacies are supplied each day. Furnishings are plush and there's a comfy quilt-covered queen-size bed.

COLONEL CROCKETT FARM INN, Whidbey Island
1012 South Fort Casey Road, Coupeville
(206) 678-3711
Inexpensive to Moderate

From the ferry dock, follow Highway 525 for 23 miles and turn left onto Highway 20. In 1.4 miles turn right onto Wanamaker Road and drive 1.7 miles. Turn left onto South Fort Casey Road and drive 0.2 mile. Watch carefully for the sign in front and turn left into the farm's driveway.

As you pull into Colonel Crockett Farm, you'll see a massive red barn that has been restored to some of its former glory and heralds the entrance to the inn. As you enter this consummate Victorian country home, you'll be impressed by its invitation to gracious living. The colors, appointments, hand-crafted wood paneling, private baths, and loving personal touches combine to assure you a sublime time away from everything except each other. The dining room is a series of small intimate tables that overlook the garden. A supreme breakfast is served here, with sumptuous egg creations and heavenly fresh-baked breads and muffins.

COUNTRY COTTAGE OF LANGLEY, Whidbey Island
215 Sixth Street, Langley
(206) 221-8709
Inexpensive

From the ferry dock, follow Highway 525 into Langley, turn right on Maxwelton Road, then bear left onto Langley Road, which becomes Cascade. Turn left on Sixth Street to reach the cottage.

This lovely, country-elegant home is located just a few blocks from town. The rooms are more like suites; a stay here promises nights filled with fantasy and days spent in country relaxation. There are two detached guest rooms with private entrances, two rooms in the main house with private baths, and a small cottage. A backyard porch overlooks the water and mountains; a large deck wraps around a well-tended garden and enjoys a similar view. The breakfast service is great.

EAGLES NEST INN, Whidbey Island
3236 East Saratoga Road, Langley
(206) 321-5331
Moderate

From the ferry dock, follow Highway 525 into Langley, turn right on Maxwelton Road, then bear left onto Langley Road, which becomes Cascade. Turn left on Second Street, which becomes East Saratoga Road.

This newly constructed home sits high on a hill on the outskirts of Langley. The views from the deck and the hot tub are, without exaggeration, spectacular. The house is huge and the four guest rooms are spacious and brightly decorated. Some have balconies, private entries, and views, and all are great places to call home for a few days of time alone. When you wake in the morning, you'll find a tray of juice and coffee waiting outside your door, followed by a home-cooked breakfast (and the cookie jar is never empty).

GARDEN PATH INN, Whidbey Island
111 First Street, Langley
(206) 221-5121
Inexpensive to Expensive

From the ferry dock, follow Highway 525 for approximately three miles and turn right onto Langley Road. Follow Langley Road, which becomes Cascade Avenue and takes you directly into the town of Langley. Take a left on First Street; the Garden Path Inn is half a block down First Street on the left, above a cluster of shops.

A picturesque brick garden path, cloaked in vines and enveloped by nature's scents, beckons to you from the pleasant prattle of the streets of Langley. As you climb the stairs that lead you to the two suites, you are promptly aware of the privacy that awaits you.

The back suite faces the street and consequently offers an uninteresting view, although the sunlight filtering through the windows of your pleasant sitting room and the simple decor are enough to make your stay pleasurable.

We preferred the front suite, which offers a view of Saratoga Passage and downtown Langley, and amenities such as a fireplace, Jacuzzi tub, VCR, dining room, living room, and ample space to enjoy the savory continental breakfast brought to your door. The Garden Path Inn is a perfect retreat for those who want the solitude of a garden hideaway and the convenience of an island town. You won't regret having chosen this path.

GUEST HOUSE BED AND BREAKFAST COTTAGES,
Whidbey Island   ◆◆◆◆
835 East Christenson Road, Greenbank
(206) 678-3115
Moderate to Expensive

From the ferry dock, follow Highway 525 north for approximately 16 miles, just past Christenson Road. The office is down the first driveway on the left in a yellow farmhouse.

This is a place I almost passed up. The unassuming yellow house is only a few feet from the main road, and from that perspective the place looked relatively uninviting and noisy. I have learned from this experience never to pass up anything based solely on its exterior appearance, because the Guest House's interior and acreage are more precious than I would have imagined. The idyllic, cozy log cabins and splendid log home set amid 25 acres of meadow and forest are some of the most outstanding kissing places I've ever seen.

These authentic log homes are like something in a storybook. Brimming with petite kitchens, fireplaces, oak furniture, stained glass windows, knotty pine walls, decks, featherbeds, VCRs, private spa tubs, and skylights, all have an abundance of charm and romantic potential. Each cabin is stocked with breakfast items, with all the ingredients fresh and abundant, including eggs from the owners' chicken coops. As if that weren't enough, there is even an outdoor hot tub and heated swimming pool on the property.

Three of the cottages are small and intimate; there are also newer units that are amazingly cozy, yet spacious, with all the amenities. The last unit to describe is a log mansion without comparison anywhere in the Northwest. This capacious home provides the ultimate in togetherness. The huge stone fireplace, large soaking tub and spa tub, antique wonders, floor-to-ceiling windows, and full gourmet kitchen are absolutely fabulous. The Guest House boasts a AAA rating and we agree wholeheartedly, though we think that a four-lips rating is far more relevant.

◆ **Romantic Outing:** One mile north of the Guest House is **WHIDBEY'S GREENBANK FARM.** This is a vineyard par excellence, with a delightful tasting room and pretty picnic grounds. If you can pull yourself away from your log cabin for a few hours, a premium afternoon is here for the sipping. The loganberry wine and liqueur can help provoke some very sweet kissing.

THE INN AT LANGLEY, Whidbey Island
400 First Street, Langley
(206) 221-3033
Moderate to Expensive

From the ferry dock follow Highway 525 toward Langley, turn right on Maxwelton Road, then bear left onto Langley Road, which becomes Cascade, which becomes First Street.

The Inn at Langley is the newest addition to this town's burgeoning list of acclaimed accommodations, and this one is the sleekest and most tempting of them all. The building is set high on a bluff overlooking Saratoga Passage so each of the 24 rooms has a glorious view of the mountains and water. Our room had a private deck, wood-burning fireplace, thick comforter, terrycloth robes, and a large tiled bathroom that I would give anything to move into my home. The deep two-person spa tub is fronted by a shower area the size of a small room, and both are precisely placed to face the view and the fire. Guests also have access to the beach below.

According to the inn's brochure, "The heart of the inn is the formal country kitchen," and this couldn't be more accurate. A generous continental breakfast is served in the morning, and a Northwest epicurean production is served on Friday and Saturday nights only to guests and visitors alike (by reservation).

INN AT PENN COVE, Whidbey Island
702 North Main Street, Coupeville
(206) 678-8000
Inexpensive to Expensive

From the ferry landing, take Highway 525 north for 28 miles to the first stoplight. Turn right and follow the main road down seven blocks. The two pink Victorian houses on the left are it.

Authenticity is important to many bed and breakfasts, particularly those trying to evoke a historical mood. The Inn at Penn Cove is convincingly Victorian. The two homes, built in the late 1800s, were renovated recently to serve as a bed and breakfast and are filled from top to bottom with antiques such as a hand-painted slate fireplace in the living room and a beautifully restored carousel horse perched in one of the guest rooms. You will marvel at the genuine Victorian mood captured here.

The rooms themselves are quite pleasant, with bay windows, fireplaces, queen-size beds, and claw-foot tubs. The time-worn common rooms are confining and smell slightly musty, which gives both houses more authenticity than you may care for.

The busy street alongside the house does detract from the inn's romantic potential, but if you are looking for a taste of history, this is the place for you. The antiques really are marvelous.

KITTLESON COVE, Whidbey Island
4891 East Bay Ridge Drive, Clinton
(206) 221-2734
Very Expensive

Call for directions.

Settled on the shores of Puget Sound, this is a serene, secluded place to reconnect with your loved one. The northeastern exposure affords a spectacular view of the Cascade Mountains and Mount Baker, providing ample proof of Pacific Northwest magnetism. There are two accommodations here, the Cove Cottage and the Beachside Suite. Both have decks overlooking the beach, plus well-stocked mini-kitchens that include already-prepared and do-it-yourself breakfast treats. If you are looking forward to keeping civilization as far away as possible, bring dinner fixings for a waterfront evening repast. The suite, although attached to the owner's home, has a private entrance. Inside, everything is airy and bright with pastel fabrics and linens. In contrast, the three-room cottage has a rustic, earthy atmosphere. A stone fireplace warms the deep green and burgundy interior, while stone floors are kept cozy with a profusion of throw rugs. (Bring slippers, the few places where the stone is uncovered can be quite chilly.) The four-poster bed with a floral bedspread and matching canopy is lovely, but the Jacuzzi tub in the bathroom is the decisive romantic touch.

◆   **Romantic Note:** You can request a "child-free" reservation, to be assured of a truly restful getaway.

LOG CASTLE, Whidbey Island
3273 East Saratoga Road, Langley
(206) 221-5483
Inexpensive to Moderate

From the ferry dock, follow Highway 525 approximately three miles and turn right on Langley Road. Follow Langley Road into Langley and take a left on East Saratoga Road. Follow Saratoga Road for a mile and a half; you will see a sign for Log Castle on your right.

Of all the castles you have read about in fairy tales, none is quite like this one. The one-of-a-kind home-grown project, perched comfortably on an isolated beach, embracing views of Mount Baker and the Cascade Mountains, has taken its owners 18 years to complete.

Each log that makes up the unique decor—including a wormwood staircase, log breakfast table, and wooden beams and doorways—has a story of origin, which the owners readily share with all who ask. The wooded ambience renders a homey charm to each of the five guest rooms.

Log houses are not significantly soundproof, but the rooms are spaced throughout the house in such a way, from the first to the third floor, that you may feel your privacy is unmarred (then again maybe you won't). Our favorite was the Ann Room, located in the third-story turret, with surrounding windows and complete views of Saratoga Passage. The Marta Suite is also engaging, with its own sun deck and porch swing perfect for two. Four of the rooms have private baths, one's bathroom is detached.

Take a walk on the beach or relax in your room and savor the lingering aroma of fresh-baked bread that permeates the house, a reminder of the three-course gourmet breakfast that awaits you in the morning.

LONE LAKE COTTAGE AND BREAKFAST,
Whidbey Island
5206 South Bayview Road, Langley
(206) 321-5325
Moderate

$110

From the ferry dock follow Highway 525 for five and a half miles and turn right onto Bayview Road. Drive one mile to the cottage, which is on the left.

Everything about Lone Lake Cottage is peaceful, enchanting, and unique. This eclectic (and I mean eclectic) assortment of accommodations, five miles outside of town, is the most inventive place to stay in Langley. One example: the innkeepers have built a striking, professionally designed aviary, complete with incubators and a waterfall, the likes of which you'd expect to see only in a zoo. There are fascinating, colorful birds from all over the world in this walk-in menagerie, and down by the lake there are black swans and exotic ducks to watch.

Two of the three units here are charming cottages, with fully equipped kitchens well stocked with breakfast treats, fireplaces, private decks overlooking the lake, VCRs, stereos, cozy eating nooks, and warm sitting areas. One unit even has a black spa tub with a skylight over it. For a real change of pace, stay on the one-of-a-kind, glass-enclosed houseboat, with its darling galley and walk-up queen-size bed. All the units have their own Jacuzzi tub and Oriental appointments. Two loving hearts need not feel alone at Lone Lake.

LOVELY COTTAGE, Whidbey Island
4130 East Lovely Road, Clinton
(206) 321-6592
Moderate

From the ferry dock, follow Highway 525 to Cultus Bay Road and turn south, staying on Cultus Bay Road until you reach Lovely Road. Then turn left to the cottage.

I dislike cute names, but in this case I'll make an exception, because Lovely Cottage is not only lovely, it is wonderful. Nestled into a two-acre oceanfront homestead, the cottage is a quaint, endearing place to spend time in total privacy. The views from your private porch, the sweeping lawn, and the gardens are nothing less than breathtaking. The snowcapped Olympics towering on the horizon and the sky's changing countenance as the sun sets are more than inspiring. There is even a huge hot tub for your own personal use in the backyard. Inside, the cottage features an eclectic blend of rustic, cozy furnishings and a full kitchen. The massive stairway down to the beach is a masterpiece of engineering ingenuity.

The owners are in the process of adding a guest suite in the main house; when complete it will have a fireplace, kitchen, two bedrooms, and a soaking tub in the tiled bathroom, which, from all appearances, will be quite beautiful. Unfortunately, this new addition will detract from the privacy of the original lone accommodation.

SEA VIEW INN, Whidbey Island
431 Anthes Street, Langley
(206) 321-1599
Moderate

From the ferry dock, go north on Highway 525 for approximately three miles to Langley Road, turn right, and drive into Langley. The inn is located in the heart of Langley on Anthes Street.

From your first glimpse of the Sea View Inn, you know you're in for something special. A colorful garden surrounding a stone-bordered pond fronts the contemporary house, which rests on a sweeping lawn overlooking the town below and the blue bay beyond. We felt enfolded in warmth and comfort the instant we set foot in the house. Light streaming through the strategically arranged windows seems to soak into the natural fir decor, radiating a warm welcome. Two wonderful guest suites with high vaulted ceilings and double spa tubs will make you want to extend your stay.

The little things have not been ignored; the fresh-baked cookies set out on the table, the blue-and-green stone fireplace, and the charm of the innkeepers, who live in a separate wing of the house, make this bed and breakfast an absolute delight.

◆ **Romantic Note:** There is a two-night minimum on weekends, April through October.

SERENITY PINES CLIFF COTTAGE, Whidbey Island
Northwest Vacation Homes
(206) 321-5005
Moderate

Call for directions.

This small, attractive, self-contained cottage is set on a forested bluff overlooking a soothing view of the Saratoga Passage and the Cascade Mountains. The contemporary interior is pretty and has all the conveniences of home, including a full kitchen, wood stove, and petite dining area. Sliding glass doors open onto a private deck with a hot tub: a warm vantage point from which you can better enjoy the view, and each other.

The cottage is managed by **NORTHWEST VACATION HOMES**; most of their other properties are better suited for families.

TWICKENHAM HOUSE, Whidbey Island
5023 South Langley Road, Langley
(206) 221-2334, (800) 874-5009
Moderate

From the ferry landing, follow Highway 525 north for four miles to Maxwelton Road. Turn right and proceed to the T intersection, where you'll see the inn.

If you've got a hankering for some real country living, head on over to the Twickenham House. The rough-hewn fence, dry dusty farmyard, hens, roosters, and sheep all add up to an authentic ranch atmosphere. Inside, the house looks more like a museum; authentic English artifacts jut out of every nook and cranny, and each has its own charming story. There are six guest rooms tucked away within this sprawling contemporary home. The rooms are distinctly plain in their simplicity, but do have private baths. In spite of the spartan decor, they are comfortable places to stay. Three of the rooms open to a casual, comfortable shared living room. A three-course breakfast is sure to fire you up for a brisk walk down the path that wends through the beautiful 10-acre wooded estate. This is where you'll find the real romance.

◆ **Romantic Note:** There is a pub in the making, which will have a giant open hearth, dartboard, classic movies, and beer on tap. The only drawback to the rustic appeal of Twickenham House is its location along a major traffic artery, where the din of cars remains insistently in the background.

THE WHIDBEY INN, Whidbey Island
106 First Street, Langley
(206) 221-7115
Moderate to Expensive

From the ferry dock, follow Highway 525 into Langley. Turn right on Maxwelton Road, then bear left on Langley Road, which becomes Cascade, which becomes First Street.

Reputedly one of Whidbey Island's finest, this inn in the heart of Langley assuredly ranks among the most interesting and elegant. Due to its bluff location, every room features serene water views to the north, west, and east. The standard rooms are pleasant, but the three romantic suites are remarkable. The Saratoga Suite, complete with bay windows, marble fireplace, and cozy but posh English furnishings, is phenomenal. Gourmet breakfasts are delivered to every room for a private, leisurely morning meal.

Restaurant Kissing

CAFÉ LANGLEY, Whidbey Island
113 First Street, Langley
(206) 221-3090
Inexpensive to Moderate

From the ferry dock, follow Highway 525 into Langley. Turn right on Maxwelton Road, then bear left on Langley Road, which becomes Cascade, which becomes First Street.

I know it seems an unlikely combination—Greek cuisine, Northwest ingredients, a country setting, and romance—but that is exactly what you'll find at Café Langley. The entrées, showcasing local fresh fish and just-picked produce, display definite Greek flair. The petite interior has white stucco walls, wood-beamed ceilings, and terra-cotta tile floors, with only a handful of oak tables and chairs. The service is friendly and attentive, and by the time dessert comes (their Russian cream dessert is phenomenal) you will be thoroughly ecstatic. The only drawback is the café's popularity, so you might have to wait for a table.

FRANCISCO'S, Whidbey Island
510 Cascade Avenue, Langley
(206) 221-2728
Moderate to Expensive

From the ferry dock, follow Highway 525 into Langley. Turn right on Maxwelton Road, then bear left on Langley Road, which becomes Cascade Avenue. The restaurant is on the water side of the road.

Francisco's is Langley's newest addition to dining out island-style. This elegant new restaurant has a premium setting on a bluff overlooking Saratoga Passage. The entire blue-gray home is wrapped in beveled glass windows that take full advantage of the magnificent location. The peach and jade interior is accented by stained glass windows, very pretty wall sconces, and ample seating. The ambience is best described as modern-Victorian, a soft mix of chic and country. Though at the time this book went to press it was still a bit early to report on the consistency of the kitchen, from all appearances, formal dining has arrived in Langley.

◆ **Romantic Warning:** Although smoking is not permitted in the restaurant, it is permitted in the adjacent small lounge, which makes for a fairly unbreathable atmosphere in that section of the restaurant.

KASTEEL FRANZEN, Whidbey Island
5861 Highway 20, Oak Harbor
(206) 675-0724
Expensive

From the ferry dock, take Highway 525 (it turns into Highway 20); the restaurant is on the right as you enter Oak Harbor.

The setting—a white house with rotating wooden water wheel, adjacent to a windmill—is reminiscent of Holland, but the food is French. Thus the name: *Kasteel Franzen* is Dutch for "French castle." In this idyllic spot, romantics can indulge their palates with luscious entrées like the Mediterranean bouillabaisse, a blend of seafood prepared in a classic French fish stock finished with saffron; the spicy Singapore prawns sautéed in cilantro; and, for the purists, escargot in puff pastry, sautéed with garlic, shallots, basil, Pernod, white wine, and mushrooms.

Despite the piano player's gallant efforts, the interior is a bit oppressive. The European Provincial dining room, with its dark wood beams, low ceilings, and dim lighting, can actually detract somewhat from the mood. But delectable cuisine and accommodating service are the reasons to dine here (and you can ask them to turn up the lights).

Outdoor Kissing

LANGLEY, Whidbey Island

The town of Langley is five miles north of the ferry dock, on Highway 525.

People with unromantic dispositions describe Langley as a one-horse town, and they're right. But that's what makes it such a terrific getaway from life in the fast lane. Langley has maintained its Northwest look and style without compromising its virtues just to attract tourists. There is nothing in the vicinity for miles around to spoil the scenery.

Langley perches on the water's edge, and its meadows and bluffs have amazing views of Mount Baker, the Cascades, and Saratoga Passage. The appeal of this town lies in the unaffected style of its buildings and shops, which are quaint and charming. Of course, over the years the main street has become a bit gentrified, but that doesn't get in the way of the original ambience. As you travel around Whidbey Island, don't let yourselves miss a visit to this delightful place.

Mount Vernon

Restaurant Kissing

WILDFLOWERS, Mount Vernon
2001 East College Way
(206) 424-9724
Moderate to Expensive

Take the College Way exit off Interstate 5. Head east for one and a half miles.

You'd never expect to find country charm anywhere near this commercialized strip of neon signs, Food Marts, and gas stations. Fortunately, you can escape the clamor and indulge your fantasies in the seclusion of a creamy white Cape Cod-style home enfolded by a garden and set back from the busy street.

Inside, the handful of tables are draped in dark blue linens and tucked intimately in the cozy alcoves of the home's original living and dining rooms. Year-round Christmas lights in the corners add a dash of warmth to the otherwise simple decor. Although the menu selection is limited, you can enjoy scrumptious and innovative seafood entrées such as butterflied grilled prawns garnished with a mango-pineapple salsa or marlin cooked with tamari, ginger, citrus, and herbs. After one candle-lit shared bite of this savory cuisine, you're likely to forget about the traffic and noise beyond and focus on matters closer to the heart and stomach.

La Conner

La Conner is the heart of the Skagit Valley's spring **TULIP FESTI-VAL**. Its soul is the 1,500 acres of prime farmland that come alive each spring, paving the landscape with huge swatches of floral glory. Although this is assuredly *the* consummate Northwest destination during the last weeks of March and early April, every season blesses the area with a romantic aura all its own. Haloed by mountains all around and with Mount Baker often visible to the north, the sweetly pastoral valley is also filled with waving cornfields, dairy farms, and acres of lush crops.

La Conner itself is a colorful, picturesque Northwest town, and a favorite springtime destination. Bordering the Swinomish Channel, it offers a remarkable selection of restaurants, antique shops, bed and breakfasts, and adundant scenery. The crowds and tour buses calm down in the late fall and winter, after the tulip lovers and vacationers leave, making this a charming corner of Puget Sound for savoring time together.

◆ **Romantic Note:** For more information about the Tulip Festival, call the **LA CONNER CHAMBER OF COMMERCE,** (206) 466-4778.

Hotel/Bed and Breakfast Kissing

CHANNEL LODGE, La Conner
205 North First Street
(206) 466-1500
Moderate to Expensive

From Washington, turn right onto First Street and go about one block to the lodge.

Settled on the dock of the Swinomish Channel, this place looks more like an upscale condominium complex than a country lodge, but it is nevertheless beautifully appointed and lavishly decorated, with all the appropriate amenities and a polished country emphasis. The formal lobby is flanked by an enormous beach-stone fireplace and floor-to-ceiling French windows that overlook the water and dock. All of the 40 immaculate rooms, although a bit on the snug side, are handsomely appointed with wood-beamed ceilings and attractive bathrooms. Some rooms have private patios or decks, but the 10 king parlor rooms are the best. Large tiled showers, Jacuzzi tubs, fireplaces, and sitting nooks combine to create an exclusive atmosphere. The exquisite dining alcove is an exceedingly romantic place to enjoy the lodge's continental breakfast.

DOWNEY HOUSE BED AND BREAKFAST, La Conner
1880 Chilberg Road
(206) 466-3207
Inexpensive to Moderate

From Interstate 5, heading north from Seattle, take Exit 221 west onto Fir Island Road, which curves north and becomes Chilberg Road. The house is on the west side of the road.

If this place weren't located on the main road into La Conner, I would give it four lips because it's an impeccable place to spend cherished moments together. But this thoroughfare can be fairly busy, especially in the summer and on weekends. All the rooms in this renovated Victorian farmhouse are country beautiful, with private baths, ample space, tremendously comfortable beds, and soothing details. The best room is the suite attached to the garage, where everything is a lush forest green and the entrance is private. (At this writing the hot tub in back is broken, which disappointed us, but not enough to significantly affect our enjoyable stay here.)

THE HERON, La Conner   ❧❧
117 Maple Avenue
(206) 466-4626
Inexpensive to Moderate

From Interstate 5, heading north from Seattle, take Exit 221 west onto Fir Island Road, which curves north and becomes Chilberg Road. As you approach the town of La Conner, look for Maple Avenue and turn left to the inn.

Each room, even the inexpensive ones, is a warm, pleasing place in which to escape the crowds during the local Tulip Festival or the flocks of summer visitors in the shops in town. The Heron is intended to be a Victorian-style inn, though the decor and exterior are a bit too modern-looking to be convincing. But inside, the rooms have antique furnishings, wooden bedsteads, beamed ceilings, and thick down comforters. All have private baths, and the most romantic have spa tubs, views, and fireplaces. An outdoor hot tub is also part of the allure. Continental breakfast is served in the formal dining room, but you are free to take yours up to the privacy of your room or out on any of the three back decks.

RAINBOW INN, La Conner   ❧❧
1075 Chilberg Road
(206) 466-4578
Inexpensive to Moderate

From Interstate 5, heading north from Seattle, take Exit 221 west onto Fir Island Road, which curves north and becomes Chilberg Road. The house is on the east side of the road.

Like Downey House, this impressively renovated Victorian farm-house is set too close to the main road. The saving graces here are the yellow blooms of mustard plants, an 85-year-old chestnut tree, and towering poplars that flank the home and the sweeping view over the valley to Mount Baker. There are three floors of country-rustic rooms, most of which have pleasant views of the valley. The preferred choices are the ones with private bath (the shared baths are not the best); the ground-floor room has a Jacuzzi tub. Outside, there is a gazebo with a hot tub. In the morning a full breakfast is served in a charming enclosed sun deck lined with tables set for two.

WHITE SWAN GUEST HOUSE, La Conner
1388 Moore Road
(206) 445-6805
Inexpensive to Moderate

From Interstate 5 take Exit 221 west and stay on Fir Island Road. In 5.3 miles you come to a yellow blinking light that leads you straight onto Moore Road.

You approach this flamboyantly renovated Victorian farmhouse from a quiet country road that passes fields of golden corn and remarkable mountain vistas. Its long driveway is lined with commanding poplars, and the grounds are filled with slightly overgrown but lush gardens. Inside the main house, the brightly painted, immaculate interior pro-vides an affable environment for a relaxing escape. Unfortunately, the three guest rooms here share a just passable small bath, which does not add up to the best romantic picture. However, total romance is to be found in the self-contained garden cottage set under huge silver maples at the back of the property. The cottage has a wraparound cedar deck, comfortable living room, floor-to-ceiling windows, separate bedroom, and a fully stocked kitchen. It isn't plush, but it can be your own country home in the middle of pristine, secluded farmland.

THE WILD IRIS, La Conner
121 Maple Avenue
(206) 466-1400
Inexpensive to Moderate

From Interstate 5, heading north from Seattle, take Exit 221 west onto Fir Island Road, which curves north and becomes Chilberg Road. As you approach the town of La Conner, look for Maple Avenue and turn left to the inn.

This brand-new inn is perfection. Every detail exudes country elegance and sumptuous bliss. Although the two-story Victorian-style exterior, with its sea green shutters and taupe siding, hugs the parking lot, it is sheer rapture inside. The inn has a total of 18 rooms, but the 12 suites are the best spots for romance. These deluxe rooms are individually decorated and have fireplaces, extra-roomy Jacuzzi tubs, wicker furnishings, wrought-iron beds, plush down comforters, and views of the mountains and valley. Some have private patios, sitting areas, unique sconces, and artwork. The Persian Suite is of particular kissing interest, with oversized pillows arranged around a plush Persian rug. A full gourmet breakfast is served at separate tables in the inn's rustic dining nook, where Greek omelets, cheese soufflés, fresh croissants, homemade granola, and fresh fruit are served buffet-style.

Restaurant Kissing

BLACK SWAN, La Conner
505 South First Street
(206) 466-3040
Expensive

On South First Street, at Washington.

There are more exciting interiors, but for miles around you are not likely to experience more exciting cuisine. Freshness is the hallmark of this restaurant, with locally grown veal, straight-off-the-boat fish, and herbs and vegetables delivered from nearby farms. Limited dinner hours and few tables make benefiting from the kitchen's skill somewhat difficult, but it's worth the effort if you care to dine in true Northwest gourmet style.

PALMER'S RESTAURANT AND PUB, La Conner
205 East Washington
(206) 466-4261
Moderate to Expensive

On the corner of Washington and Second streets.

Palmer's attractive wood-beamed dining room is simply appointed with hunter green carpeting, lace-covered windows, and wood tables. At lunch the Brie hamburger and wilted spinach salad with smoked duck are both impressive. Dinner choices consist of fresh meats, fish, and pastas, all finished with a savory flair. King salmon with a Pernod and tarragon cream sauce and the fresh lamb shank with caramelized onions are both delicious.

Anacortes

Hotel/Bed and Breakfast Kissing

MAJESTIC HOTEL, Anacortes
419 Commercial Avenue
(206) 293-3355
Inexpensive to Expensive

Entering Anacortes on Commercial Avenue, follow Commercial to Fourth Street. The Majestic is on the corner on your right.

Many travelers like to use the active town of Anacortes as a stopover on their way to and from the San Juan Islands. If you plan a brief encounter with this Northwest port of call, the Majestic Hotel offers abundant warmth and elegance. The grand four-story white building, built in 1889, stands fast in the midst of the industrial jostle of Commercial Avenue. You enter through French doors into a pleasant lobby with high ceilings and European decor. Each of the 23 rooms is graced with pastel carpeting, down comforters, and a mixture of antiques and classic white wicker furniture. The Superior, Deluxe, and Majestic suites have wet bars and refrigerators; some of the more expensive suites also have oversized soaking tubs and private decks that overlook the courtyard gardens, gazebo, and trellis. As you climb the open winding staircase to the mezzanine level for continental breakfast, look up at the expansive stained-glass skylight.

◆ **Romantic Note: JANOT'S BISTRO AND PUB,** (206) 299-9163, (Moderate), connected to the Majestic, is a great place to have lunch or dinner. The spacious, airy dining room has high ceilings and a wall of windows that offer a lovely view of the courtyard gardens.

CHANNEL HOUSE, Anacortes
2902 Oakes Avenue
(206) 293-9382
Very Inexpensive to Moderate

Following Commercial Avenue into Anacortes, take a left on 12th Street, which becomes Oakes Avenue. Channel House is on the right.

You might bypass this nondescript beige farmhouse on your way to the ferry. Given the chance, however, the Channel House could convince you to stay in Anacortes longer than you anticipated. The hardwood floors, Oriental rugs, wood-faced fireplaces, modest decor, and grand downstairs dining room lend a historical aura to the building, which was originally built for an Italian count in 1902.

There are four guest rooms in the main house, two of which share a bathroom. None of the four is romantic or worth a stay. An outside walkway lined with flowers and plants (passing the not-so-private hot tub) leads you to the two connecting cottage suites that are the Channel House's finest offerings. The Victorian Rose will probably be your preference, with its four-poster bed, whirlpool tub, and French doors that open to a view of the water. The Country Rose has a glaring, bright yellow color scheme and none of the charm of its neighbor. It also feels somewhat confining without a view.

The kindly hosts are sure to warm you with a scrumptious full breakfast of French toast stuffed with fruit and other delectable morning delicacies.

Bow

Restaurant Kissing

OYSTER BAR, Bow
240 Chuckanut Drive
(206) 766-6185
Expensive to Very Expensive

On Chuckanut Drive, a short drive from Bellingham.

This refined, very French restaurant is a culinary milepost along famous Chuckanut Drive. Only 12 tables adorn the pocket-size, knotty-pine dining room, lined with scintillating, legendary views of Samish Bay through the floor-to-ceiling windows. The menu changes with the seasons, but the salmon is always exquisitely prepared and delicately sauced, with interesting side dishes like a fresh fruit salsa or a vegetable pâte. Of course, the oysters are remarkable, particularly when served with caviar and a wine-garlic-butter sauce.

OYSTER CREEK INN, Bow
190 Chuckanut Drive
(206) 766-6179
Moderate

On Chuckanut Drive, a short drive from Bellingham.

Enveloped by forest, set above a stone-studded flowing creek, the Oyster Creek Inn provides a relaxing environment for lunch or dinner. The restaurant is only a minute's drive north of The Oyster Bar, but a far greater distance in mood and style. The casual interior is all wood, with wraparound windows that bring the outside in. The spirit here is informal and unhurried. The menu offers classic Northwest seafood with all the fixings; the staff is friendly and attentive. Fresh halibut, prawns, and oysters are flavorful and precisely prepared. A salad of assorted fresh greens or oyster soup comes with the entrées, and both are exceptional.

Outdoor Kissing

CHUCKANUT DRIVE

From Interstate 5, exit outside of Bellingham or Burlington to Highway 11, following the signs for Chuckanut Drive.

From the moment you embark upon this landmark coastal drive, the visual delights begin. If you're heading south, the exhibition starts with forested cliffs that reach down to the water's edge. On the horizon lies the silhouette of Lummi Island, and in the distance the rugged coastline of Chuckanut Bay. As you continue south, the varying patterns of islands, forest, and meadows form a dazzling panorama. **LARRABEE STATE PARK**, eight miles south of Bellingham, is a wonderful place to stop and walk along the chiseled beach and see the sights up close.

Bellingham

Hotel/Bed and Breakfast Kissing

BIG TREES BED AND BREAKFAST, Bellingham
4840 Fremont Street
(206) 647-2850
Inexpensive

From Interstate 5, take the Lakeway Drive exit heading east. Stay to the right and it becomes Cable Street, and then Lake Whatcom Boulevard; turn right on Coronado, then cross Fremont, and the house is down the first driveway on the right.

In some ways this is a traditional bed and breakfast—not particularly unique, more like visiting grandma's house. But on the whole, this is an intriguing spot for quiet moments and true relaxation. The handsome original woodwork inside this turn-of-the-century Craftsman-style home is worth a long look. The wood-beamed ceilings and the built-in cabinetry are lovely. Two acres of old-growth fir trees, at least 200 years old, surround the gray shingled home, along with a perfect lawn, pleasant gardens, and a flowing creek. The innkeeper attends to all the details, including immaculate rooms with televisions, phones, beautiful handstitched quilts, down comforters, featherbeds, and roomy private baths. Breakfast in the morning is a hearty assortment of fresh-baked scones, fresh fruit (which may include mangoes filled with strawberries), fresh-squeezed orange juice, and Dutch baby pancakes dusted with powdered sugar and covered with fresh fruit.

SCHNAUZER CROSSING, Bellingham
4421 Lakeway Drive
(206) 733-0055
Inexpensive to Moderate

From Interstate 5 heading north, take the Lakeway Drive exit, go east for three miles, and then turn left onto Lakeway Drive. Watch for the signs that lead to the house.

The impressively renovated Fairhaven District, the spectacular start of Chuckanut Drive, and the spellbinding slopes of Mount Baker only an hour's drive to the east make Bellingham a consummate romantic destination. And Schnauzer Crossing sets the standard for other bed and breakfasts to aspire to. Every detail necessary for an intimate getaway is attended to by the friendly, professional innkeeper.

Set on a bluff overlooking Lake Whatcom, this contemporary home with wood-beamed cathedral ceilings, floor-to-ceiling windows, sweeping lawns, and lush gardens is a dream-come-true. The Master Suite is like a small apartment. It has a private entrance through a tree-framed garden, a king-size bed, an alcove sitting area, stereo, wood-burning fireplace, and a huge bathroom with a sizable spa tub and roomy double-head shower. Believe me, you will step into this suite and not want to leave. The other room is nice and comfortable, with its own bath, terrycloth robes, and views of the lake, but it doesn't compare to the Master Suite. The new picture-perfect cottage features a very private wraparound deck, hardwood floors, large Jacuzzi spa, green-tiled bath, gas fireplace, small kitchenette, and sheer comfort. Ahh, what pleasure!

Breakfast, a lavish presentation of gourmet delights, might include sweet rhubarb crisp with hazelnut cream dribbled on top, triple sec French toast with three kinds of syrup, and fresh muffins. As good as it sounds, it tastes even better. If you can pull yourselves away from your room, or the breakfast table, venture down to the lake for some sailing, canoeing, fishing, or swimming, and afterwards you can take a good long steamy soak in the outdoor hot tub, tucked behind the house under towering fir trees.

SUNRISE BAY, Bellingham
2141 North Shore Road
(206) 647-0376
Inexpensive

Call for directions.

Two simple but pretty rooms, both with private entrance, private bath, skylights, TV and VCR, telephone, and soft floral linens, are part of the appeal of this lakeside bed and breakfast. But the real allure is the outdoor hot tub, heated swimming pool, and large cedar deck overlooking the water and foothills. The interior of the main house is wrapped in floor-to-ceiling windows and is an attractive place for the elaborate morning meal.

Restaurant Kissing

CAFÉ TOULOUSE, Bellingham
114 West Magnolia
(206) 733-8996
Inexpensive

On Magnolia near Cornwall.

Excellent food, a small contemporary setting, and outstanding des-serts are responsible for this café's distinguished reputation. The casual interior (something between a lunch counter and an upscale café) fronts a fairly serious kitchen that adds cilantro pesto to their perfect chili verde and enhances multileafed salads with fresh fruit vinaigrettes.

IL FIASCO, Bellingham   ❖❖❖
1309 Commercial Street
(206) 676-9136
Moderate to Expensive

On Commercial between Holly and Magnolia.

Il Fiasco is Bellingham's premier dining location, and it lives up to its reputation nightly. The attractive interior of brick walls, wood tables, and exposed heating ducts provides a polished atmosphere in which to savor outstanding Italian creations. Your attentive waitperson and the accomplished kitchen staff will help make your meal a special event. The four-cheese lasagne in a garlic cream sauce is as rich and delicious as it sounds, and the pasta with garlic, sun-dried tomatoes, and arti-chokes mixed with fresh tuna and salmon is flawless. Romance may not be the primary reason to come to Il Fiasco, but after you eat a superlative meal here it will surely be on your mind.

PACIFIC CAFÉ, Bellingham   ❖❖
100 North Commercial Street
(206) 647-0800
Moderate to Expensive

On the corner of Commercial and Champion streets, in the Mount Baker Theater building.

A soothing interior of blond wood tables, shoji screens, and Japanese-style overhead lights is what you will find at this attractive downtown restaurant. The lunch and dinner menus are quite similar, so at either meal you can dine on fresh fish, such as Hawaiian ono served with a generous chanterelle mushroom sauce, pasta dishes such as light creamy seafood linguine, and a very good chicken teriyaki.

Lummi Island

Hotel/Bed and Breakfast Kissing

LOGANITA, Lummi Island
2825 West Shore Drive
(206) 758-2651
Moderate to Very Expensive

Take the Lummi Island ferry, just north of Bellingham, following the signs to the ferry landing or the Lummi Casino. The ferry leaves on the hour between 6 A.M. and 12 P.M. After docking, turn right on Nugent Road, which becomes West Shore Drive.

You will be embraced with warmhearted attention by the gregarious, fastidious innkeeper of this Northwest island estate. (Stop reading and call now for the next available summer weekend. Trust me.) A grassy knoll blesses the white frame country house with unobstructed views of the water, islands, and mainland. Outside, a multitiered deck provides ample space to linger over the breathtaking scenery. The immense knotty-pine rooms on the ground floor are common areas for the guests; two stone fireplaces, abundant cushy seating, grand piano, popular kitchen area, and floor-to-ceiling windows at the front of the house create an inspiring setting for whiling the day and night away.

Down comforters, floral fabrics, wicker furniture, silver ice buckets, antique champagne glasses, bay windows, and impressive Northwest artwork grace each of the rooms. All have standard private baths, some with attractive blue tiling. Three of the rooms, although extremely attractive, are a bit small. The one upstairs suite (with a separate snuggling alcove) and the two self-contained cottages (one adjoins the main house) all have fireplaces, sitting areas, comfortable furnishings, soothing to exhilarating views, and are superior. A generous full breakfast is served buffet-style in the great room and features a silver platter filled with fresh fruit, walnut cake, smoked salmon, and eggs. Casual luxury best describes Loganita, and the setting makes it irresistible.

THE WILLOWS INN, Lummi Island
2579 West Shore Drive
(206) 758-2620
Moderate to Very Expensive

Take the Lummi Island ferry just north of Bellingham, following the signs to the ferry landing or the Lummi Casino. The ferry leaves on the hour between 6 A.M. and 12 P.M. After docking, turn right on Nugent Road, which becomes West Shore Drive.

All of your senses will be enlivened and beautifully tended to at this unique waterfront retreat with scintillating views of the Strait of Georgia, the forested hills of nearby San Juan Island, and Vancouver Island in the distance. The inn is embraced by rose arbors, vegetable patches, and herb gardens. In the main house you'll find four basic guest rooms, two with private baths and two that share a bath accessed down a flight of stairs. That isn't great, but be patient—I'm getting to the good part. Out back, behind the main house, stand two detached cottages. The smaller one is adorable and affords delicious serenity and comfort. The larger is particularly enticing, with two sumptuous bedrooms, white down quilts, Jacuzzi tub, oversized tiled shower, designer kitchen, cozy living room with gas fireplace, stereo, TV and VCR, and views of the spectacular scenery. The price tag is steep on this one, but two couples traveling together make it almost reasonable. (It is rented only to people who know each other.)

The last illustrious component of The Willows is the kitchen's skill at preparing lavish breakfasts, high teas, and four-course dinners; all are feats of culinary excellence. Meals are served only when the bed and breakfast is open, Thursday through Sunday, in the glass-enclosed formal dining room. Breakfast is an elaborate presentation of fresh breads, soufflés, and a perfect stuffed French toast with homemade syrups. Afternoon high tea features the best shortbreads you'll ever taste and a premier selection of cakes and delicacies such as an exquisite nectarine-cream cheese tart. At night the conversation is hushed as a bounty of the freshest food possible is presented and savored. Tomato-orange-cilantro soup, a hearty seafood Provencal, king salmon with sorrel sauce, and chanterelle mushrooms in a puffed pastry shell are some of the delectable selections you may find on the menu. Intoxicating double chocolate pecan pie or a chocolate silk pie will melt any resistance you might have considered.

SEATTLE AND ENVIRONS

Seattle is a big city with a small-town mentality. Its many neighborhoods are fiercely individualistic, almost like separate little villages with distinct personalities reflected in the homes, shops, and people. Despite this diversity, Seattle residents have much in common. This is a town where no one jaywalks or honks their horn (except the new arrivals, although they are quick to adapt). A true passion for the outdoors is evident in everything the locals do, from bicycling, hiking, and skating to boating, windsurfing, and skiing. Outdoor recreation is a serious, year-round pursuit here.

Seattle's striking setting amid lakes and bays, verdant hillsides, and rugged mountain peaks gives it a serene, beguiling environment with mesmerizing views. Several popular movies, television shows, and national magazine articles have enhanced Seattle's reputation, but the city's growing popularity has taken some of the glitter off this previously untarnishable stone. Traffic can be a living nightmare, housing prices have skyrocketed, and there are days when smog hovers over the area. But those drawbacks can't diminish or end the honeymoon Seattleites have with their city—the ski slopes are still only an hour's drive east of downtown; excellent theater, jazz, opera, comedy clubs, and dance thrive here; island getaways are an hour or two away; and the hiking country is stupendous. There are also enough *kissing* places here to keep two people preoccupied with romance for a lifetime.

Hotel/Bed and Breakfast Kissing

ALEXIS HOTEL, Seattle
1007 First Avenue
(206) 624-4844
Expensive to Very Expensive

Six blocks south of the Pike Place Market, on First Avenue between Spring and Madison.

Like many downtown hotels, this is a very exclusive and very expensive place to stay. Where the Alexis parts company with other hotels is that it is also the epitome of luxury. For sumptuous detailing and ample space you can't do much better, particularly if you are willing to go the extra mile and reserve one of the six suites with a wood-burning fireplace, tall ceilings, oversized windows, spa tub, and formal living room. These lavish accommodations are beautifully appointed and comfortable. Complimentary continental breakfast is served in the hotel's handsome restaurant (see the Romantic Suggestion). There are no crowds milling about at the Alexis; with only 54 rooms, it can feel quite intimate. So order room service, light the fire, set your shoes out to be shined, and get ready for a very special evening.

◆ **Romantic Suggestion:** Whether or not you are staying overnight at the Alexis Hotel, take time to have breakfast, lunch, or dinner at **THE PAINTED TABLE**, (206) 624-3646, (Inexpensive to Moderate). The room is a showpiece: wood paneling, pillars, a large transom skylight, and high ceilings contrast with grand contemporary chandeliers, art-deco sconces, and a gallery's worth of work by local artists. The setting is more business-oriented than intimate, but the peach-colored stucco walls add warmth, and the effect is impressive. The food is excellent, with a few exceptions: the pastas were too oily and the cheese was overdone. Other than that, everything was delicious. The portions are generous and the staff is politely attentive.

THE GASLIGHT INN, Seattle
1727 15th Avenue
(206) 325-3654
Inexpensive to Moderate

Head east on Denny Way to Capitol Hill. Veer left onto Olive Street, which shortly becomes East John and eventually terminates at 15th Avenue East. Turn right on 15th Avenue East and go several blocks. The Gaslight Inn is on the right-hand side of the street.

The Gaslight Inn, located in Capitol Hill's busy 15th Avenue neighborhood, attracts mainly businesspeople who are weary of staying in the 500-unit hotels available downtown. The Gaslight has nine striking rooms, six with private baths. One is filled with Indian artifacts, while another, with its wood-paneled walls and a deer head above the bed, has the flavor of a Northwest hunter's library. Two of the rooms have decks that overlook the backyard pool and the Seattle skyline. None of the rooms is frilly, but all have benefited from a high-quality renovation. The plaster walls and ceiling in each room are smooth perfection, painted with coat after coat of deep, rich color until virtually flawless.

It's clear to me that the handsome decor isn't all that attracts the downtown business crowd to this inn; the efficient manner in which things are run and the consistent attention to detail are also major drawing points. The bottom line for The Gaslight Inn is this: whether you're conducting business or pleasure in the Seattle area, if you want your lodging to be as gracious as possible, this place fits the bill.

HAINSWORTH HOUSE, Seattle
2657 37th Avenue Southwest
(206) 938-1020
Inexpensive

From Interstate 5 go west on the West Seattle Freeway. Take the Admiral Way exit and continue on Admiral to the top of the hill. Turn left on Olga. The Hainsworth House is at the intersection of Olga and 37th Avenue Southwest.

Built in the early 19th century, this mammoth Tudor-style mansion has an atmosphere of relaxed luxury and comfort. The Victorian decor is impressive, but also homey enough to make one feel compelled to curl up on the soft couch in the TV room and spend a lazy evening watching old Garbo flicks. Only two rooms are set aside as guest chambers; both have Victorian-style decor, an abundance of English country floral prints, private decks, and private baths. The larger room is by far the nicer, with a fireplace, king-size bed, and an outstanding view of downtown Seattle from the deck on a summer evening or through the large bay windows on a cloudy but cozy Northwest day. The smaller room has a spacious deck overlooking the garden. Regardless of the weather, the ever-changing Puget Sound offers the ultimate in soothing scenery. In the morning you wake to a formal gourmet champagne breakfast.

HOTEL VINTAGE PARK, Seattle
1100 Fifth Avenue
(206) 624-8000, (800) 624-4433
Expensive to Unbelievably Expensive

In downtown Seattle on Fifth Avenue near Spring.

Tastefully appointed, comfortable rooms with canopied crown beds, stately period furnishings, and attractive bathrooms are the hallmark of this newly renovated downtown hotel. Rich color schemes of hunter green, plum, and taupe; original artwork; and 24-hour room service from the adjacent **TULIO** restaurant make this a premium addition to Seattle's hotels. Every evening in the petite fireside lobby, there is a wine tasting featuring selections from Washington wineries.

INN AT THE MARKET, Seattle
86 Pine Street
(206) 443-3600
Moderate to Expensive

Located in the Pike Place Market, at the corner of First and Pine.

To many, the most romantic setting in Seattle is the Pike Place Market. If you would like to stay right in the center of town, you can do so in style at the Inn at the Market. Although the room decorations are fairly plain, each room has nice touches like large armoires and French country furnishings. Breakfast is not served, but the market, with its stalls and restaurants, is steps away. For those who want proximity to the best of Seattle's landmarks, there's no place like this one.

FOUR SEASONS OLYMPIC HOTEL, Seattle
411 University Street
(206) 621-1700
Expensive to Unbelievably Expensive

On University between Fourth and Fifth avenues.

This ultra-posh downtown hotel features more than 400 luxuriously renovated rooms in a centrally located landmark building. The rooms (some with separate sitting parlors) are graciously decorated, but essentially just nice hotel rooms. They won't spark romance in and of themselves. What will sweep you away, though, are the restaurants, health club, and lobby area, which are all simply sensational. Once you arrive at The Four Seasons you'll have no reason to go anywhere else to fulfill your amorous requirements. While you're enjoying the facilities at the complimentary health club—a lap pool, a 20-person spa tub (which never seems to be in use), a modest workout room, and an outdoor lounge—you can arrange for poolside service of fresh coffee and eggs Florentine.

Downstairs, the **GARDEN COURT LOUNGE** is a radiant composite of tea room, lounge, bistro, and ballroom. It is an immense hall, arrayed with a bevy of trees, marble floors, 40-foot-tall windows, a petite waterfall cascading into a marble pond, and well-spaced groupings of settees, cushioned chairs, and glass coffee tables. This prodigious dining room changes appearance as the day progresses: Sunday-morning brunch, savory lunch, authentic afternoon tea service, evening cocktails, and late-evening dancing to a small band every Friday and Saturday night (piano dancing Tuesday through Thursday).

THE GEORGIAN ROOM (reviewed elsewhere in this section) is one of the most superlative dining spots in all of Seattle, and not to be missed for an ultra-special celebration when price is not a consideration.

All in all, when you talk about a grand stay in Seattle, you're talking about The Four Seasons Olympic.

◆   **Romantic Note:** Ask the hotel about its specially priced romantic weekend packages.

LAKE UNION BED AND BREAKFAST, Seattle
2217 North 36th Street
(206) 547-9965
Moderate to Expensive

Call for reservations and directions.

I must caution you about two problems with this bed and breakfast. First, even if you have good directions and know Seattle, the home is tricky to find, so be sure to ask for *very* specific directions. Second, the privacy of the smaller of the two bedrooms is limited due to the downstairs location of the bathroom. In spite of that, you will be impressed with this contemporary three-story wood-and-brick home overlooking the north end of Lake Union. You enter through a landscaped garden enclosed by a six-foot-tall brick wall. The modest-size interior has thick white carpeting, interesting art pieces, and overstuffed white chairs flanking a marble fireplace.

The house can accommodate two couples. The penthouse is a huge room adorned by willow furniture and a fireplace of brown marble. The bathroom has a large spa tub with a superb view of the lake and city, and there are control-heated tile floors that flow into a sun-drenched solarium with the same wonderful view. The other upstairs bedroom, which is much less expensive, is simple and comfortable and has a bathroom located down on the main floor. That would automatically be a romantic no-no if the bathroom didn't contain a glass-brick-enclosed sauna, piped-in music, and a large tiled shower. And, yes, the breakfast: a mouthwatering presentation of soufflés, pastries, fruits, granola, egg dishes, and anything else the owner/chef thinks of, served on Lenox china and Baccarat crystal.

SALISBURY HOUSE, Seattle
750 16th Avenue East
(206) 328-8682
Inexpensive

On Capitol Hill, on the corner of Aloha and Sixteenth Avenue.

This charmer of a bed and breakfast is located in an old, established neighborhood on Capitol Hill filled with venerable homes. The inviting Prairie-style home provides its guests with a peaceful oasis from the area's colorful but sometimes overwhelmingly busy atmosphere. The decor is simple and homey, but surprisingly elegant. Comfortable furniture, wraparound windows, polished maple floors, fireplaces in the common rooms, and a glass-enclosed sun room with wicker furniture are lovely enhancements. All the guest rooms have attractively renovated baths and a truly gracious feeling. Full breakfast is served in the morning in the formal living room.

SORRENTO HOTEL, Seattle
900 Madison Street
(206) 622-6400
Expensive to Unbelievably Expensive

At Madison and Terry streets, about six blocks east of downtown Seattle.

The Sorrento has one of the most handsome, not to mention *the* most romantic, lobby lounges in the city. The **FIRESIDE ROOM** piano bar holds a stunning, albeit formal, assortment of settees, sofas, and chairs arranged around an imposing hand-painted tile-and-stone fireplace. It is an inviting spot for an early-evening conversation or an after-dinner aperitif. But that is only the beginning; the award-winning **HUNT**

CLUB restaurant (reviewed elsewhere in this section) is here and it is a radiant setting for dining.

Of the hotel's 76 rooms, the suites are the best, with their exceedingly plush furnishings, large windows, stereos, and formal fabrics. Unfortunately, the bathrooms are dull and the standard rooms are just OK, but everything else is exemplary. Turn-down service includes a hot water bottle placed under the sheets for a warm evening snuggle.

Very little about the Sorrento bears any resemblance to a typical city hotel. You need only one visit to convince you of that.

Restaurant Kissing

ADRIATICA, Seattle
1107 Dexter Avenue North
(206) 285-5000
Expensive

Call for directions.

This stately house, perched on a hillside overlooking Lake Union, looks out of place amongst its industrial neighbors. But when the sun has gone down and the surrounding area is obscured by nightfall, the Adriatica appears regal and refined. The third-floor bar is a perfect place to have a quiet drink. Even on Saturday nights, you will find very few people up here, and you are sure to find a table with a glimpse of Lake Union, plus some privacy.

The restaurant is on the second floor of the house, and requires some renovation. Instead of candlelight, the tables are adorned with flimsy pink lamps, and the unique elegance of the house is undercut by the stark, almost bare walls and plain white tablecloths. Regrettably, the wait staff was aloof (bordering on rude), and the food was only mediocre. One evening the people at the table next to us returned their salmon, and the chicken we ordered was greasy and burnt. The baked mozzarella cheese appetizer with basil and tomato was delicious, as were the prawns on angel-hair pasta and the chocolate soufflé. That means you have a 50-50 chance; at these prices not great dining odds.

The most romantic spot here is an atrium filled with colorful flowers and plants, set in back of the building.

AL BOCCALINO, Seattle
1 Yesler Way
(206) 622-7688
Inexpensive to Moderate

From downtown, go south on First Avenue to Pioneer Square. Turn right on
Yesler. Al Boccalino is on the left side of the street at the very end of Yesler Way.

It can get boisterous at lunch and sometimes at dinner, but this tiny
brick-walled restaurant is still a find. A vintage building, typical of many
in the Pioneer Square area, houses the restaurant. Floral curtains are
strung across the middle of wrought-iron-caged windows. The floor is
covered with institutional green tiles with multicolored flecks that
reminded me of my elementary school hallway. In contrast, the white
tablecloths are starched to perfection, and dignified turn-of-the-century lamps hang from the ceiling and shed soft light throughout the
restaurant. The hodge-podge gains charm as you peruse the menu.
Classic and unusual Italian dishes are offered here. If you're looking for
some of the city's finest Italian cuisine and a subdued, intimate,
neighborhood atmosphere, Al Boccalino should be first on your list.

THE BYZANTION, Seattle
601 Broadway East
(206) 325-7580
Inexpensive to Moderate

On the corner of Broadway East and East Mercer.

Seattle's Broadway district is no match for its New York namesake, yet
this promenade of boutiques, cafés, and restaurants is a magnet for
devotees of almost every life-style. A half-mile walk down this street of
glitzy variety can be fun and educational for anyone in the mood to
browse the shops and watch the people. After you've had your fill, head
for the north end of Broadway, where this demure, cozy Greek restaurant
promotes intimate dining. The cuisine is mostly traditional Greek and
remarkably tasty, including several vegetarian dishes. The staff is
patient and unusually considerate.

◆ **Romantic Note:** The restaurant serves a health-aware breakfast
and Sunday brunch of whole-wheat pancakes and waffles, with fresh-
roasted coffee and fresh-squeezed juices.

CAFÉ DILETTANTE, Seattle
1600 Post Alley
(206) 728-9144
and
416 Broadway East
(206) 329-6463
Inexpensive

In the Pike Place Market, just off Pine Street between First and Pike, or on Broadway East, between East Republican and East Harrison.

All right, I admit it, I'm a chocolate lover, and even if this place weren't charming I'd still be a fan. The Dilettante's chocolates are the stuff of dreams (and outrageous temptations to excess). Café Dilettante on Broadway has charming wood tables and a dimly lit chocolate-brown interior; the one downtown in the Pike Place Market has marble tabletops arced around a glass showcase of creamy morsels. The Capitol Hill location is actually the more romantic in design, but the crowds here often interrupt the mood. This is particularly regrettable in the evening, when sharing a torte covered in the Dilettante's fabulously rich Ephemere Sauce is the best way to say goodnight—except for a kiss, that is. The café in the Market is, for some reason, rarely full, and as a result is always romantic.

CAFÉ SOPHIE, Seattle
1921 First Avenue
(206) 441-6139
Inexpensive to Moderate

Café Sophie is located in downtown Seattle, about half a block north of the Pike Place Market, between Stewart and Virginia.

Sophisticated elegance coexists here with romantic coziness and casual comfort. The restaurant's high gold-trimmed ceilings and starched white linen tablecloths are softened by the inviting forest green color scheme. The walls are covered with gold-leaf mirrors that reflect glowing light from delicate lamps on each table. One wall of the restaurant is lined with booths framed by rich, gold-tasseled green curtains. In back there's a room called the Library, which is worth requesting when making reservations because of its sweeping view of Puget Sound. In addition, the fireplace, burgundy velvet seats, tapestry cushions, and book-lined shelves make comfort and elegance the closest of companions. As if this ideal atmosphere weren't enough, the food is truly superior; soups with unique Northwest seasonings and fresh pastas and seafood are prepared with the utmost care. What's more, Café Sophie has the best desserts and most romantic breakfasts in Seattle. That alone warrants your serious consideration.

CAMPAGNE, Seattle
86 Pine Street
(206) 728-2800
Expensive

In the Pike Place Market off Pine Street, in the courtyard of the Inn at the Market.

Situated ideally in Seattle's famous Pike Place Market, Campagne serves superb lunches and dinners. The creative menu will satisfy even the most distinguished gourmet. In summer there is outdoor seating in the courtyard, and at night flickering candles give off a dreamy, dim light. Considered by some to be the best and most romantic restaurant in Seattle, Campagne could inspire a kissing-intensive experience.

CHEZ SHEA, Seattle
94 Pike Street, #34
(206) 467-9990
Moderate to Expensive

Chez Shea is located in the upstairs of a Pike Place Market building that houses Left Bank Books, on the corner of First and Pike.

At night, after you've walked through the deserted market and quietly watched the sky turn from vivid blue to glowing crimson, you can climb the wooden stairs that lead to Chez Shea and share an unforgettable gourmet dinner. The restaurant is small, so all tables afford a view of Puget Sound and West Seattle, but try to sit near a window so that you can also look down on the happenings in the street below.

This restaurant's dark wood floors, creamy cinnamon-colored walls, white arched windows, high ceilings, and period character set the stage for the ultimate romantic evening. The menu at Chez Shea features five different five-course meals. The food is French and creatively prepared each night: a roulade of prosciutto, figs, and Stilton and goat cheese with a port glaze; scallops in champagne sauce served in a potato basket; and blackberry mousse are just a few examples. This is the perfect place to take someone special if you both love the market and want ambience oozing with character and charm.

DAHLIA LOUNGE, Seattle
1904 Fourth Avenue
(206) 682-4142
Expensive

In downtown Seattle on Fourth between Stewart and Virginia.

Touches of theatrical detailing mingle with a formal atmosphere at this popular Seattle restaurant. Striking sconces, tall ceilings, vividly colored walls, dramatic lighting, and cushy booths are part of this elegant setting. The creative menu lists entrées such as petrale sole stuffed with scallops, matzutaki mushrooms, and sake butter, and sashimi-grade tuna charred rare and served over a delicious pasta puttanesca. The king salmon is accompanied by a rich three-cheese polenta and marjoram salsa. It is all tantalizing and surprisingly consistent.

THE GEORGIAN ROOM, Seattle
411 University Street, in the Four Seasons Olympic Hotel
(206) 621-1700
Expensive to Unbelievably Expensive

On University between Fourth and Fifth avenues.

Every facet of this distinguished dining room is luxurious and regal. Ornate crystal chandeliers, monumental floral arrangements, two-story Palladian windows, and subdued, sensuous lighting create a captivating, sensual atmosphere in which to enjoy very posh breakfasts and lunches and exquisite five-star dinners. The cuisine shows eclectic Pacific Rim influences, and is served with an emphasis on presentation and flawless kid-glove service. Tantalizing dishes such as dandelion-geoduck soup with smoked cod crêpes, wild rice and Greek oregano consommé with lamb meatballs, poached scallops in hazelnut broth, and guinea fowl dabbed with rhubarb wine sauce are all impeccably prepared. Desserts are magnificent; the Grand Marnier soufflé is unsurpassed.

THE HUNT CLUB, Seattle
900 Madison Street
(206) 622-6400
Expensive to Unbelievably Expensive

At Madison and Terry streets, about six blocks east of downtown Seattle.

Oozing with romance is this seductively lit (bordering on dark) dining room with Honduran-mahogany paneling framing brick walls. The service is attentive and the food is exceptionally creative and carefully prepared. Your every need will be obligingly met, including privacy. Fresh pheasant, perfect salmon, and remarkable sauces are typical of this superlative dining revelry. Breakfasts are more affordable, but still memorable.

IL TERRAZZO CARMINE, Seattle
411 First Avenue South
(206) 467-7797
Expensive

In Seattle's Pioneer Square, on First Avenue between Jackson and King streets.

A poetic city nightspot, right in the middle of what is not the prettiest part of Pioneer Square. You enter through a brick archway, past a ceramic aqua-blue tiled fountain cascading into a series of spotlighted ponds. Strategically placed backlighting reflects off the water and makes the patio shimmer and gleam in the night air. This is the restaurant's backyard, where tables are set during the summer. Inside, romantic details are evident in the pretty dining room, replete with comfortable rattan chairs, crystal, and floral-patterned china, all arranged to encourage close encounters.

Rest assured that the food lives up to the atmosphere. The kitchen prepares a combination of traditional and daring Italian dishes, with an exceptional antipasto presentation. Your evening can easily be centered around the delicious cuisine and glowing ambience of Il Terrazzo Carmine.

LA DOLCE VITA, Seattle
3426 Northeast 55th Street
(206) 523-3313
Moderate

At the intersection of 35th Avenue Northeast and Northeast 55th Street.

As authentically Italian as it is thoroughly amorous, *la dolce vita* describes what you'll find here in the food and atmosphere. Terra-cotta-tiled floors, soft lighting from wrought-iron chandeliers, Romanesque-style art and wall hangings, floor-to-ceiling windows, and well-spaced seating are all part of the warm, attractive setting. Hearty, deftly prepared, and perfectly seasoned pasta, meat, and fish dishes are served here. Every bite is a flavorful sensation. The very Italian owners bring a joyous, friendly warmth to the elegant surroundings, and this combination makes for one of the most wonderful dining experiences we've ever had in Seattle.

◆ **Romantic Note:** Live classical music is performed on Friday and Saturday evenings at La Dolce Vita. It is a unique, although sometimes distracting, accompaniment to a passionate Italian dinner.

MAXIMILIEN-IN-THE-MARKET, Seattle
81-A Pike Street
(206) 682-7270
Inexpensive to Moderate

In the Pike Place Market, at the south end of the arcade, facing the water. Look for the entrance in the shop area to the south of the clock.

This is almost the quintessential romantic Seattle breakfast place. At Maximilien there's a relaxed atmosphere at all meals, but especially at breakfast. This modest restaurant, with its small array of wooden tables, walls covered with antique mirrors, and a mesmerizing view of Elliott Bay and the Olympics, serves very French and sometimes tasty morning meals. The soufflés are iffy and the pastries often don't taste fresh, but the coffee, view, and quiet setting are always fine. Maximilien also serves good French dinners that are reasonably priced and feature the Olympics changing color in harmony with the setting sun.

QUEEN MARY CONFECTIONERS, Seattle ◆◆◆◆
2912 Northeast 55th Street
(206) 527-2770
Inexpensive

On Northeast 55th Street between 29th and 30th Avenues Northeast.

It is easy to drive past this small storefront restaurant, though it is probably the most romantic restaurant in Seattle. Once inside, you will feel as if you've been transported to the English countryside. This exceedingly charming, polished restaurant has a beautiful interior with wood paneling, pleated floral fabric lining the walls and entrance, English-lace-covered windows and comfortable wicker chairs placed around a handful of tables set for two. Fastidious attention to detail and freshness is to be found here at every meal. Breakfast is an elaborate display of fresh pastries, granolas, and breads; midday brings light, flaky quiches and generous sandwiches; and dinner is an elegant gourmet event. Roast leg of lamb stuffed with red and yellow peppers, and pasta with artichokes and smoked salmon in a heavenly cream sauce were both sumptuous. High tea is also a daily offering, and you will be properly impressed with this ritual. But I've left the best for last: dessert. The most outrageous, luscious cakes, tortes, and mousses are made fresh here daily. Chocolate cake with Amaretto mousse, marbled cheesecake, and fresh fruit tarts were only a few of the selections available the night we fell in love with Queen Mary.

REINER'S, Seattle
1106 Eighth Avenue
(206) 624-2222
Moderate to Expensive

On Eighth Avenue between Spring and Seneca.

It's not in the most romantic location, crammed between two city buildings, but you'll find yourself drawn off the street into a colorful garden entryway shaded by trees. As you enter the small dining room, you notice that every last corner is filled with polished detail. The tables, draped in white linen, set beneath an arched dome ceiling, are surrounded by modern tapestries. Venerable antiques, crystal chandeliers, and lace-curtained windows convey a sense of refined intimacy. Although the tables are arranged somewhat snugly, your privacy is kept intact by the rich ambience of the room. Whether you dine on the extremely fresh grilled king salmon or take advantage of the three-course pre-theater prix fixe meal served nightly (guaranteed to have you out before the curtain goes up), you are sure to satisfy your palate and whet your romantic appetite.

ROVER'S, Seattle
2808 East Madison
(206) 325-7442
Expensive to Very Expensive

Near the corner of Madison and 28th Street.

An unassuming neighborhood setting, a discreet interior, subtly dramatic lighting, white walls covered with pastel art, and some of the most sumptuous continental cuisine you will ever taste are waiting for you at Rover's. Perhaps the decor is a bit stark to be considered cozy or charming, but sophisticated, elegant dining is also enticing for a personal celebration. The chef here is incredibly skilled, and proves it with dishes such as quenelles of salmon with tomato fondue in a dry vermouth sauce, filo filled with goat cheese, tomato concasse with a goat cheese sauce, steamed lobster with a black truffle sauce, and rabbit served with caramelized garlic and huckleberry sauce. Outstanding!

SEATTLE ART MUSEUM AND CAFÉ
100 University Street
(206) 654-3100
Inexpensive

Located in downtown Seattle, on both First Avenue and Second Avenue at University Street.

A stroll through the permanent museum collections and special exhibitions is a stimulating way to spend a leisurely afternoon stirring your cultural passions. Although the location of the Seattle Art Museum might bother some tourists, don't let the seedy area discourage you—what waits inside is worth checking out. Vast windows line the main floor, allowing light to pour through onto provocative architecture, hand-carved statues, marble floors, and a small, contemporary café. This eatery offers a variety of specialty sandwiches that might surprise you. The vegetarian club sandwich can hardly be eaten without a fork, piled high as it is with grilled eggplant, roasted peppers, cucumbers, sprouts, tomato, and a special onion spread. The warm spinach salad comes lightly steamed in a pancetta-sherry vinaigrette, which would have been perfect but the dressing was too oily. For couples who aren't very hungry, it is still a great place to enjoy a latte and each other's company surrounded by the best in Northwest art. The tables are well spaced, and it is possible to feel intimate in this bright, open café.

SOSTANZA, Seattle
1927 43rd Avenue East
(206) 324-9701
Moderate to Expensive

From downtown Seattle take Madison Street all the way to Lake Washington and turn left on 43rd. The restaurant is the second storefront.

Madison Park is a charmingly sophisticated, entirely gentrified Seattle neighborhood, but it isn't so slick that you will feel out of place without your power suit or running clothes. For those who want to enjoy the village-like atmosphere only a stone's throw from the lake, there are kissing possibilities to be found. Sostanza is a delightful dining spot with a tender blend of elegant and country-rustic touches. Amber stucco walls, wood-beamed ceiling, soft lighting, a crackling fireplace, and nicely spaced tables fill this Italian trattoria with warmth and comfort. The food is remarkable and consistent, evoking a delightful sensory visit to the Italian countryside.

SPACE NEEDLE RESTAURANT, Seattle
219 Fourth Avenue North
(206) 443-2150
Expensive

Just go to the Seattle Center (Fifth Avenue and Broad Street) and look up.

I remember the first time I went to the Space Needle on a clear day. All of the region's glories were astonishingly evident, from the Olympics to the Puget Sound islands to the green-haloed neighborhoods of Seattle to the Cascades. I also remember wishing it wasn't so touristy and tacky, and that the food was better. Well, it's still touristy but it's no longer tacky, and the food is actually quite good. It is still the sort of place you take your out-of-town relatives to for a special occasion, but the tables are arranged for surprising privacy and the service is excellent. Nighttime, sunset, candlelight, and fresh king salmon with this view are worthy of more kisses than I care to count.

SZMANIA'S, Seattle
3321 West McGraw
(206) 284-7305
Moderate to Expensive

Head east on Denny Way until it turns north and becomes Elliott Avenue, then take the Magnolia Bridge exit and cross over the bridge. Stay straight until you reach West McGraw and turn left.

How I wish that this restaurant, located near Magnolia Bluff and Discovery Park, in the charming Magnolia neighborhood, had a more romantic atmosphere. Almost all the necessary ingredients are here for an enticing, sensual repast: soft lighting, a sleek interior, and an open kitchen with the most enticing aromas wafting through the two dining rooms. Unfortunately, the tone here is slightly too casual and exuberant, plus parents who can afford to are encouraged to bring their children, and they do. Oh, well. None of that has an effect on the truly remarkable skills of the chef. Fresh fish is magnificently prepared, with every succulent, mouth-watering nuance intact. Our white king salmon baked in a crispy potato crust and served with an olive-pesto sauce, and lingcod with sweet balsamic butter accompanied by three different fresh pastas tossed in an ultra-light cream sauce, were delicious. Their Caesar salad is one of the best and most authentic in the city. And if the ambience doesn't drive you to ecstasy, the dessert selection will. A perfect crème brûlée, strawberry shortcake, or white and dark chocolate mousse can prove almost too wicked. But what's a little decadence between friends?

Outdoor Kissing

ALKI BEACH, West Seattle

Take Interstate 5 to the West Seattle Freeway exit and the West Seattle Bridge. Cross the bridge and follow Harbor Avenue to the beach and around to Beach Drive.

The waterfront neighborhoods of West Seattle are only a few minutes from downtown Seattle. The area near **LINCOLN PARK** looks out to a spectacular view due west, but Alki Beach, with its northwesterly exposure, has the most expansive sensational scenery of them all. A long stretch of sandy beach with exquisite profiles of the snowcapped Olympics and the cool dark waters of Puget Sound is an incredible place to stroll hand-in-hand almost anytime of year. Unfortunately, a warm summer day can change this flawless stretch of land into a mass of urban congestion. During the spring, fall, or winter, when things are quieter, couples can find gentle moments here watching the sky and mountains change expressions with the passing hours.

◆   **Romantic Viewpoint: HAMILTON VIEWPOINT** in West Seattle, just off California Avenue Southwest, is a nicely designed turnoff, facing the downtown skyline of Seattle. From here you can watch the reflections of the buildings' twinkling lights in the cobalt blue water and the moon's golden glow over the surface. This is also a rare vantage point from which to watch sunrise above Seattle. Of course, you won't be the only couple embracing in the moonlight, but you will probably be the only ones snuggling in the early light of dawn.

◆   **Romantic Suggestion:** The **B & O Espresso** on Capitol Hill is not a place one would go for an intimate encounter. An encounter with the '60s maybe, but not with romance. But **THE PEACE CAFÉ** (formerly a branch of B & O ESPRESSO), 2352 California Avenue Southwest, (206) 935-1540, (Inexpensive), in West Seattle is exceptionally romantic, and a most inviting place to stop for a latte and a rich death-by-chocolate dessert. Jade green columns, small wrought-iron tables with marble tabletops, a lofty ceiling, pretty wall sconces, and subdued lighting create a lovely, warm setting.

"BHY" KRACKE PARK

Located on southeast Queen Anne Hill, north of downtown, at the intersection of Fifth Avenue North and Highland. It is also known as Comstock Park.

Unless you've read the first edition of *The Best Places To Kiss* or live nearby, you may not have heard of this park with the funny name. As you drive through the unpretentious neighborhood, you'll probably think nothing of the small, unobtrusive playground on your left. But stop and take another look. "Bhy" Kracke Park starts off as an innocent playground, less than a block long, at the bottom of a hill. On either side of it, landscaped walkways begin angling upwards, meet, then curve around and up, and around and up, to the top of the hill. As you follow the course upward you find five tiers of grassy vistas; park benches, surrounded by dense hedges and vines, all face a startling city view.

Around each turn is another glimpse of the city, building up to what lies at the top. Unbelievable!

◆ **Romantic Note:** If you don't want to walk up, drive to the park entrance on Comstock, at the top of the hill, and walk down one tier.

DISCOVERY PARK SAND CLIFFS, Seattle

The park is in northwest Magnolia. To enter the park from Magnolia Boulevard, take the Magnolia Bridge exit off Elliott Avenue and stay to your left. At the first stop sign, turn left onto Magnolia Boulevard and follow it till it dead-ends at the park's southeast entrance.

Discovery Park is an unusual area with an amazing variety of trails and terrain. You can hike through dense woods or along sandy cliffs above Puget Sound with unmarred exposure to everything due north, south, and west. Or take the wooden steps leading down to the shore and ramble over driftwood, rocky shoreline, and sandy beach. While wandering through your new romantic discovery (pun intended), look for the sand cliffs on the southwest side of the park. During the winter, when sundown occurs in the late afternoon, come stand atop these golden dunes for an intoxicating view of day passing into night.

◆ **Romantic Note: MAGNOLIA BOULEVARD** snakes around the edge of the Magnolia area of Seattle on the way to Discovery Park. This urban thoroughfare is blessed by a majestic 180-degree view of the sound. The cliffs along its southwest border showcase the city and the Olympics. As you follow the drive, you will notice several obvious places to pull off and park. The panoramas from these areas are spectacular but, unfortunately, no privacy is afforded there. However, if you walk from the grass-lined curb down to the edge of the cliff overlooking the water, the street is no longer visible. A wool blanket will help make the damp grass more comfortable.

HIGHLAND DRIVE, Seattle

From Roy Street on lower Queen Anne, turn onto the steep part of Queen Anne Avenue North. Two blocks up, turn left onto West Highland Drive and follow it along the southwestern slope of the hill.

This exclusive street, lined with mansions and classic older apartment buildings, has a prominent southwestern view from below the summit of Queen Anne Hill. At the intersection of Seventh Avenue

West, Eighth Place West, and West Highland, you will discover a grand panoramic vista. There is a grassy knoll up here with benches from which you'll have the most sweeping, complete view of the city skyline and the Olympic Mountains. With a picnic basket in tow, you can spend an entire summer afternoon up here in each other's arms.

HOT-AIR BALLOONING

Two balloon companies to consider in the Seattle area are Balloon Depot, Redmond, (206) 881-9699; and Climb on a Rainbow, Woodinville, (206) 364-0995.

If you're thinking that a hot-air balloon ride sounds like a frivolous, expensive, childish sort of excursion, you're right. It is a Mary Poppins lift-off into fantasy land. After an evening balloon ride, the term "carried away" will suddenly have new meaning.

Usually you depart just before sunset. Your first impression will be astonishment at the enormous mass of billowing material overhead and the dragon fire that fills it with air. As you step into the gondola, your heart will begin to flutter with expectation. Once aloft, as the wind guides your craft above the countryside, the world will seem more peaceful than you ever thought possible. You will also be startled at the splendor of sunset from way up here as twilight covers the mountains with muted color and warmth. A caress while floating above the world on a cloudless summer evening can be a thoroughly heavenly experience.

◆ **Romantic Note:** Some balloon companies serve champagne and a light picnic brunch after the flight.

WASHINGTON STATE FERRY RIDE
Very Inexpensive (Next to Nothing)

Most departures are from the Seattle Ferry Terminal, on Marion and Alaskan Way. For information on schedules and directions, call the Washington State Ferries at (206) 464-6400 or toll-free at (800) 843-3779.

Utilitarian types may use the Washington State Ferries only as a means of transportation to and from work, but we romantics take a different approach. What better way is there to get a sweeping view of the majestic mountains surrounding the Seattle area or the many islands scattered throughout the Puget Sound? Granted, it's no *Love Boat*—the decor is tacky and privacy is lacking—but for very little money, you and yours can bundle up for a stroll on the open deck and enjoy a glowing sunset. The crisp sea air is bound to inspire some snuggling. Or another option is to make a day of it: bring a picnic, comfortable walking shoes, and a sense of adventure to explore some of the ports of call, which include Bainbridge Island, Bremerton, Kingston, and Vashon Island.

The romance rating of this outing definitely depends on how romantic you want to make it. During rush hour or peak tourist season, lines can be long and crowds can be abundant; at those times you may want to use the ferry only as a means of transportation. Don't worry, though, you aren't turning into a *utilitarian* type, because you'll be headed for a different romantic getaway—one mentioned in this book, of course.

WATERFALL GARDEN, Seattle

Just north of the Kingdome, at the northwest corner of Washington and Main streets. The park closes around 9:00 P.M.

United Parcel Service built this lush urban garden as a gift to the citizens of Seattle, and it is a unique city hideaway. This cloistered downtown oasis is enclosed by stone walls and a wrought-iron gate. A large rushing waterfall tumbles over boulders at the back of the garden, its pleasantly noisy rush helping to drown out any evidence that civilization is right next door. Tables and chairs are scattered about, making it a convenient place for a refreshing afternoon picnic. You can also use the garden for a rendezvous with someone special before a football game, dinner, or the theater. Except at lunchtime, you're likely to be quite alone together here.

Woodinville

Outdoor Kissing

CHATEAU STE. MICHELLE WINERY, Woodinville
14111 Northeast 145th
(206) 488-1133

From Interstate 405 North, take the Wenatchee/Monroe exit. Follow Highway 522 east and take the Woodinville exit. Keep right and at the second stoplight turn right onto 175th. At the four-way stop, turn left onto Highway 202. Go two miles to the winery, which is on the right-hand side.

Built in the style of a French country chateau, this well-known winery offers more than superior Northwest wines to its visitors. The 87 acres of manicured grounds are ideal for lazy strolls after a complimentary wine tasting and a cellar tour, particularly during the fall harvesting season. There is also a summer-long series of moderately priced performances, ranging from jazz to Shakespeare, in the outdoor amphitheater. The winery's wine shop offers meats, cheeses, exquisite wines, and truffles—all the essentials for a perfect picnic.

Carnation

Hotel/Bed and Breakfast Kissing

IDYL INN, Carnation   ♥
4548 Tolt River Road
(206) 333-4262
Inexpensive to Expensive

Call for reservations and directions.

This contemporary home rests on a secluded seven-acre organic hobby farm, near the banks of the Tolt River. While the town of Carnation is not the first place you'd think to come to for a romantic exploit, Idyl Inn provides its guests with a multitude of relaxing activities and a serene, restful atmosphere. The solar-heated indoor pool, sauna, hot tub, and outdoor patio are ideal for two lovers interested in a healthy hideaway.

Of the three rooms here, two are fairly small, share a bathroom, and are plainly decorated. The third room is the only room I recommend. Although it is not elegant, it has all the amenities you need: a refrigerator filled with fresh juices and mineral water, thick terrycloth robes, a coffee maker, king-size bed, and a shower big enough to be a fourth room. The bed is covered with a creamy lace spread that complements the mauve and soft rose color scheme. When you look out the window you see the Tolt River rushing by (how much it's rushing depends on the time of year) and the organic hobby farm, which looks more like an unkempt garden.

Snoqualmie

Hotel/Bed and Breakfast Kissing

SALISH LODGE, Snoqualmie
37807 Southeast Fall City-Snoqualmie Road
(206) 888-2556
Expensive to Very Expensive

From Interstate 90, going east from Seattle, take the Snoqualmie Falls exit (Highway 202) and follow the signs to the lodge at the head of the falls.

Salish Lodge has almost everything going for it: a well-respected name, a celebrated location at the head of Snoqualmie Falls, and outstanding, thoroughly romantic accommodations. Each of the plush guest rooms has furnishings that ooze comfort and invite tenderness, a spa tub, and a well-stocked wood-burning fireplace. The popular dining room here is elegantly appointed, with views of the falls from almost every seat. Table 5, with a ringside view of the falls, is of particular romantic interest, but you can't reserve it in advance. The five-star chef here cooks up some of the most savory Northwest dishes you'll ever taste. Soups are delectable, the fresh salmon and halibut are perfectly prepared and delicately sauced, and the desserts are superb. Sunday brunch is an event.

The major drawback to this stellar location is the throngs of tourists that invade the place day in and day out, particularly on weekends. Also, only a handful of these exquisite rooms have views of the falls; the rest look out to the road or the power plant upstream.

Fall City

Restaurant Kissing

THE HERBFARM, Fall City
32804 Southeast Issaquah-Fall City Road
(206) 784-2222
Moderate

Call for reservations and directions.

I almost didn't include this restaurant because reservations are practically impossible to obtain. Bookings for the fall/winter season are taken during the last week in August and are snatched up immediately through January; summer reservations are taken the third week in April and the entire season is full by the end of the first day. Now, if that doesn't whet your curiosity and appetite, I don't know what will.

This farm restaurant, set in the middle of a forested suburban neighborhood, serves some of the most exotic Northwest cuisine you will ever taste. Part restaurant, part herb garden, part gift and plant shop—the main theme here is reverence toward the earth and sustenance of life. The small, charming dining room is graced with skylights and an open kitchen. It's a bit eccentric, but adorable. Delectable concoctions such as a parfait mousse of wild mushrooms, king salmon in a zucchini blossom, herb sorbets, and rosemary shortbread cookies are paragons of flavor. If you are lucky enough to get a reservation, dinner for two here is more than romantic—it's irresistible.

WASHINGTON CASCADES

Cascade Range

Washington's stretch of the Cascade Range is nothing less than spectacular. To the north, Mount Baker's glacial peak stands guard near the U.S.-Canadian border. South of Mount Baker, for 300 miles, is a mesmerizing wilderness that includes national forests, parks, and mountain passes, with startling views of the volcanic giants: Mount Rainier, Mount St. Helens, and Mount Adams. This chain of mountains is patterned with old-growth evergreens, snow-covered cliffs, and countless plummeting waterfalls and spirited rivers. In contrast to the wet, vivid greenery on the west side of the Cascades, the east side of the mountains is authentic Marlboro country—awash in hues of gold, bathed in hot sunshine in summer, and blasted by snowy cold in winter. Almost every square foot of this expanse is magnificent.

The most popular and accessible route through the region is the **CASCADE LOOP,** a series of connecting highways through the northern section of the mountains. Begin the loop just south of Everett, where Highway 2 heads east across Stevens Pass to the town of Leavenworth on the east side of the mountains. Just before Wenatchee, take Highway 97 north to Chelan, where you continue heading north on Highway 153 toward the towns of Twisp and Winthrop. From there you take Highway 20 west toward Mazama, heading back across the Cascades to Interstate 5. (The loop officially continues out to La Conner and down through Whidbey Island, finishing with a ferryboat ride to Mukilteo, just south of Everett.)

Driving is the fastest, but not the most intimate, way to experience this area. There are stimulating hikes to consider. Contact the **NATIONAL PARK SERVICE,** 2105 Highway 20, Sedro Woolley, Washington 98284, (206) 856-5700, to request an informational packet and catalog on how to get hiking maps of the area. There is a network of graveled dirt roads off the main highways that lead to the paths less taken. These are treks of the heart for pleasure and adventure.

◆ **Romantic Prelude:** If you are heading east to the Cascades from Seattle on Interstate 90 and you want a remarkable look at the scenery you'll be traveling through, consider stopping at **SNOQUALMIE WINERY**, 1000 Winery Road, Snoqualmie, (206) 888-4000 (watch for the signs next to the Snoqualmie Falls exit). The view of the mountains from the tasting room is unbelievable.

Rockport

Outdoor Kissing

EAGLE WATCHING, Rockport
For information, call the Department of Wildlife
(206) 775-1311

Viewing is possible along Highway 20 between the towns of Concrete and Marblemount during December and January.

Bleak gray skies, negligible daylight, and the mist of Northwest rain can make the heart of the Cascades moderately dreary during the months of winter. Yet in the middle of this inclement weather, December and January are made vibrant when hundreds of bald eagles migrate to the Skagit River during salmon spawning season. (Salmon die after spawning, which makes the river an eagle's gourmet delight.) All along its path, eagles soar overhead or perch in clear sight on exposed alpine branches. This profound assemblage is one of the largest in the lower 48 states, and viewing is possible from many points along the road and through eagle-oriented rafting excursions. By mid-March, after all the fish have been eaten and the eagles have dispersed, the Cascades are once again ready for spring renewal.

◆ **Romantic Suggestion:** There is little in the way of accommodations out here except for the **CASCADE MOUNTAIN INN**, 3840 Pioneer Lane, Concrete, (206) 826-4333, (Inexpensive to Moderate). Efficiency and relaxation are the trademarks of this well-established bed and breakfast (open between May and September and during eagle season). Encompassed by pasture land and mountains, the setting is truly lovely. Six unpretentious (somewhat spartan) rooms with ordinary private baths are perfect for hikers coming to see the eagles or longing for Cascade beauty. The breakfasts are exceptionally fresh and generous.

RIVER RAFTING
Northern Wilderness River Riders
23312 77th Avenue, Woodinville
(206) 448-RAFT
Expensive

If you are interested in traveling any of the rivers in the region, call for information and directions on where to rendezvous with your guide.

The Skykomish, Klickitat, Methow, White Salmon, Toutle, and Chiwawa rivers are visually exciting and relentlessly tumultuous. If you're in an adventurous mood, there are several river-rafting companies in the Northwest that will provide professional guides to take you down these rivers. Northern Wilderness is a good, safe company that will provide you with solid information as well as one of their clever brochures.

Once you've decided which river you want to negotiate, the rest is, if you will, all downstream. As you follow the tendril-like course the water has etched through the land, each coiling turn exposes a sudden change in perspective on the landscape. One turn reveals grassy woods adjoining the quiet flow of peaceful water; another magically manifests a rocky tableau penetrated by a bursting mass of energy called white water. The raft's roller-coaster motion accentuates the thrill and glory of the landscape. And the sensation of cold water against your skin as you wildly paddle over and through a whirlpool can make your heart pound and your senses spin.

Mazama

Hotel/Bed and Breakfast Kissing

THE MAZAMA COUNTRY INN, Mazama
1 Mazama Road
(509) 996-2681
Inexpensive to Moderate

Fourteen miles north of Winthrop, just off Highway 20, watch for the signs to the inn.

The Mazama Inn is in the middle of nowhere, and that is one of its most attractive points. Set in the heart of a forest at the foot of a mountain, the inn has a handful of units that are simple, austere, and clean, which would be a romantic drawback if it weren't for their sensational views and the amenities available both winter and summer. Everything is here for you: horseback riding, helicopter skiing, cross-country skiing, mountain biking, windsurfing, sleigh riding, a sauna, a hot tub nestled in a garden setting, and a country-style restaurant. (During the winter, the meals are included in one reasonably priced package.) The soothing dining room has a view of gently swaying boughs through the tall windows, and a floor-to-ceiling stone fireplace keeps the room toasty warm. The Mazama Country Inn is an easy, casual setting for playing and getting away from it all.

Winthrop

Hotel/Bed and Breakfast Kissing

SUN MOUNTAIN LODGE, Winthrop
Patterson Lake Road
(509) 996-2211
Inexpensive to Expensive

Follow Highway 97 north toward Pateros. At Pateros, turn northwest onto Highway 153 and follow the Methow River toward Twisp. Take Highway 20 through Twisp and on to Winthrop. From there follow the signs to the lodge.

Every facet of Sun Mountain Lodge is remarkable and stunning, including the drive there. The winding road up to this mountaintop resort offers sweeping views of rugged, sculpted peaks and the golden Methow Valley below.

The renovated main building and lobby area are made out of massive timbers and stone, and the interior is graced by immense wrought-iron chandeliers, stone flooring, and rock-clad fireplaces. All of the rooms in the main lodge are beautifully appointed, though a bit hotel-like, and most have windows that face the dramatic panorama (although some overlook the roof). The suites, in a separate wing across from the lodge, are impeccable. Each unit has its own fireplace, stone patio, sliding glass doors, willow furnishings, and lush comforters; in winter, you can cross-country ski out your back door. The views from here are mesmerizing. The lodge's other stellar amenities include two heated pools, hiking trails, horseback riding, exercise equipment, mountain bikes, and the most effortless tranquillity imaginable.

If you've decided not to take advantage of the premium accommodations, at least take the time to stop for a while at the restaurant, which is housed in the original section of the lodge. The developers were wise enough to leave well enough alone, because this part of the lodge was and is flawless. From every position you can allow your eyes to feast on surroundings that are food for the soul. The deck wraps around the outside and brings you face to face with the grandeur of the area. Surprisingly, the menu is impressive, the service excellent, and the entrées and desserts delicious. The kitchen is famous for its applewood-smoked duck. Hold hands tightly; this place, from kiss to kiss, is truly amazing.

◆ **Romantic Note:** Sun Mountain Lodge offers totally outrageous, thoroughly intoxicating helicopter-skiing packages for both downhill and cross-country skiers. There are virgin powder runs that will leave you breathless for months to come. At the end of the day, you will need to cuddle very close and review your feats of athletic prowess.

Stehekin

Take Highway 2 heading east past Leavenworth, toward Wenatchee. Follow the signs for Highway 97 North, which will take you to the town of Chelan, where you can catch the boat to Stehekin. For information on scheduled departures, call (509) 682-3503 or (800)-4-CHELAN. Hikers will want to check with the North Cascades National Park Service, (206) 856-5700, for the backpacking route to Stehekin.

Stehekin is a geographically unique town, accessible only by ferryboat (no cars) from Chelan or a hike over the mountains via highcountry trails. Lake Chelan is renowned for its glorious, dramatic scenery. Jagged mountains line this 55-mile lake and are breathtakingly reflected in the cool blue of the glacier-fed waters. The exquisite ferry ride takes approximately four hours, and there is only one round-trip excursion a day. Stehekin tends to be a bit crowded with ferry passengers in the afternoon, but most of them stay only for the day. Once the boat leaves, in the late afternoon, only the romantics remain, and the town is serenely peaceful once more.

Hotel/Bed and Breakfast Kissing

SILVER BAY INN LODGING, Stehekin
(509) 682-2212
Moderate

Call for directions.

Silver Bay Inn, the local bed and breakfast, is a special place to stay—
and not just because of its solar window construction, the cozy, win-
dowed breakfast nook, the wondrous views from its deck and rooms, the
soaking tub in the master suite, or the tempting continental espresso
breakfasts. It's special because of the extreme isolation of the location,
which makes this spot a Northwest must for those who want to get away
from it all.

Cashmere

Hotel/Bed and Breakfast Kissing

CASHMERE COUNTRY INN, Cashmere
5801 Pioneer Drive
(509) 782-4212
Inexpensive

From Highway 2 take the Cashmere exit, which puts you on Division Street.
Continue to Pioneer Street and turn right.

Aplets and Cotlets are notoriously sweet confections that stick to
your teeth and help dentists send their kids to college. They are also
Cashmere's claim to fame. Well, I guess every town needs something,
and doesn't everyone's aunt love this stuff? However, if the town is
looking for a new trademark, it could turn to this affable inn as an
alternative. The location isn't the best—across from some tract housing—but this immaculate and affectionately renovated farm home is
surrounded by meticulously groomed gardens, an acre of apple orchards,
and plum trees. Inside, the four guest rooms, a tad on the small side, are
beautifully decorated and have private baths. There is a nice-sized tile
swimming pool out back and a hot tub.

The innkeeper is a gourmet cook, and breakfasts are lavish. One morning you may wake to French toast stuffed with cream cheese, peach schnapps and nectarines, apple spice muffins, and cantaloupe slices drizzled with homemade mint syrup. Cashmere is a better romantic destination because of this bed and breakfast.

Restaurant Kissing

THE PEWTER POT, Cashmere
124 ½ Cottage Avenue
(509) 782-2036
Moderate

In the town of Cashmere on Cottage Avenue, just off Division Street.

Pretty as an English postcard is this small countryside restaurant, but the cuisine is almost entirely American. Lace-covered windows, a handful of tables, and attentive service are the overture, but the talent of the kitchen is the symphony. Hearty, wonderfully prepared down-home cooking is the essence of the menu. Beef pot pie, turkey dinner with all the trimmings (even when it isn't Thanksgiving), and country ham served with rum-raisin sauce are maybe even a little better than Mom made. The deep-dish apple pie is beyond delicious and large enough for two. Authentic English afternoon tea is served every afternoon, and the fresh tarts and pastries are excellent.

Leavenworth

In many ways Leavenworth is not a romantic destination. My misgivings are due to the town's blatantly repetitive Bavarian theme and tourist-oriented atmosphere. The Germanic ski-lodge influence is robust in a beer-fest, crowds-galore sort of way, but it doesn't leave much room for tender snuggling or quiet moments. And this town can get crowded. Still, Leavenworth has something for everyone, and you'll find some romantic alternatives that enable the softer side of the town to be yours—including cross-country skiing, hiking, white-water rafting, daydreaming, quiet restaurants, picnics, and more.

Hotel/Bed and Breakfast Kissing

ALL SEASONS RIVER INN, Leavenworth
8751 Icicle Road
(509) 548-1425
Inexpensive to Moderate

From Highway 2 at the west edge of town, turn south onto Icicle Road.

An unassuming exterior houses this professionally run, country-elegant bed and breakfast. Nestled on a bluff overlooking the Wenatchee River and tree-covered mountains, the inn has plenty of room inside for snuggling and relaxing. Five lovely, spacious rooms are here, most with private decks or patios, Jacuzzi tubs, king-size beds, handmade quilts, sitting areas with period love seats, and views all around. Breakfast in the morning is a sumptuous spread of homemade granola, fresh zucchini bread, ham slices with apricot glaze, potato pancakes, and a chile soufflé. Ask for the innkeeper's recipe book if you'd like to take some of this superb living home with you.

HAUS LORELEI BED AND BREAKFAST, Leavenworth
347 Division Street
(509) 548-5726
Inexpensive to Moderate

From Highway 2, as you enter the town of Leavenworth from the west, turn south onto Ninth Street. Go two blocks and turn east onto Commercial and then south again onto Division. Division dead-ends at Haus Lorelei.

At Haus Lorelei the best of two worlds is available: you can be at the edge of Leavenworth's lively town center, yet have no evidence that it's only moments away. From the moment you enter this European-style beach-stone country mansion, you'll sense that relaxation is at hand and the stress of the world is somewhere else. This bed and breakfast offers an easygoing, informal winter or summer sojourn.

The dining and living room areas are partitioned by a massive, beach-stone fireplace. A huge screened porch overlooking the expansive lawn and the Wenatchee River below is where a simple, but elegant breakfast is served. The three downstairs bedrooms are huge, comfortable, and decorated with magnificent antiques imported from Germany. These rooms have simple private baths. There are three more rooms upstairs, two of which are suitable for families or groups. The third room, the River's Edge, has a mesmerizing view from anywhere in the room, including the bed, and is my favorite. The eccentric, although attentive hostess (or her helpful sons, one of whom has Tourette's Syndrome) can help you plan a rewarding day.

◆ **Romantic Note:** Haus Lorelei specializes in weddings. They cater everything themselves and set up white chairs, tables, and flowers in the gardens, with the mountains and river as backdrop.

LEAVENWORTH VILLAGE INN, Leavenworth
1016 Commercial Street
(509) 548-6620, (800) 343-8198
Inexpensive to Expensive

On Commercial near 12th Street.

In some ways, this is just another Swiss-style motel—except for the three huge suites that have deluxe furnishings and plush comforts. Hunter green and wine accessories fill the two-room suites. Each has a large Jacuzzi tub surrounded by white pillars, gas fireplace, comfortable living and dining room area, wood four-poster bed, a microwave, and a small refrigerator. There isn't a view or an interesting location here, but if you don't open the curtains you can find plenty of romance and solitude at this inn. A light continental breakfast is served in a small dining room next to the lobby.

MOUNTAIN HOME LODGE, Leavenworth
8201-9 Mountain Home Road
(509) 548-7077
Inexpensive to Expensive

Take Highway 2 to Leavenworth. East of town, immediately past the bridge over the Wenatchee River, turn right on Duncan Road. Duncan Road connects with Mountain Home Road, which will take you directly to the lodge. In winter the prearranged pickup area is just west of Duncan Road; call for specific directions.

If seclusion is something you dream about and being taken care of is what you crave, you can come to Mountain Home Lodge and find the perfect balance of the two. The substantial wood lodge is cradled atop a private mountain meadow, and the staff here will graciously tend to all your needs. The only way to reach it during the winter is via prearranged snowcat pickup at a rendezvous point just outside Leavenworth. The slow, half-hour journey up offers views of the quiet river valley twinkling with lights from the shops and streets of Leavenworth. Be prepared for a quiet ascent punctuated only by the sounds of crunching snow and your "oohs" and "aahs" of amazement.

If you arrive during winter, the mountain and meadow will be completely covered by snow; the steam from the hot tub will drift lazily into the air and disappear. The rooms are unassuming though very comfortable, with views of the surrounding landscape. The fireplace in the shared living area is next to the small dining room where you will be served three mountain-fresh, country-style meals every day. Wall-to-wall windows allow you to watch the winter weather in its full white glory as you soak up the warmth and hospitality of the interior. Cross-country skiing, snowmobiling, and sledding are all at your doorstep.

During the summer months, Mountain Home Lodge is easily accessible but just as private and exciting. Without the snow's enchanting limitations, horseback riding, restaurants, and hiking are nearby.

◆ **Romantic Note:** During the winter there is no safe way to drive here, so the restaurant is for guests only and meals are included in the price of accommodations. During the summer anyone can make reservations for meals here, even without staying overnight.

PENSION ANNA, Leavenworth
926 Commercial Street
(509) 548-6273
Inexpensive to Expensive

From Highway 2 in the town of Leavenworth, turn left on Ninth Street, then left again onto Commercial. The pension is on the corner of Ninth and Commercial.

The Bavarian farmhouse design of this bed and breakfast is one more cliché in a town where every other storefront manifests the same theme. For those who can take only so much theme living, once inside this immaculate pensione all the triteness dissolves and you are escorted to a stately (although spartan) room. The suites come complete with thick down comforters, down pillows, lush carpeting, stately armoires, tiled private baths, plenty of space, spa tubs, fireplaces, and sitting areas. Even without spas and fireplaces, the other rooms are very comfortable. An

Austrian-style continental breakfast (cheeses, meats, and breads) is served in a congenial room on the main floor where tables for two and carved wood chairs are placed around a wood banquette.

New to Pension Anna is the addition of two rooms in the impeccably renovated former Catholic church adjacent to the main building. The cathedral ceilings and arched windows are intact, and the furnishings are appropriately baronial and plush. I know this sounds a bit unconventional, and it is, but these rooms are sumptuous and without question very good places to kiss. Unless, of course, you are feeling guilty about something you need to confess.

RUN OF THE RIVER BED AND BREAKFAST, Leavenworth
9308 East Leavenworth Road
(509) 548-7171
Moderate to Expensive

Call for reservations and directions.

Probably the finest bed and breakfast in Leavenworth, this is an exceptional place to spend treasured moments together. Every romantic and practical detail is seen to with great care and discernment. The pale gray contemporary log home has cathedral ceilings and is surrounded by a picturesque garden bursting with wildflowers, and a stone rockery. A deck with a spectacular view of the Cascades and the winding Icicle River is close to each room. The distinctive rooms feature handcrafted log beds, antique quilts, terrycloth robes, loft cuddling nooks, private decks with wood swings, and every imaginable amenity, including binoculars. Two of the rooms downstairs have wood stoves and large beach-stone-framed Jacuzzi baths. The Rose Suite upstairs also has a private spa bath. There is a huge hot tub set near the river in a log pavilion at the back of the house.

One possible drawback here is the lack of comfortable or ample seating in the common areas, but the rooms are almost too inviting to leave anyway. Breakfast is served around one large table in the dining room and is a bountiful presentation of fresh fruit, vegetable frittata, organic sausages, and apple cobbler. This used to be a hidden jewel in Leavenworth, but it isn't so hidden anymore. How could anyone possibly not want to come back?

Restaurant Kissing

EDEL HAUS INN, Leavenworth
320 Ninth Street
(509) 548-4412
Inexpensive to Moderate

At the edge of town, turn left on Front Street to Ninth.

An anomaly in a town of faux Bavarian chalets, although a welcome change of pace, is this charming country restaurant located on the edge of town in a hobbit-like white stucco house with red trim. The interior is neatly arrayed with linen-draped tables and blond wood chairs. Plentiful patio dining is enfolded by forest and lit with torches in the evening. Salads, pizza, and fresh pastas are all excellent. The spicy turkey sausage pizza with sun-dried tomatoes and Gouda cheese, and the mesquite-grilled fresh halibut in a sesame sauce are delicious. It isn't elegant dining, but it is consistently good.

◆   **Romantic Note:** Edel Haus Inn also offers accommodations that I would call "bed and lunch/dinner." Breakfast is not provided, but you get a 50% discount off both lunch and dinner at the restaurant. The three upstairs rooms share a small bath, and although nice are not worth recommending in this context. What is of interest, and a great kissing bargain, is the Jacuzzi suite on the ground floor with a private entrance. This is a very comfortable, cozy spot for $90 a night.

THE TERRACE BISTRO, Leavenworth   ◆
200 Eighth Street
(509) 548-4193
Inexpensive to Moderate

Just off Eighth Street, in the alley between Commercial and Front streets.

Reputations take a long time to die—both good and bad. Considered by many to be the best in Leavenworth, this handsome, cozy rooftop dining room can't compare to what it once was. The pasta I ordered was swimming in oil, the packaged rolls were barely passable, and the salad was meager and soggy with dressing. Service can be abrupt and discourteous. The Bavarian decor—high-backed chairs with scarlet cushions, floral carpeting, and white stucco walls—still creates a rich atmosphere, but unless you stick with the fresh meats (which can sometimes be overcooked) and the very good desserts, you are better off kissing somewhere else.

Outdoor Kissing

ICICLE OUTFITTERS AND GUIDES, Leavenworth
2800 Icicle Road
(509) 784-1145, (800) 497-3912
Moderate

Call for a brochure, reservations, and directions to their location on the south shore of Lake Wenatchee.

A great way to encounter this area is to take a trek on horseback, and Icicle Outfitters and Guides provides everything from one hour rides to an overnight pack trip. Overnight journeys come complete with meals, pack horses, saddle horses, a well-seasoned wrangler, cook, tents, and the entire camp setup necessary for a two-to-seven-day expedition. This is one unbelievable adventure. You'll cross unspoiled wilderness where pure mountain lakes and streams glisten in the sunshine, the wind rushes through the trees, hawks soar overhead, and the snowcapped peaks tower above. As you warm yourself around the roaring campfire at night, after the hearty, freshly cooked dinner is served and cleared, you will find yourselves at peace with each other and the world.

◆　**Romantic Alternative: EAGLE CREEK RANCH,** 7951 Eagle Creek Road, Leavenworth, (509) 548-7798, is another well-respected, full-service horse ranch that offers sleigh, buggy, hay, and trail rides and backcountry hiking journeys.

Mount Rainier

For area information, call (206) 569-2211. Many roads lead to Mount Rainier National Park. From Enumclaw to the north and Yakima to the east, take Highway 410 into the park. Highway 12 from both the southeast and southwest intersects with Highway 123, which will also take you into the park. On the southwest side of the park, Highway 7 intersects with Highway 706 at the town of Elbe. Highway 706 goes right into the park and takes you straight to Paradise, literally and figuratively.

Using poetic words to describe Mount Rainier is best left to the laureates. For the kissing purposes of this book, suffice it to say that almost every inch of this mountain is quintessentially romantic and outrageously exquisite. From its dormant volcanic heart to its eternally glacier-covered peaks, Mount Rainier is guaranteed to provide superlative panoramic views, memorable hikes, and lasting memories. If it's Northwest drama and passion you yearn for, this mountain has it.

Several park roads, including some of the main routes onto the mountain, are closed during the winter, so always check for seasonal accessibility. Excellent hiking books are available for this region from Mountaineers Books. For their catalog, write to 1011 Southwest Klickitat Way, Suite 107, Seattle, WA 98134, or phone (206) 223-6303.

Hotel/Bed and Breakfast Kissing

ALEXANDER'S COUNTRY INN, Ashford
37515 State Road
(206) 569-2300, (800) 654-7615

Follow Highway 161 through Eatonville and Elbe until it becomes Highway 706. Follow this through the town of Ashford, just outside of Mount Rainier; the inn is several miles east of town on the left-hand side of the road.

Nestled on the edge of old-growth forest (and unfortunately next to the two-lane highway that leads you to Mount Rainier), you'll find a quaint blue country inn surrounded by a lush green lawn with winding walkways and wooden benches enclosed in a white picket fence.

Before you settle into a room for the night, you might decide on dinner in the restaurant downstairs. Cozy up in a casual wooden booth with soft cushions, savor the warmth of the wood-burning fireplace, and peek out of the lace-curtained windows that overlook the old wooden waterwheel and surrounding yard (and, in the distance, traffic). Request the fresh trout, typically caught the very same day in the backyard pond, or try the hearty stuffed green peppers. The excellent entrées are accompanied by fresh-baked sourdough bread; the service is attentive. Finally, satiate your sweet tooth with a chocolate torte covered in a light raspberry sauce. Now, with a full stomach, you can head upstairs.

The inn's spacious common room has a homey fireplace, but is still somewhat disappointing due to sparse furnishings and dim lighting. Some of the guest rooms are much the same, even slightly gloomy, but there are two rooms occupying the tower that you'll be sure to appreciate. The first is the upstairs tower suite, a double-decker room with a bright sitting room, furnished with attractive antiques. Carpeted stairs lead you to the loft bedroom and sunlight filters through the large windows. Located in the bottom half of the tower is another two-room guest suite. The octagonal bedroom has redwood paneling and wraparound windows. All of the rooms throughout the inn have unique stained glass windows, which add a colorful flair to the accommodations.

Complete your evening with a soak in the intimate hot tub (test the temperature with your toes first—it was too hot to get in the night we were there), sheltered in a half-enclosed gazebo that overlooks a well-lit pond. Watch the trout jump across the water's surface, leaving ripples in the silhouetted reflections of the trees, and enjoy the quiet, sweet-smelling breeze emanating from the nearby forest.

PARADISE INN, Mount Rainier
55106 Kernahan Road East, Ashford
(206) 569-2275
Inexpensive to Moderate

Nineteen miles inside the southwest entrance of the park.

Paradise Inn is the only lodge available at the top of the mountain. The view from up here is truly remarkable and well worth the drive, but the accommodations at the inn are disappointing, to say the least. Don't be fooled by the lobby, which is an airy, beautiful, open-beamed room built from logs. Large fireplaces and cozy tables and chairs are scattered throughout, providing many tempting places to snuggle up together with a hot drink. Unfortunately, the numerous guest rooms are situated along dismal, decaying hallways, and the rooms themselves are at best claustrophobic, with small windows and dilapidated furniture, and sorely in need of renovation. It's a shame they don't do more with this prime property. Until they do, I strongly suggest that you spend the night in the valley and save Paradise for daily excursions.

Outdoor Kissing

CHINOOK PASS, Mount Rainier

If you're in the Mount Baker-Snoqualmie National Forest on the east side of Mount Rainier, Highway 410 will take you through the pass.

On a fall afternoon, Chinook Pass becomes almost too glorious. You'll be so excited by the scenery, you might finish touring and forget to kiss. Take a moment to conjure up the image of golden light bathing hills and lakes. Notice the vivid shades of red and amber that embellish the trees and meadows. Feel the fall air brush your skin while the sun's heat tempers that chill. Sigh... This is a visual gift to share with each other.

◆   **Romantic Note:** The drive through the pass is loaded with vista turnoffs, hikes with dizzying switchbacks, and meadows that you can explore side by side. The only caution is to travel prepared. Comfortable hiking shoes, munchies (lots of munchies), water bottle, tissues, and a day pack will make Chinook Pass a more passable experience. Also, be considerate of the wilderness. Trails are for people; the rest of the area is for the animals and plants. Considerate behavior on the part of all visitors will keep the beauty intact for many more years to come.

PARADISE, Mount Rainier
Mount Rainier National Park
$5 entry fee

Nineteen miles inside the southwest entrance of the park.

A scenic climb by car through lush old-growth evergreens, the spellbinding roar of waterfalls rushing down jagged mountain rocks, nimble deer foraging for greens at the side of the road, brightly hued blue jays, mountain goats, eagles, lumbering elk, and wildflowers of all kinds make for an unforgettable romantic interlude. Mount Rainier looms before you, draped in majestic snowy white, growing larger and more magnificent the farther you drive up the windy curves toward its peak. Take advantage of the various scenic stops with vantage points of the mountain beyond and the surrounding park. Get out of your car and lean (carefully) over the edge of the stone railings and marvel at the heights to which you've come together. Sunset over the valley of trees below is astonishingly surreal. It's no wonder they call this Paradise.

SUNRISE, Mount Rainier

*From the north or east, take Highway 410 into Mount Rainier National Park
and follow the park map to Sunrise.*

If you've always wondered what it must be like at the top of the world,
come to Sunrise and fulfill your fantasy, for this is as close to the top of
the world as you can drive in the continental United States. When you
arrive, there are so many inspiring trails (some relatively easy) that
choosing one might be harder than you'd like. Your day hike can be a
level, leisurely stroll or a strenuous trek up a mountain path, far away
from everyone and everything except each other. You will never hear
such silence.

Trout Lake

Hotel/Bed and Breakfast Kissing

MIO AMORE PENSIONE, Trout Lake
53 Little Mountain Road
(509) 395-2264
Moderate

*From Highway 14 on the north side of the Columbia River Gorge, near White
Salmon, head north on Highway 141 to Trout Lake. As you enter the town,
watch for the signs to Mio Amore.*

For some reason, Mount Adams isn't lauded as much as the other
sights in the Cascades. Yet this inactive volcano is in a unique position
at the south end of Washington state, juxtaposed between the green,
lush forests of the western half and the rain shadow of the eastern half.
This is wine country, and the base of the mountain is surrounded with
manicured vineyards. The endless recreational opportunities here provide all the outdoor entertainment requisite for a Northwest escape.

Mio Amore Pensione rests at the foot of Mount Adams, whose
snowcapped peaks and rolling hills tower over its backyard. This
Victorian home has been renovated into a wonderful bed and breakfast,
with attractive rooms and tender touches all about. (Only one room has
a private bath; the other two share a bath.) Adjacent to the house is the

original turn-of-the-century ice house, which has been renovated into a loft cottage. It is still somewhat chilly, with stone walls and sparse furnishings. The highlight of your stay will be the gourmet morning meal and four-course dinner served by the innkeepers every day.

Breakfast is complimentary for those staying at the pension. This eye-opening meal is graciously served and consists of luscious homemade tortes, breads, and special Italian baked dishes. Dinner features exotic meats and fresh fish, selected on a daily basis by the first couple to book their reservation. Mio Amore is one of the few places where you can combine mountain exploration with gourmet feasting, and it's a relaxing place in which to pamper yourselves in proverbial Northwest style and seclusion.

◆ **Romantic Note:** Reservations for dinner are accepted even if you are not staying overnight. Be aware that the home is small, and if you are not participating in dinner, you will hear the experience from the upstairs rooms between 7:00 P.M. and 9:30 P.M. Also, a new romantic drawback is the parking lot next door to the pension, with an adjacent barbecue area that can accommodate up to 150 people. There is also a stage for outdoor theatrical productions by local theater groups. This little place is likely to be terribly busy during the summer.

Restaurant Kissing

SERENITY'S, Trout Lake
Highway 141
(509) 395-2500
Inexpensive

Heading toward Trout Lake, northbound on Highway 141, watch for the signs. The restaurant is on the left.

Serenity isn't always this easy to come by, especially at these prices. A wooden barn converted into a restaurant, unfortunately set directly off Highway 141, offers a pleasant site to enjoy distant views of Mount Adams while sampling continental cuisine. Although none of the windows face the highway, it is hard to forget. The wood-and-stone interior is cozy and casual, warmed by a wood stove and adorned with floral-printed linen tablecloths and fresh flower arrangements on each table. Share bites of baked Icelandic cod fillet served with drawn butter, or try the breast of chicken Kiev with wild rice dressing. Dally over dessert and savor the scenery; this dinner is only the prelude for more to come.

Husum

Outdoor Kissing

CHARLES HOOPER FAMILY WINERY, Husum
196 Spring Creek Road
(509) 493-2324

Call for directions and seasonal hours.

On your way to or from Mount Adams, be certain to stop at the Charles Hooper Family Winery. A picnic or a stroll through the vineyards treats you to one of the most exquisite views you'll behold anywhere. A large, wood-framed building with enormous wood doors was recently added; this is where the wine is made and can be tasted. Take time for this one; your eyes, palates, and hearts will be forever grateful.

White Salmon

Hotel/Bed and Breakfast Kissing

INN OF THE WHITE SALMON, White Salmon
172 West Jewett
(509) 493-2335
Moderate

From Highway 14, follow Highway 141 a short distance to the town of White Salmon. The inn is at the north end of town on the right-hand side of the road.

A testimony to the fruits of a little T.L.C., this remodeled 1937 brick hotel welcomes you with fashionable warmth. Previously we recommended that you only have breakfast here, a delightful four-lip presentation of more than 20 European-style pastries and breads, including baklava and strudel. Choose from six savory breakfast entrées, including the Hungarian *hauf* (ham baked with Swiss cheese and green onions, seasoned with caraway) or the artichoke frittata, with marinated artichoke hearts, jack cheese, green onions, black olives, and fresh tomato. Feast on this incomparable breakfast in the elegant dining room, highlighted with lace tablecloths and curtains, and bright floral wallpaper.

The surrounding rundown section of town has not changed, but under new management the accommodations here have dramatically improved (fortunately, the inn's cuisine remains consistently excellent.) The inn now exudes an authentic European charm; its lobby and hallways are decorated with old wood, refurbished Victorian lamps, framed turn-of-the-century photographs, and time-worn patterned wallpaper. Put your feet up in the roomy red sunken parlor, warmed by a gas fireplace, and enjoy the magnificent antiques while nibbling on home-made cookies available for guests at the front desk.

A wooden walkway in the backyard rambles past a hillside bursting with colorful terraced gardens and carpeted with creeping phlox. Dip your toes in the spacious nearby hot tub, well lit at night and enclosed in an attractive lattice-work fence.

The inn itself successfully blends size (16 rooms) and intimate potential. Most of the guest rooms have small windows without views and are therefore somewhat dark, but even so, several have been endowed with affectionate touches that make them more conducive to romance. The honeymoon suite has plush new carpeting, an enormous king-size bed covered in lush white linens, and a cozy sitting room lit by an intricate metal Victorian lamp, the likes of which you've never seen before. Just down the hall, you'll find a suite with a sweeping canopy that drapes over the queen-size brass bed covered by a hunter green floral comforter. All of the rooms have private baths, several with lovely wood paneling. Not all of the rooms are up to these standards yet, so you might have to hunt for just the right one.

Goldendale

THREE CREEKS LODGE, Goldendale
2120 Highway 97, Satus Pass
(509) 773-4026
Expensive to Very Expensive

Follow Highway 141 east along the Columbia Gorge. At Biggs Junction turn onto Highway 97 and follow it for 15 miles or so. Three Creeks Lodge is on the left; look for signs.

Part of the romantic appeal of this retreat is the drive that takes you here. The Columbia Gorge is beyond breathtaking, with rugged, parched cliffs and wondrous rolling hills ascending on both sides of the surging river. The lodge itself is sufficiently isolated, sheltered by woods and bordering a creek that runs close by many of the cabins. The chalet rooms, both creekside and woodside, and the rooms with enclosed decks and outdoor spas are adequate, although sparse in decor. The deluxe chalet and the creek houses are more luxurious, with glass skywalls, private decks and spas, hand-crafted furniture, and views of the burbling creek. Once you're cozied up in the room of your choice or lounging in the privacy of your own outdoor Jacuzzi, you'll know you made the right decision. Miles from the world at large, nature beckons for you to unleash yourself. Splash a little, frolic in the woods, and enjoy the abundant privacy. (For those in buildings that share accommodations, be aware that the walls are quite thin.)

The lodge offers two romantic packages, appropriately named "Memorable Evening" and "Romantic Evening." Both include a stay at the secluded deluxe chalet, creekside private chalet, or hillside creek house, in addition to an exquisite seven-course dinner served in the exceedingly romantic dining room. Speaking of dinner, you're sure to relish the cuisine. Your hosts encourage you to take your time between courses and you can wander over to the lounge, or even outside, to let your stomach settle before you embark on another delectable course. Cleanse your palate with a cool sorbet served between entrées and then settle down to sautéed prawns, flambéed at your table by the competent and gracious staff. Romance is undoubtedly Three Creeks Lodge's forte.

SOUTHERN WASHINGTON COAST

Hoquiam

Hotel/Bed and Breakfast Kissing

LYTLE HOUSE, Hoquiam
509 Chenault
(206) 533-2320
Moderate

From Olympia go west on Highway 101, which becomes Highway 8, then Highway 12, then 101 again, and takes you into Hoquiam. The Lytle House is located next door to the historic Hoquiam Castle. Just follow the signs as you enter Hoquiam.

Admittedly, Hoquiam is the last place you'd go for romance, but since there aren't any bed and breakfasts worth mentioning in or even near Ocean Shores, you might consider staying here, just a 20-minute drive from the ocean. Immerse yourselves in the elegance of the Victorian era in a beautifully restored 1900 Queen Anne mansion set grandly on a hilltop overlooking Grays Harbor. From your room you can gaze in wonder over a colorful collage of rooftops in the town below.

Much of the house has been kept extraordinarily intact, and its circular second-floor sun deck, majestic front porch, various shaped windows, and peaked awnings look much as they did in 1900. The house recalls its early years with authentic details: stained glass windows, hardwood floors, kerosene lamp chandeliers, a coal-burning firebox, and, in the living room, an original mural painted for the bride for whom the house was first built.

All but two of the eight guest rooms have private baths, but even those with shared baths are pleasant (robes are provided) and offer something unique: the third-floor shared bath has a claw-foot European tub filled with live goldfish. (Don't worry, there's a shower for the guests' use.) Our favorites were the Rose Room, which embraces you in sunlight and elegant lace, and the Windsor Room, which opens onto a private balcony with a view of Grays Harbor. The Garden Suite is spacious, with two queen-size beds, a living room, kitchen, and bath. The decor is historically tasteful, graced throughout with beautiful antiques.

Your hosts take pride in serving an abundant full breakfast in the plush, deep-red dining room, at your own individual table draped in white lace. Choose from a six-item menu that includes specialty omelets, French toast, granola, yogurt, and other standard breakfast items. Without doubt, this is the best place to stay in the immediate area.

Moclips

Hotel/Bed and Breakfast Kissing

OCEAN CREST RESORT, Moclips   ❤❤
Highway 109
(206) 276-4465
Inexpensive to Expensive   *Not B & B*

Follow Highway 109 out of Aberdeen, past Ocean Shores, and into Moclips. The resort is on the left, one mile north of Pacific Beach.

It's surprising that there are so few bed and breakfasts along this segment of the Washington coast, because the serene stretches of sandy beach and careening white-capped surf are truly exquisite. Nevertheless, you can share the glory in this resort nestled in a grove of spruce trees, perched high on a bluff with an unparalleled view of the Pacific Ocean. From the parking lot, the two four-story buildings resemble a standard hotel, with unsightly blue doors marking each of the 45 guest rooms and cars whizzing by on the highway behind you. Don't be deceived; there is much waiting for you inside.

The accommodations range from comfortable large studios with small refrigerators to spacious two-bedroom apartments with full kitchens; all have fireplaces or wood stoves. The rooms are done in a fairly typical hotel decor, although the studios in Building 5 have attractive cedar paneling, soft colors, queen-size beds, and newer furnishings. What really makes this place worth your while are the breathtaking views from the large windows and decks found in most of the rooms. (You won't even know you're near a highway—I promise.) And it doesn't stop there. Wind down a beautifully constructed 133-step staircase through a wooded ravine to the beach, which extends for miles in either direction. If you get tired on the way back up, stop and share a kiss in the shade on one of several benches along the way built for just this purpose.

You can luxuriate in the sauna, hot tub, swimming pool, or massage parlor in the recreational facilities, which are located across the street in a contemporary wooden building with high-vaulted ceilings, skylights, and three tiers of windows. (Remember, these facilities are available to all of the guests, so don't expect much privacy.)

Breakfast is not included in your stay. Although the dining room has spectacular views, the food and service are mediocre at best, so you'd be better off eating elsewhere. But for coffee or a cocktail, and a sunset chaser, you could find yourselves engaged in some serious kissing.

Copalis Beach

Hotel/Bed and Breakfast Kissing

IRON SPRINGS OCEAN BEACH RESORT, Copalis Beach ◆◆
Highway 109
(206) 276-4230
Inexpensive to Expensive

Follow Highway 109 north from Aberdeen; Iron Springs is three miles north of Copalis Beach.

Nature enthusiasts are sure to feel at home in one of the 27 cabins tucked amidst 100 acres of spruce trees on a low-lying bluff overlooking the Pacific Ocean. The pastel pink and beige cottages scattered across the property are sheltered by trees and spaced adequately apart, giving each cottage ample privacy and a sense of isolation, perfect for a tranquil weekend getaway. Several of the cabins have direct beach access, and you can wander barefoot from your cabin right into the surf. The cabins range in size from one-bedroom studios to apartments that can accommodate up to four people. Each is fully equipped with full kitchen, cooking supplies, fireplace, electric heat for those who prefer it, and fresh linens. Large windows and decks provide wonderful views of the ocean and the surrounding woodland. The interiors are plain but comfortable, done primarily in pastels accented with colorful throw rugs, brass lamps, simple artwork, and antiques. Several cabins have been renovated in a more pleasing modern decor, with interesting color schemes, leather couches, and newer decks.

Get heart-healthy together and hike along a trail that meanders through the forest. Those not daring enough to brave the ocean's cold can take a dip in the covered heated pool open to guests. Later, treat yourselves to a cinnamon roll and clam chowder, available in the gift shop near the registration office.

The only potential drawback to this ocean hideaway is its popularity with families in the summertime. Your cabin should provide enough privacy so that the only sound you'll hear is the gentle roar of the ocean. But just in case, you might want to consider coming in the off-season.

Nahcotta

Restaurant Kissing

ARK RESTAURANT, Nahcotta
273rd and Sandridge Road
(206) 665-4133
Moderate to Expensive

Call for directions.

Don't let the nearby oyster farm's industrial equipment, trucks, and buildings deter you from a romantic evening at the Ark. Once inside the small red-painted building jutting out into Willapa Bay, you'll understand why. The restaurant is enclosed by views of the water on all sides, with a wide selection of window tables to choose from. The wood-and-brick interior and large stone fireplace make for a casual but pleasing atmosphere, accented with white tablecloths; colorful flags and knick-knacks hang from dark wood beams overhead.

The real reason to come to the Ark is the superb cuisine. Considered one of the finest restaurants on the peninsula, the Ark serves fresh local items such as salmon glazed with scotch and orange juice, laced with Drambuie, and garnished with crème fraîche, and lightly breaded, grilled oysters harvested right out of Willapa Bay. Save room for espresso or tea and the seductive selections of their silver dessert tray. Then sit back and watch as the twinkling stars emerge from the sky beyond your window.

◆ **Romantic Note:** The restaurant is closed Monday and Tuesday, and closed entirely January through March. Be sure to ask about their popular summer Garlic Festival before they close for the winter. Reservations for this epicurean festival are accepted only after midnight on Valentine's Day (after all your romantic kissing is done). The menu features every possible (and impossible) appetizer, entrée, and, yes, even dessert, accented with more garlic than you can imagine. Definitely for garlic lovers only.

Long Beach

Hotel/Bed and Breakfast Kissing

BOREAS BED AND BREAKFAST, Long Beach
607 North Boulevard
(206) 642-8069
Inexpensive to Moderate

Follow Pacific Highway into Long Beach and take a left on North Sixth, then a right on North Boulevard.

The mystery and magnificence of the open sea have drawn dreamers, poets, and lovers to its shores for centuries, and Long Beach is no exception. Unfortunately, as you pass through the various small towns dotting this peninsula, you cannot help but wonder how the magnificence became entangled with the endless succession of shops, gas stations, restaurants, motels, and urban advertising that line either side of Pacific Highway. Don't let this distract you; the ocean and the sprawling dunes are just moments away.

Just one block west of the unsightly highway in Long Beach, you can park your car and take refuge in a quaint and delightfully renovated beach house ensconced in grass-covered dunes, with a sweeping, undisturbed view of the Pacific Ocean. Unwind in comfortable common areas filled with an eclectic assortment of antique furnishings and glowing fireplaces. Listen to a favorite recording from the owners' extensive collection, or ease into the spacious hot tub in the sun room, where there is also a sauna in the making. The pleasant kitchen, done up in attractive black and white tile, is open to the guests, and you can help yourselves to tea and coffee or fresh-baked muffins at any time.

Choose from four gracious guest rooms with ocean views, two of which have private baths. A favorite is the upstairs room with private bath, high vaulted ceilings, skylights, whitewashed walls, snuggly floral comforters, and bountiful sunlight.

A delicious full breakfast, complete with hot-out-of-the-oven fresh breads, baked egg dishes, and fresh fruit, is served at the dining room table. Although you don't get much intimacy eating *toutes ensemble*, you probably won't mind. Your hosts help to make conversation lively, and the food is plentiful. Besides, after breakfast you can always take a walk, just the two of you, through the dunes to the water's edge.

◆ **Romantic Note:** Next door you'll find a weathered cabin available for rent. It is sparsely furnished and not nearly as well kept as the bed and breakfast, but it does have three bedrooms, a kitchen, one and a half baths, and a working fireplace. A perfect getaway for those seeking affordable, roomy, and exclusive privacy with beach access.

Restaurant Kissing

PASTIMES COFFEE AND COLLECTIBLES, Long Beach ❤
South Fifth and Pacific Highway, in the Oceanic Building
(206) 642-8303
Very Inexpensive

Located on Pacific Highway, on the corner of South Fifth.

Not only is Pastimes the peninsula's only espresso bar, a necessity for many Northwesterners, it is also a lovely and casual place for quiet conversation. On the ground floor of an attractive renovated house, in the heart of Long Beach, you can sit at the wooden espresso bar and sip a hot latte or challenge each other to a game of chess at one of the tables arranged throughout the sunlit, cheery room. Wander about and take notice of the collection of unusual antiques: turn-of-the century photos of Long Beach, an antique wedding dress, and an intricately carved wooden bird cage, among other curious items. Although the windows face the bustling street, the soft jazz playing in the background and the congenial ambience, not to mention the coffee, provide the perfect energy boost for a romantic day at the beach.

Outdoor Kissing

LEADBETTER POINT STATE PARK

Take Pacific Highway to the northernmost tip of the peninsula.

There are lots of romantic places to walk hand-in-hand on this peninsula, the most obvious being the beach and dunes themselves. Other options are the **NORTH HEAD LIGHTHOUSE** or the **CAPE DISAPPOINTMENT LIGHTHOUSE**, both located in Ilwaco, just minutes from Long Beach; the latter is a somewhat steeper proposition. You also might consider going to the northern tip of the peninsula to **LEADBETTER STATE PARK**, where you can be assured of privacy throughout the year. You can wander all day and not run into anybody. But don't wander too far; people have been known to get lost in the wilderness up here. Also, the seasonal appearance of large, aggressive black flies can yield an unforeseen kissing obstacle.

Ocean Park

Hotel/Bed and Breakfast Kissing

COAST WATCH BED AND BREAKFAST, Ocean Park ◆◆◆
Unmarked, private road
(206) 665-6774
Inexpensive to Expensive

Call for directions and specific address.

City dwellers often forget how beautiful sunset or a star-filled sky can actually be, but a weekend at Coast Watch can reacquaint you with nature's abundant splendor. Escape to one of two spacious suites in this weathered gray-blue cabin set in the dunes, yards from the ocean. Both suites are full of sunlight, one providing a dazzling view of the ocean and dunes, the other a northerly view of the surrounding natural scenery. We preferred the suite with the ocean view, which also has a large deck that is perfect for enjoying sunsets, but both suites are pleasant, roomy, and plain with simple lines and colors and modest wicker furnishings.

The conscientious host takes pride in the smallest of details, from the fresh-cut rose on your pillow to the delectable fruit-platter breakfast served at your convenience in your private suite. She has even been known to drive for miles, from store to store, to find quality fruits to ensure her guests' satisfaction. (No kidding!)

This unique bed and breakfast has no common areas for guests outside of their individual suites, which assures unlimited privacy. Additionally, because there are only two suites, you'll feel as if the expanse of beach and grass-covered dunes is yours for the taking. Stroll at dusk and let the waves wash over your feet or wait until the sun has set and let the stars above enfold you. The only drawback to a weekend at Coast Watch will be your reluctance to go back to the real world.

◆ **Romantic Note:** There is a two-night minimum on weekends.

Seaview

Hotel/Bed and Breakfast Kissing

THE SHELBURNE COUNTRY INN, Seaview
4415 Pacific Way
(206) 642-2442
Moderate to Expensive

From Aberdeen, take U.S. 101 south to Route 103 and turn north. The inn is on the left side of the street, at the corner of Route 103 (Pacific Way) and J Street.

Even though it lacks an ocean view, romantic couples from all over the Northwest think of the Shelburne first when they want a seaside getaway. And no wonder—the 15 rooms and suites in this restored turn-of-the-century inn are all furnished with elegant European antiques, lace pillows, handmade patchwork quilts, crocheted bedspreads, private bathrooms, and plenty of Victorian atmosphere. Many also feature a balcony or deck. Of course, not all rooms are created equal. Some have queen beds, some have doubles; some face the charming kitchen garden, some have less inspiring street views. A favorite is the corner suite with a separate sitting area and an old-fashioned claw-foot tub.

Guests are greeted with a plate of astonishingly rich cookies fresh from a bakery down the street, but the real appetite pleaser is breakfast. The Shelburne's gourmet breakfasts are like works of art, designed for eye appeal as well as savory flavor. Feast on treats such as a three-cheese omelet with red salmon caviar or waffles with fresh fruit. Plates are decorated with edible flowers and herbs. After this indulgence, you can hike through a series of dunes to reach the long, smooth beach, which tends to be less crowded here.

◆ **Romantic Alternative: NENDEL'S EDGEWATER**, 409 Southwest 10th Street South, Long Beach, (206) 642-2311, (Inexpensive), is an ordinary chain motel in an extraordinary location: at the end of the dunes, facing the roaring surf. A nearby quarter-mile boardwalk allows lovers a chance to stroll through the fragile dunes without harming them and provides a fine ocean overlook.

Restaurant Kissing

THE SHOALWATER RESTAURANT, Seaview
4415 Pacific Way, in the Shelburne Inn
(206) 642-4142
Moderate to Expensive

See directions to the Shelburne Inn.

Can food be wildly romantic? At the Shoalwater, the proof is in the pudding, or perhaps we should say it's in the rose geranium sorbet. No matter what you choose from the imaginative and wide-ranging menu, it will be utterly fresh and delicious. Sautéed mushrooms with Dijon mustard, fresh dill, and sour cream; baked halibut with dill pesto, melon relish, and cucumber mayonnaise; roasted pork tenderloin with pecans in a Dijon mustard sauce and an apricot glaze—need we say more? The desserts more than live up to the rest of the meal.

Even if the food at the Shoalwater were merely mediocre, the setting alone would win it at least a lip. The restaurant takes up much of the bottom floor of a turn-of-the-century house that long ago became part of the Shelburne Inn, and it features stained and leaded glass windows, high ceilings, and well-spaced antique wooden tables and chairs in a warm, country Victorian atmosphere.

◆ **Romantic Note:** The Shoalwater offers a series of "Northwest Winemakers Dinners" that feature special vintages from individual wineries, talks with the winemaker, and dishes specially designed to complement each bottling. Unforgettable!

◆ **Romantic Alternative:** The owners of the Shoalwater also operate the **LIGHTSHIP RESTAURANT**, 409 Southwest 10th Street,

Long Beach, (206) 642-3252, (Inexpensive to Moderate), which features more casual dining in a room with sweeping ocean and coast views.

Chinook

Restaurant Kissing

SANCTUARY RESTAURANT
Highway 101 and Hazel Street
(206) 777-8380
Moderate to Expensive

South of Long Beach, just off Highway 101.

In the sanctuary of a renovated former church, you can sit in actual pews and marvel at your surroundings, including stained glass windows and other structural remnants of the building's past. The food is outstanding, especially the local seafood and a vast array of homemade desserts. This distinctive setting might just be the perfect spot for you to make your vows all over again.

> *"Press yourself into a drop of wine, and pour yourself into the purest flame."*
>
> Rainier Maria Rilke

Oregon State

PORTLAND AND ENVIRONS

Once you visit Portland, you are likely to become an enthusiast. This growing municipality has two distinct personalities—one is urban and the other is rural. There is an impressive amount of greenery here, and an amazing variety of terrain for walking, hiking, and dawdling. Gardens, parks, forests, and rivers blanket the landscape, and all are beautiful and meticulously maintained. Then there's the urban side of Portland's character: the upscale charm of Nob Hill, a charming refurbished neighborhood teeming with restaurants and shops; the growing downtown dotted with art deco buildings and glass skyscrapers; a restored old-town area with all its vintage charm left intact; and the recently developed, affluent riverfront area called RiverPlace. And both these personalities are in perfect balance. This is what makes Portland so remarkable: city life is tolerated only if it doesn't get in the way of the countryside. Whether you are visiting for a day or a week, this city's earthy appeal is bound to make a loving impression.

Hotel/Bed and Breakfast Kissing

GOVERNOR HOTEL, Portland ❤️❤️
611 Southwest 10th
(503) 224-3400, (800) 554-3456
Expensive to Unbelievably Expensive

Call for directions.

You don't have to be a governor to appreciate the stellar accommodations at this refined, historic downtown Portland hotel, although you might need a governor's pocketbook. A harmonious mixture of turn-of-the-century decorum and modernistic appointments fills the grand lobby. Fascinating hand-painted murals, found throughout the hotel, pay tribute to Lewis and Clark and the Native Americans they encountered while exploring the Oregon Territory. The subtle, soft hues of the artwork and original mahogany wood furnishings make for a smooth introduction to your interlude.

Some of the standard guest rooms, which are the least costly, are less than enchanting, with simple furnishings and somber tones. The deluxe guest rooms, which are just slightly more expensive, offer considerably more warmth and comfort, with skylights that fill the room with sunshine, plus Northwest art, gas fireplaces, and cozy love seats. Moving even farther up, you can choose from several penthouse suites, which have an abundance of skylights, quiet seclusion, and generous space. The decor varies slightly from room to room, but maintains its fairly conservative composure, even at the top. Those with narrow budgets might consider looking elsewhere for something less sedate and more affordable.

◆ **Romantic Suggestion:** The impressive **CELILO RESTAURANT**, (503) 241-2100, (Moderate to Expensive), adjacent to the hotel lobby downstairs, supplies old-world ambience. Share an intimate conversation in a window booth glancing over the busy city streets. Reminiscent of a Parisian brasserie, the interior is an inviting blend of dark wood pillars and beams, and elegant tables draped in white. King salmon, the house specialty, is served three delectable ways: steamed in rice paper, grilled gravlax, or baked on a smoking alder plank. The other enticing entrées are equally delicious.

THE HERON HAUS, Portland
2545 Northwest Westover Road
(503) 274-1846
Moderate to Very Expensive

Call for directions.

Bed and breakfasts are known for being cozy, warm, and congenial. Nothing is quite so affection-producing as a stay in a home where the owners diligently tend to their guests' hearts and senses with such amenities as the wafting aroma of just-baked morning pastries, a roaring fireplace, cushy furnishings, snuggly quilts covering oversized pillows, and a conspicuous amount of tender loving care. The Heron Haus has all this and more.

The home is a huge (7,500 square feet), attractively furnished mansion almost entirely given over to the guests. Features include a sun deck, a pool, and four spacious sun-filled suites with cozy sitting areas. The bathrooms are so spectacular that you may decide to stay in yours and forget about returning to bed. One suite has an ample spa tub that overlooks the city, and another has a shower with seven nozzles that will cover every inch of you with pulsating water. With space to spare, Heron Haus can accommodate couples who want to emerge clean, giggling, and inseparable.

THE HEATHMAN HOTEL, Portland
1009 Broadway
(503) 241-4100
Expensive

Call the hotel for directions.

When you walk into the lobby of the Heathman, your first reaction will be Northwest skepticism. While the geometric art and marble detailing fill the interior with a distinguished and striking appearance, the modern design and hard finishes make a cold, stark impression. Perhaps the coziest part of the hotel is the **TEA COURT**. The classic decor, solid teak paneling, large fireplace, and genial quiet make this a suitable place for an afternoon of thoughtful conversation and warm gazes. Upstairs there is a library lounge next to the hotel's bar, with elegant cozy sofas and chairs to snuggle in. This is definitely the warmest section of the entire hotel.

As you might expect, the rooms are handsome and appropriately first class, with all the pertinent amenities. Subtle tones of pale green and rose, marble fixtures in the bathrooms, rattan-and-leather chairs, plush draperies, and original Northwest artwork enrich the basic hotel style of the elegant (though small) rooms.

◆ **Romantic Highlight:** The **HEATHMAN HOTEL RESTAU-RANT** is considered to be one of the finest around. Attentive service and skillfully prepared dishes make for a memorable evening of fine dining. Breakfasts are also elegant, as carefully created as the dinners. The only drawback here is the business conversations taking place around you. But after dinner, when you retire to your room, there will no longer be a need for suits, ties, heels, or briefcases, and then you can really let your hair down.

◆   **Romantic Alternative: THE BENSON**, 309 Southwest Broadway, (503) 228-2000, (Expensive), is a grand old hotel with one of the most massive, ornate lobbies you will see anywhere in the Northwest. The chandeliered, wood-paneled interior is stunning and the lounge seating intimate and quiet. But even after a well-publicized $16 million renovation, that's still all there is. The rooms are disappointing and drab. For this kind of money they could have done much better. How is it possible to misspend so much money? What a kissing shame.

HOTEL VINTAGE PLAZA, Portland
422 Southwest Broadway
(503) 228-1212
Expensive

On Broadway, between Washington and Stark.

While everybody else is submitting to the hoopla of the newly renovated and outlandishly expensive Benson and RiverPlace hotels, you can find affordable romance in the bountiful luxury of Hotel Vintage Plaza. The open lobby envelopes you in classic, elegant style with dark wood paneling, marble pillars, grandiose fresh bouquets, and sumptuous sofas. Lift your eyes skyward and take notice of the upstairs hallways, wraparound balconies, and a solarium roof that draws the sunlight in, giving the entire expanse an airy distinction.

In amorous style you can escape the city in any of the Starlight Rooms, located on the top floor and featuring extensive conservatory windows. Gaze at the sky from the comfort of your plush bed, warmed with handsome down comforters. If you need more space, the two-story townhouse suites are beautiful, with loft bedrooms, winding staircases, full kitchens and living rooms downstairs, private entrances for both floors, and jetted Fuji soaking tubs.

Start your evening tasting the complimentary local wines served nightly in the lobby. A decidedly warm overture to a quiet evening in the lap of luxury.

◆   **Romantic Note: PAZZO**, (503) 228-1515, (Moderate to Expensive), is the restaurant adjoining the hotel's lobby. The mood here contrasts sharply with the refined elegance of the hotel, embracing you instead with vivid colors and patterns, numerous tables, and steady, lively chatter. Even so, the service is prompt and the Italian cuisine is of the finest quality.

JOHN PALMER HOUSE, Portland
4314 North Mississippi Avenue
(503) 284-5893
Inexpensive to Expensive

Call for directions.

Don't get caught in this tourist attraction on summer weekends. Registered as a national historic monument, this bed and breakfast has been well publicized in the Portland area and beyond. The gleaming yellow-gold gabled 1890 Victorian house was built as a showcase and it still fulfills its role, reveling in a multitude of original antiques. The immaculate grounds, bordering flower gardens, and seasonal decorations are charming, although somewhat commercial. For the authentic Victorian experience, I recommend the distinctive three-room bridal suite, adorned with lace and an extravagant display of antiques: the hand-carved Eastlake antique double bed in the master bedroom, the "consumption porch" providing fresh air and views of Portland, and the library sitting room give lovers a taste of grand living. Peruse the wooden bookshelves for old classics, and sink into a plush, old-fashioned sofa.

Don a robe and tiptoe to the hot tub in the cottage next door. When you are fully relaxed, assuage your appetite with excellent dishes selected from a specially designed menu and complemented with wines from the Tualatin Vineyards. Weekend or nightly packages are available, which can include your own private butler or maid, a horse-and-carriage ride with Lady C.J. (the horse), a five-course gourmet dinner served in the formal dining room, champagne toasts, and/or a formal high tea. Make a reservation early, preferably off-season, for a more enjoyable and intimate stay. Once you have indulged in the many luxuries here, you'll understand why the inn has gained its popularity.

MACMASTER HOUSE BED AND BREAKFAST, Portland
1041 Southwest Vista Avenue
(503) 223-7362
Inexpensive to Moderate

Call for reservations and directions.

Many things about this turn-of-the-century mansion are impressive and reminiscent of grand old-world living. Some things could stand a bit of sprucing up. As you walk up to the house, the formal portico, with its

Doric columns and Palladian windows of leaded glass, looks a bit rundown and in need of paint and landscaping. Once inside, however, there is a bright, airy feeling all around, and everything is elegant, grand, and well maintained. The suites are all handsome and lush, four have fireplaces, and most have separate sitting areas. The MacMaster Suite has a deck with a view; the Safari Room, with its unusual four-poster bamboo bed, is the largest and most attractive suite in the house. The rooms with private baths are definitely the best.

PORTLAND'S WHITE HOUSE, Portland
1914 Northeast 22nd Avenue
(503) 287-7131
Inexpensive to Moderate

Call for directions.

Political addresses are not romantic, but everything here is totally bipartisan, so don't worry. Greek columns, a fountain, a circular drive-way, and a white exterior with a west wing and an east wing give this White House an impressive resemblance to its Washington, D.C., namesake. Inside the similarities stop, but the bed-and-breakfast refine-ment continues. Still, the real reason to come here is not so much for the guest rooms on the second floor, even though they are nice enough and scrupulously maintained. Come instead for your wedding, so that the reception can happen on the lower levels and the bridal party can take over the rooms upstairs. The owner of the White House is a catering specialist, and turns her house over for special parties three times a month. If you do want to stay just for the bed and breakfast, the accommodations are gracious and the morning breakfast is wonderful. Weekends can prove a bit hectic when an event is taking place, but during the week everything is sedate and composed.

Restaurant Kissing

ATWATER'S RESTAURANT, Portland
111 Southwest Fifth Avenue, in the U.S. Bancorp Tower
(503) 220-3629
Very Expensive

On Fifth and Burnside in downtown Portland, on the 30th floor of the U.S. Bancorp Tower. From Highway 405, take the City Center exit to Fourth Avenue. Turn north on Fourth Avenue and west on Pine Street. This will take you to a parking garage under the building.

Atwater's Restaurant, atop Portland's tallest building, is designed to look like an exclusive uptown residence. From the Oriental-style elevator doors to the silver service, marble floors, and other extravagant finishing touches, it is clear that this is an ultra-formal dining establishment. The service is attentive, almost to the point of hovering, but the food is superior (they serve a lavish Sunday brunch) and artistically served. From this vantage point on cloud nine, you can watch the downtown buildings reflect the sun's light until only a silhouette of mountains is visible through the floor-to-ceiling windows.

CAFÉ DES AMIS, Portland
1987 Northwest Kearney Street
(503) 295-6487
Moderate to Expensive

Take Northwest Lovejoy west to 19th Avenue and turn south for one block to Kearney Street. The café is at the intersection of Kearney and 19th.

Café des Amis, an effective blend of Northwest atmosphere with epicurean French cuisine, is considered one of the best dinner spots in Portland. The room is simply appointed with wood tables well spaced from each other, white walls, and starched white linen tablecloths. There's a cordiality about the place that makes for a totally romantic experience, and the food is a gastronomic treat. The pâtés are delicious; the duck, quail, and salmon are perfectly prepared; and the New York steak is the thickest and tenderest you may ever have. The delectable desserts are a master stroke.

CODY'S CAFÉ, Portland
115 Northwest 22nd Avenue
(503) 248-9311
Moderate

One half block north of Burnside Street.

Café hardly describes what you'll find when you literally step into a contemporary, artistic rendition of ancient Rome. Terra-cotta floors, stately white columns, classical Romanesque sculptured art, and dome ceilings surround floral-patterned booths that are cozy, yet sophisticated. The mahogany tables are numerous but well spaced, leaving an appreciated degree of privacy. Both lunch and dinner offer superb entrées, ranging from the Mediterranean shish kebab to grilled, boneless bluefin tuna served with papaya salsa. For a creative change of taste and style, you have to celebrate at least one special occasion at Cody's.

PAISLEY'S, Portland
1204 Northwest 21st Avenue
(503) 243-2403
Moderate

From downtown Portland, go west on Northwest Lovejoy Street to Northwest 21st Avenue and turn left. Paisley's is at the intersection of Northrup Street and 21st.

Paisley's is located in the heart of Portland's Nob Hill, which is blessed with more than 40 lovingly renovated neighborhood shops and restaurants, each more interesting than the next and several among the best Portland has to offer. Paisley's lives up to this area's reputation with its dedication to fine cooking in a relaxed setting. The attention the new owner has given to maintaining an attractive, unpretentious place is reflected in the modest interior filled with wood tables, finished wood floors, pastel artwork, and soft lighting. Outdoor seating is available on the front porch. Breakfast, lunch, and dinner are all well done and graciously served. Save room for the desserts here, which are almost as delicious to hear described as they are to eat. The aroma of robust cappuccino and delicate soufflés, tortes, tarts, and brûlées will sweep you off your feet.

GENOA, Portland
2832 Southeast Belmont Street
(503) 238-1464
Expensive

On Southeast Belmont between 28th and 29th avenues.

Genoa's has the distinction of being rated one of the best dining experiences in the Northwest. Quite a reputation to live up to, but the skilled kitchen consistently produces culinary feats of excellence. If discreet, epicurean dining is what you're looking for in Portland, come to this small storefront location in a less-than-interesting section of the city. You can't see inside; cranberry-colored window coverings keep outsiders out and insiders from seeing anything of the outside world—including light. Once you adapt to the sultry lighting, you'll find a seven-course parade of Italian delicacies that will keep your attention throughout the entire evening.

LA MIRABELLE, Portland
1126 Southwest 18th Avenue
(503) 223-7113
Expensive

On Southwest 18th between Main and Jefferson streets.

The rundown exterior of this old building gives no indication of the gracious world that lies within. Lace-covered windows seem incongruous from the outside, but inside you'll find a luxurious Renaissance-style atmosphere and exquisite French food. Banquettes in floral upholstery line the wall, and starched white linen tablecloths set with fine china and crystal sparkle against the whitewashed walls. There are three small dining salons at La Mirabelle, and though the service can be a bit pompous it is efficient. The entire experience is exceptional. Open Wednesday through Saturday evenings only.

WESTMORELAND BISTRO, Portland
7015 Southeast Milwaukie
(503) 236-6457
Moderate to Expensive

Call for directions.

If you want a fine dining experience in a warm casual atmosphere you can look forward to an evening or afternoon at Westmoreland's Bistro. The older neighborhood setting has a certain amount of charm and an unruffled personality. Inside, soft lighting, tables for two, and simple decor set the scene for both lunch and dinner. The international menu covers everything from Middle Eastern cuisine to ample hamburgers, puff pastry stuffed with mushrooms, and a warm spinach salad with goat cheese and a cherry vinaigrette. All are wonderfully prepared. Of particular interest to romantic enophiles is the wine selection; more than 200 labels are available for retail purchase, and you can enjoy one with dinner for only $1 extra. A definite kissing bargain.

Outdoor Kissing

MACLEAY PARK, Portland

Macleay Park is one of many entrances to Portland's Forest Park. You can enter Macleay off the Thurman Bridge near Franklin and 32nd Street Northwest, or at the end of Forest Park in northwest Portland off Cornell Road.

Macleay Park is a park within a park, and a gorgeous example of nature's ability to thrive in the midst of a city. This lush green wilderness, strewn with surging creeks and hiking trails, is just one of the almost limitless doorways into Portland's immense backyard, also known as Forest Park. Forest Park is regarded as the largest city wilderness in the United States. It affords so many kissing places that if you're not careful, you'll risk a lip or two.

◆ **Romantic Note: COLLINS' SANCTUARY**, run by the Portland Audubon Society, 5151 Northwest Cornell Road, (503) 292-6855, is another doorway into Forest Park, and not very well known even though its secluded beauty is near the heart of the city. There are trails and paths that will lead you to private corners of this 67-acre wildlife area.

RIVERPLACE, Portland

From downtown Portland take Southwest Market Street east to the river, where it dead-ends at Riverplace.

Personally, I don't find RiverPlace the least bit romantic. How can a half-mile-long arcade of condominiums, stores, and restaurants be intimate and endearing? But when I visited this Willamette River development I saw so many couples strolling hand-in-hand that I decided to include RiverPlace anyway. I'll try to give you a romantic perspective on this place, out of a sense of fairness.

RiverPlace begins with the European refinement and poshness of the **RIVERPLACE HOTEL**, 1510 Southwest Harbor Way, (503) 228-3233, (Very Expensive and Beyond), at the northern tip of the walk. Here you have an exquisite European-style building with nice, hotel-like but overpriced accommodations.

I would, however, encourage you to try the distinctive, much-admired restaurant adjacent to the lobby called **ESPLANADE**, 1510 Southwest Harbor Way, (503) 288-3233, (Expensive). The bright yellow decor, interlaced with soft maroon and blue, enhanced by modern art-deco mosaics, reflects a contemporary, festive mood. Celebrate the ambience with sautéed halibut with wasabi hollandaise and wild rice, or grilled ahi with peppered mango puree and cucumber salsa. Kissing and dining should always be this good.

The lobby bar here is also one of the most romantic in town. As you continue walking you'll have the water on one side and a series of handsome condominiums on the other, with a dozen or so boutiques and eateries. Farther down are more restaurants with water views.

Admittedly, this is a lovely development and there are enough options here to offer something for everyone regardless of taste or budget. Romantic or not, RiverPlace is worth a stroll and perhaps a stop somewhere along the way for a glass of wine or a shot of espresso, a quick disco beat, or whatever else may be alive and happening.

SAUVIE ISLAND

Go north on Highway 30 to the Sauvie Island Bridge, about 11 miles from downtown Portland. There is a small day-use fee for a visit to the island.

When you feel the need for wide-open empty space, take a drive to this vast pastoral oasis. Sauvie Island is a popular Portland getaway, but its size prevents it from ever feeling crowded. There are relatively isolated beaches and numerous hiking trails through wetlands, pasture, oak woodlands, and spotty sections of coniferous forest. Oak Island is a much smaller land mass, attached by a natural bridge at the northeast end of Sauvie Island, where stretches of sandy beach are available.

◆ **Romantic Warning:** Sauvie Island can be covered in smog when other parts of the area are clear. Check the horizon before setting out for the island. No drinking water or gasoline is available here.

SKYLINE DRIVE, Portland

Portland's Forest Park is a vast wilderness on the west side of the Willamette River. At the park's south end, Cornell Road intersects with Skyline Drive. Skyline Drive borders the east side of the park.

Is it possible for city roads or highways to spiral up and around to celestial splendor? If so, Skyline Drive is a likely candidate, and a quick or slow cruise over this winding road will help you cast a deciding vote. Three miles of fascinating vistas outline the eastern boundary of Forest Park. At the crest you can view the contours of the Cascades, the Willamette Valley awash in shades of green, the gentle forms of the Coastal Range, and the skyline of downtown Portland. If you want to get up and away without having to go far from the city, cruise Skyline Drive any time of day or night.

TRYON CREEK STATE PARK, Portland

Head south from Portland on Interstate 5 to the Terwilliger exit. Travel two and a half miles due south on Southwest Terwilliger Boulevard to get to the park.

This is the place for easy walks along gently rolling red-bark paths through thick forestland. Don't expect wide vistas or places to sit in the sun; it is almost always shady and moist here, not to mention a little muddy in the winter. But whether you walk for miles or just a few hundred feet, the two of you will feel safe, unhurried, and alone here.

WASHINGTON PARK ROSE GARDENS, Portland

From downtown Portland, drive west on West Burnside, following the signs to the gardens.

Washington Park Rose Gardens is a perfect lover's-lane hideout. The road to the tree-shaded parking area winds up a long, steep hill to a summit where the park itself reigns supreme over the city and the Willamette Valley. From the fragrant, endless rows of rosebushes to the exotic Japanese gardens to the unhindered view of Portland and the mountains beyond, this is pure embracing territory, acre after magnificent acre. It's a perfect place to come for quiet afternoons, brilliant sunsets, or twinkling evening lights.

◆ **Romantic Note:** Although the **PITTOCK MANSION**, 3229 Northwest Pittock Avenue, (503) 823-3623, is essentially a museum, the well-kept grounds beautifully frame the view of Portland beyond, seemingly nestled in an abundance of distant trees. Stroll the grand walkways behind the mansion, and cherish the sunset in the shadows of fine architecture.

WINE COUNTRY/
WILLAMETTE VALLEY

Newberg

Start from the town of Newberg on Highway 99W, and proceed along this route down to Eugene.

A 25-minute drive southwest from Portland brings you into the Willamette Valley, home of the famous Oregon wineries. Embraced on the west by the gentle countenance of the Coastal Range and to the east by the glacial peaks of the Cascades, this area has much to treasure. You could call this region the Sonoma Valley of the Northwest, but that wouldn't do it justice. The Willamette Valley is far more stunning, and the wineries, although young, offer an acclaimed selection of wines any enophile would appreciate.

A large number of wineries are scattered within this picturesque area, each with its own attitude regarding the art of winemaking. Many of the wineries feature vineyard-draped hillsides, a rathskeller-style tasting room, or a reposeful country setting. Still others are plain buildings at roadside that lack atmosphere, but make up for it in their wine selection. Whether you choose to visit one or all, and whether you choose to imbibe or not, your entire winery-hopping tour will be an intoxicating joy.

To better acquaint yourselves with the myriad wineries in the region, the **OREGON WINEGROWERS' ASSOCIATION**, 1200 Northwest Front Avenue, Suite 400, Portland, OR 97209, (503) 228-8403, publishes an excellent brochure called *Discover Oregon Wineries* that will help you with your tour.

◆ **Romantic Suggestions:** TUALATIN VINEYARDS, on Seavey Road, Route 1, Box 339, Forest Grove, (503) 357-5005; **ELK COVE VINEYARDS**, on 27751 Northwest Olson Road, Gaston, (503) 985-7760; and **REX HILL VINEYARDS**, 30835 North Highway 99W, Newberg, (503) 538-0666, are only a sampling of the more than 50 wineries in this area. Tualatin has a picnic area shaded by cherry trees that overlooks the valley and vineyards. Elk Cove has breathtaking views from its attractive tasting room, and picnic tables set on a grassy knoll. Rex Hill has a wonderful tasting room and setting.

Hotel/Bed and Breakfast Kissing

SPRINGBROOK HAZELNUT FARM, Newberg
30295 North Highway 99W
(503) 538-4606
Inexpensive

From Portland, take Interstate 5 south to the Tigard exit. Continue west on 99W about 14 miles to milepost 21. You should see a sign for the farm on the road.

Many aspects of this bed and breakfast are delightful: 60 acres of prolific hazelnut trees, expansive flower gardens, a large vegetable and herb garden, swimming pool, tennis court, and an 8,000-square-foot farmhouse. The problem is that the swimming pool looks rather murky, the gardens are in only OK condition, the tennis court is a bit rundown, and most of the home is in need of a great deal of renovation. So where's the romance? In the completely restored carriage-house apartment in the orchard. The fully functional apartment has a bright, soothing, contemporary interior with a lovely kitchen. A full breakfast is stocked in the refrigerator, including homemade jams, muffins, eggs, pancake batter, and sausages for you to whip at your convenience. If you are touring the wine country, this is a delightful spot to set up temporary amorous housekeeping. The landscaping can use some work, but from this vantage point it has a certain amount of rustic charm.

Restaurant Kissing

THE COFFEE COTTAGE, Newberg
808 East Hancock
(503) 538-5126
Inexpensive

In the town of Newberg, on Highway 99W heading south, on the east side of the street.

No self-respecting Northwesterner can go very long without the requisite latte, cappuccino, or mocha. There are literally hundreds of places to imbibe this dark roasted aromatic liquid, in some of the most out-of-the way locations you can imagine. In the wine country, the Coffee Cottage is a very affectionate spot for taking an unhurried coffee break. The wood-frame home also has an outdoor garden patio where you can enjoy a warm day, iced lattes, and great desserts.

Dayton

Hotel/Bed and Breakfast Kissing

WINE COUNTRY FARM BED AND BREAKFAST, Dayton ❤❤
6855 Breyman Orchards Road
(503) 864-3446
Inexpensive

From Highway 99W, turn west on McDougall Road and then north on Breyman Orchard Road.

Spend some time walking through the stables where the Arabian horses are kept, or relax on the porch of this renovated 1910 stucco farmhouse and take in the all-encompassing view of the valley, mountains, and vineyards. Morning brings a generous breakfast. Of the four bedrooms here, two have private baths and are comfortable. This isn't fancy or refined, but it is another secluded part of the world where civilization seems very away.

McMinnville

Hotel/Bed and Breakfast Kissing

ORCHARD VIEW INN, McMinnville
16540 Northwest Orchard View Road
(503) 472-0165
Inexpensive

Call for directions.

You may wish to extend your tryst in the tasting rooms by staying at Orchard View Inn. This octagonal home is nestled in a country neighborhood where deer prance around the backyard. Outside, a deck surrounds the entire home; inside you'll find vaulted ceilings, large windows, and skylights. The large rooms are simple and homey and the house is entirely for the use of the guests. It isn't elegant, but it is secluded and relaxing.

YOUNGBERG HILL FARM BED AND BREAKFAST, McMinnville
10660 Youngberg Hill Road
(503) 472-2727
Inexpensive

Call for directions.

I can't think of a better base for touring the wine country than this elegant country mansion set on a hilltop surrounded by vineyards and pristine farmland. A winding gravel road brings you up to an illustrious view of the valley, mountains, and rolling hills. The entire house is surrounded by wide decks. Each of the five rooms is simply furnished and has a private bath. They are nice, but not great. What is great is their commanding view of the area. A full hearty breakfast is served in the formal dining room at a common table with floor-to-ceiling windows all around.

OREGON COAST

Follow Highway 101 south from Astoria, near the Washington state border, to Brookings, near the California state border.

It is probably safe to say that no other state has a span of highway quite like Highway 101 in Oregon. This road hugs large sections of the coast and almost every mile is filled with incredible scenery. The drive is literally breathtaking. Thank goodness there are many turnoffs, parks, hikes, undiscovered coves, rocky inlets, and ravines where you can stop and drink in the view at your own leisurely pace.

The boundless drama of this area is enhanced by the constant, temperamental mood swings of the weather. At times the mixture of fog and sea mist creates a diffuse screen through which the world appears like an apparition. Other moments bring a disturbing quiet as a tempest brews on the horizon, where ocean and sky meet and bond as one. Yet even on the calmest of summer days, the unbridled energy and the siren song of the waves unleashing their power against beaches, headlands, and haystack rocks have a spellbinding impact. The Oregon coast is so beautiful that it can rekindle your relationship with each other and the world.

Not only is the scenery stupendous, but the two of you can also share in a multitude of activities such as hiking through coastal rain forest, beachcombing, hunting for agates, clamming, exploring tide pools, kite flying, and whale watching. Until you've attempted each of these, you haven't truly experienced the Oregon coast.

After whetting your appetite with all these heartfelt images, I must tell you of a drawback: like all stunning locations in the Northwest, most weekends and almost every day during the summer here can be maddeningly crowded. Most days produce traffic jams reminiscent of any big city, while the beaches can be overflowing with civilization instead of sea gulls and crustaceans. All of the places recommended in this collection take the concept of solitude and seclusion quite seriously, but there is only so much we can do. It is essential you keep the popularity of the area in mind when planning your getaway. This way you have a better chance of getting away from it all instead of finding it *all* there when you arrive.

◆ **Romantic Note:** For information on **OREGON COAST PARKS AND RECREATION** areas, call (503) 378-6305. For up-to-the-minute camping information from March through Labor Day, call (800) 452-5687 or (503) 731-3411. Be sure to bring along proper beach attire and gear: bathing suits in the summer, jeans and warm sweaters during the rest of the year, plenty of towels and a blanket, a bucket with shovel for clamming or agate hunting. There are hundreds of secluded, totally accessible beaches along the road that you will want to take full advantage of. Be prepared so that when the moment strikes your fancy to splash in the surf or walk hand-in-hand through the sand, there won't be anything stopping you.

◆ **Romantic Warning:** Although this might sound like an exaggeration, it isn't: there is an almost interminable procession of motels bordering the coast and abutting Highway 101. Most of these are appropriately labeled "motel," but some call themselves "inn," "cottages," and "resort." Several of them do have alluring views, real fireplaces, and efficient kitchens, but by any name they are still motels, assuredly OK places to stay, but by the standards of this book not the least bit romantic. For a list of these places for the entire state, write to the **OREGON LODGING ASSOCIATION**, 12724 Southeast Stark Street, Portland, OR 97233, (503) 255-5135, for their concise guide, *Where To Stay In Oregon.*

Gearhart

Hotel/Bed and Breakfast Kissing

GEARHART OCEAN INN, Gearhart
67 North Cottage
(503) 738-7373
Inexpensive

From Highway 101 turn west on Pacific Way and then right on North Cottage to the inn.

Probably more a motel than an inn, this modest white frame building houses 11 cottage-style rooms. Some of the units have kitchens; all are clean and comfortable, with wicker furniture and attractive linens. Unfortunately, the inn wraps around a courtyard that also happens to be the parking lot. Not great, but the location in the heart of Gearhart is the primary focus and worth a stay. The beach is only a short walk away and the privacy there is supreme.

Restaurant Kissing

OCEANSIDE RESTAURANT, Gearhart
1200 North Marion Drive
(503) 738-7789
Moderate

From Highway 101 turn west on Pacific Way and then right on North Marion to the restaurant.

The town of Gearhart is one long parade of breathtaking beach and fabulous designer seaside homes. This is one of the few communities along the Oregon coast that, for the most part, feels like a refined, affluent neighborhood. There is nothing that even vaguely resembles a tourist attraction, except directly behind the Oceanside Restaurant, but once you pass the sprawling condominium vacation complex called Gearhart by the Sea and enter the lone building that houses the restaurant, you won't be aware of anything but the beach and good food. The window-enclosed dining room—complete with oversized chandeliers, vaulted cedar-beamed ceiling, and a handful of tables—faces grass-covered sand dunes with the sparkling Pacific Ocean in the distance. What a view! Lunch is OK, but the dinner entrées are very good. The angel-hair pasta with fresh crab and shrimp in a rich pesto sauce and the fresh salmon, both enjoyed with an aperitif of sunset, are our favorites.

PACIFIC WAY BAKERY AND CAFÉ, Gearhart
601 Pacific Way
(503) 738-0245
Inexpensive to Moderate

From Highway 101 turn west on Pacific Way to Cottage. The café is at the corner of Cottage and Pacific.

If you want to taste some of the most sensational baked goods this side of the Rockies, then this unassuming café is the place for hot espresso, fresh cinnamon rolls, and you. The outside is set off by green-striped awnings, white wood, and gray weathered shingles. Inside you will find a casual setting of cranberry-colored tables with hunter green chairs surrounding a wood-burning fireplace. In spite of the laid-back nature of the staff, everything is immaculate and nicely presented. Lunch and dinner, surprisingly, are as good as the breakfasts, with generous portions and exact seasonings. The lunch menu has a great selection of sandwiches, while dinner offers mostly fresh pastas and seasonal fish. All this and the beaches of Gearhart only a stone's throw away.

◆ **Romantic Note:** Call to check on the café's seasonal hours.

Seaside

Hotel/Bed and Breakfast Kissing

BEACHWOOD BED AND BREAKFAST, Seaside ◆◆◆◆
671 Beach Drive
(503) 738-9585
Inexpensive

From Highway 101 head into the town of Seaside on Avenue G and continue to Beach Drive. The bed and breakfast is on the corner of Avenue G and Beach Drive.

In the past I would have said that there is almost nothing romantic about Seaside, a town where much of the ocean has been obscured by hyperactive motel developers with no sensitivity to the landscape, where arcades and boardwalks are teeming with kids. However, you can find space to breathe at the expansive beaches to the north or south of town, and at the Beachwood Bed and Breakfast.

The innkeepers paid attention to all the right details when they went about renovating this gabled Craftsman-style home. Despite its proximity to the center of town, the setting feels surprisingly remote and quiet. Inside, hunter green carpeting, whitewashed walls, stately antique furnishings, leaded glass windows, lace curtains, and country fabrics grace every room. There are only three guest rooms here, and all are filled with romantic possibilities. The Halladay Suite is the premier spot, with a brick gas-burning fireplace and two-person spa tub. The Lewis and Clark Room, with a private detached bath, is also charming. Breakfast is served in the formal dining room and the menu is outstanding. Pumpkin pancakes, Spanish-style eggs served with fresh salsa, and

French toast stuffed with cream cheese are a few of the entrées you may find upon awakening.

Did I mention that the Beachwood Bed and Breakfast is only a block from the beach? This place is truly a find!

GILBERT INN, Seaside
341 Beach Drive
(503) 738-9770
Inexpensive

Turn west off Highway 101 onto Avenue B, continue to Beach Drive, and turn right.

Move this wonderful bed and breakfast to almost any other beachfront setting in the Northwest and you would automatically have a four-lip place to spend exquisite time together. Because it is located on a busy intersection in downtown Seaside, it loses a couple of lips. Other than that, everything at this immaculate Victorian is cozy and snug. All 10 rooms are delightfully renovated and have plenty of comfort and appeal. The new wing, added in 1989, contains a series of brightly done rooms with private bathrooms that are decorated to blend creatively with each suite's inviting decor. Wicker furniture, handsome wood armoires, and country fabrics dress up each room.

The generous morning meal (not gourmet, but definitely hearty) is served at white wrought-iron tables set in a lovely pink breakfast nook that you enter through white French doors. There aren't enough tables for each room, so you might have to wait your turn, but if you have a late breakfast you will be all alone, a notable romantic asset. So what if the town of Seaside isn't all that romantic? The beach is only a block away, and the Gilbert Inn can even out the rough edges.

RIVERSIDE INN, Seaside
430 South Holladay
(503) 738-8254, (800) 826-6151
Very Inexpensive

On South Holladay, the main street of Seaside, between Avenues E and G.

The Riverside Inn is one of the better kissing bargains I've found along the coast. There are a few romantic warnings, but at these prices and with the innkeepers' attention to detail, particularly the generous breakfast, none of them matter much. First, this inn is on the main street through Seaside; second, the surroundings are mostly stores and some rundown houses; third, some of the 11 rooms are really small. OK, now that's out of the way. The reason to stay here is the Riverview Annex, in the back of the main building, which faces the river. The rooms here are large, with small kitchens, a tile counter for dining, sliding glass doors, decks, and comfortable furnishings. It may not be fancy, but it is relaxing, particularly the large communal deck perched over the river, a great place to catch up on long discussions you've been too busy to make time for.

◆ **Romantic Alternative: SUMMER HOUSE,** 1221 North Franklin, (503) 738-5740, (Inexpensive), is a small bed and breakfast with four very attractive and cozy guest rooms, all done in peach and gray with floral linens, queen-size beds, and private white-tiled baths. Summer House feels bright and cheerful, and it is only one block from the beach. Breakfast is served in the fire-warmed dining room, or on the flower-filled deck when the weather permits.

Cannon Beach

Cannon Beach is just west of Highway 101. Take Highway 26 from Portland west to Highway 101 and head south to Cannon Beach. Highway 30 from the north also leads to Highway 101.

As you approach Cannon Beach, you may not believe your eyes—the cliffs and ocean here seem to stretch out to infinity. There are more than seven miles of beach, with firm sand and rolling waves that beckon dreamers and lovers to roll up their jeans and stroll along the shore hand-in-hand. The seascape is crowded with massive rock outcroppings, a key feature of this coastline. The hallmark of Cannon Beach is a freestanding monolith called Haystack Rock, the third-largest of its kind in the world and a true natural wonder. At low tide you can stand at its base and feel humbled by its towering dimensions.

The nickname for the entire Oregon coast is "Sunset Empire," a most descriptive title. As the sun begins to settle into the ocean, brilliant colors radiate from the horizon, filling the sky like a golden aurora borealis. At first the light penetrates the clouds as a pale lavender-blue haze, transforming suddenly into an intense yellow-amber, and culminating in a blazing red that seems to set the sky on fire. Then, as dusk finalizes its entrance, the clouds fade to steel-blue-gray and the sky changes its countenance from cobalt blue to indigo. Slowly the moon takes a central place in the evening heavens, reflecting its presence on the surface of the water in platinum rays. When the weather cooperates, this performance occurs nightly at Cannon Beach and along the entire Oregon coast.

◆ **Romantic Options: ECOLA STATE PARK** and **INDIAN BEACH** are just to the north of Cannon Beach off Highway 101. Usually state parks are not considered good places for conducting affectionate business. Though they may be well kept and offer supreme scenery, they also tend to be crowded and inundated with RVs and kids. But the character of this area is so exceptional, the potency of the sights so remarkable, you'll not notice anyone but yourselves and the splendor of nature.

◆ **Romantic Warning:** On warm summer days Cannon Beach is very crowded, with traffic and congestion that seem out of place in such a serene, tranquil setting. Consider the quiet towns of Manzanita or Oceanside (both described in this section) farther south along the coast as alternatives to Cannon Beach on crowded summer weekends.

Hotel/Bed and Breakfast Kissing

THE ARGONAUTA INN, Cannon Beach   💋
188 Second Street
(503) 436-2601
Inexpensive to Expensive

In Cannon Beach, turn west off Highway 101 onto Sunset. Drive to Hemlock Street and turn south. At First Street turn west and then south again onto Larch Street. The Argonauta Inn is to the right of the dead end.

For imaginative, rustic accommodations, The Argonauta Inn stands alone. The inn is a weathered seaside complex that houses three small, cozy apartments and a large oceanfront beach house set right at the center of everything Cannon Beach has to offer. The shore is at your front door and the town is at your back. Most of the details are too good to be true: glass-enclosed patios, fireplaces, complete kitchens, antiques, powerful panoramas. But then there are the drawbacks: saggy beds, mildewy smells, and tacky touches that are more secondhand than homey. Nevertheless, mostly because of location, this is still one of the most interesting places to stay in Cannon Beach.

CANNON BEACH HOTEL AND RESTAURANT, Cannon Beach
1116 South Hemlock
(503) 436-1392
Inexpensive to Moderate

On South Hemlock in the heart of Cannon Beach.

If only this were directly on the beach, it would be a rare find, but it is on the main street of Cannon Beach and as a result can get quite noisy. The brochure says it is a European-style hotel, and in some regards that's true. The striking exterior is framed in weathered shingles with green awnings and shutters, the lobby has an inviting sitting area, and the rooms are quite handsome. Some of the more expensive rooms have couches, small dining tables, gas fireplaces, king-size beds, and, unfortunately, single-person spa tubs. The decor is done in a handsome combination of hunter green and taupe.

Continental breakfast is served in the adjacent restaurant, which is also a wonderful spot for a simple breakfast, a casual lunch, or a romantic dinner. The kitchen really knows what it is doing, so you won't be disappointed.

SURFSAND RESORT, Cannon Beach
Hemlock and Gower
(503) 436-2274
Moderate to Expensive

From Highway 101 follow the Cannon Beach Loop Drive to Hemlock Street and watch for the sign on the west side of the street.

Can it be possible that I am about to describe the romantic details of a Best Western motel? Such places are usually my model for describing what is *not* romantic about a particular location or accommodation. But the Surfsand Best Western is pretty darned good and rates all of those lips I have given it. Now let me explain why.

Our room was spacious, decorated in soft shades of mauve and gray. Its outdoor deck had a perfect view of Haystack Rock (it also had a view of the parking lot, which wasn't perfect but still pretty good). A huge spa tub in the bedroom area provided a welcome, leisurely soak near the gas fireplace, which again wasn't perfect, but it warmed the room quickly and there was no fuss or bother with wood and kindling. The large bathroom, attractively done in white tiles, was outfitted with colorful oversized towels. And in the adjoining building there was even a large indoor pool and enormous hot tub. Other, less glamorous units in the older section of the property have a ringside ocean view of everything due west to the horizon. For location and quality, this place is definitely one to consider; just ignore the name.

◆ **Romantic Note:** Surfsand Resort also manages oceanside rental properties in the area. Some of these are the most enviable places to stay on the coast. Imagine a handsome traditional Oregon coast home that fronts the crashing surf with scintillating views of the awesome scenery (and awesome is an understatement). Prices vary from Moderate to Very Expensive, but most properties are large enough for at least two couples traveling together.

◆ **Romantic Consideration: THE WAYFARER RESTAURANT,** 1190 Pacific Drive, (503) 436-1108, (Inexpensive to Moderate), owned by the Surfsand Resort, has one of the best view dining rooms in Cannon Beach, and is entirely smoke-free. The interior is done in the same mauve and gray color scheme as the resort. The food is pretty good, though you'll do best if you stick to the fresh-broiled selections or steamed clams and mussels. Breakfast is quite good; the early mornings are peaceful and calm and the espresso is hot and fresh.

TURK'S HOUSE AND COTTAGE, Cannon Beach
Highway 101
(503) 436-1809
Expensive to Unbelievably Expensive

Call for directions.

A few well-written articles by travel writers, placed in some notable publications, have made Turk's House and Cottage *the* place to stay in Cannon Beach. You have to forgive travel writers, though; after all, we are only doing our job, even though the results can mean that some choice places become so popular it's difficult to get reservations.

For starters, you get the entire run of this 1,800-square-foot home settled on a forested hill with a compelling view of the Oregon coastline.

The uniquely crafted building is supported by stilts on one side and built over the western slope of the hill on the other. The exterior is of rough-cut spruce and fir, with a wraparound deck on the ocean side of the house. The interior is a stunning display with towering pine ceilings, floor-to-ceiling windows, and a massive stone fireplace; the spacious two-level master bedroom has a generous spa tub, an open tile shower, and exercise equipment. Breakfast is a private affair, stocked every morning in your own kitchen. From top to bottom you will be delighted with your stay here. Just remember to book months in advance to assure yourselves your share of ecstasy.

THE WAVES MOTEL, Cannon Beach
188 West Second Street
(503) 436-2205
Inexpensive to Moderate

Take the first Cannon Beach exit, then turn right on Second Street. The Waves is to the right just before the dead end.

This assortment of beach accommodations is as eclectic as it gets. Located just behind The Argonauta Inn, The Waves Motel is a hodgepodge: some rooms have scintillating views of the ocean, most have kitchens, many have fireplaces, some sleep two, some sleep six. The interiors are mostly plain yet quite comfortable, except for a few ultra-rustic cottages that aren't recommended at all. A newer, modern wing has units that have neither fireplace, view, nor kitchen, but they're brand spanking new and extremely comfortable and attractive.

While none of that sounds particularly endearing, if you choose one of the units with an ocean view and fireplace—particularly in the Flagship Buildings—now we're talking cozy and warm. The resonant sound of the surf against the steadfast shore is a welcome reminder of just how far behind you've left city life.

THE WHITE HERON LODGE, Cannon Beach
356 North Spruce
(503) 436-2205
Moderate

Call for reservations and directions. Reservations are handled by The Waves Motel.

The White Heron Lodge is located on the beachfront just north of the main village of Cannon Beach. Even though the lodge is close to town, in this part of the world it is far enough to make a difference in the peacefulness of your surroundings. Sea grass grows nearby as the sand eventually gives way to a well-kept lawn. The modern construction consists of one Victorian-style fourplex with comfortably appointed, fully equipped apartments, and a contemporary duplex that is spacious enough for five. There are decks that look out to the shore, fireplaces that crackle with inviting warmth, a spa tub, and lots of space to feel right at home while you spoil yourselves in utter relaxation and quiet.

Restaurant Kissing

CAFÉ DE LA MER, Cannon Beach
1287 South Hemlock Street
(503) 436-1179
Expensive

Just off the main street of Cannon Beach, near Dawes Street. Dinners only, Thursday through Sunday.

The small rustic interior has been simply but pleasantly put together, and the attentive staff consistently delivers enticing dinners and superior service in a relaxing atmosphere. Pink tablecloths, forest green walls, and rather tight seating comprise the setting, but the kitchen's efforts highlight the evening. What a welcome change of pace from the dining fare you usually find along the coast.

PULICCI'S RESTAURANT, Cannon Beach
988 South Hemlock Street
(503) 436-1279
Inexpensive to Moderate

On South Hemlock Street in the heart of Cannon Beach.

This unassuming little restaurant, and I mean little, is filled with fragrant aromas and excellent Italian food. In the summer you have the option of dining outdoors in a white-fenced, flower-bedecked courtyard. Otherwise, you can sit in the very small, sparse interior at one of six wood tables and admire the mosaic leaded-glass windows. "Intimate" is the operative word here. There isn't much of a wine list and the interior can be snug, but the food and the ambience make this place special.

Tolovana Park

Hotel/Bed and Breakfast Kissing

THE HEARTHSTONE INN, Tolovana Park
107 East Jackson
(503) 436-2266
Inexpensive

Call for directions.

For a coastal change of pace, particularly if the summer pace of the beach is a bit much for you and you want to be near the surf but not too near, the Hearthstone Inn is your answer. Located in an out-of-the-way corner of Tolovana Park, this unobtrusive contemporary wood building, hidden by gently swaying willow trees, looks more like a residence than a lodging. Inside are four generous studios with vaulted cedar ceilings, beach-rock fireplaces, skylights, stained glass windows, and fully equipped kitchens. The shore is a short walk away and accessible for an invigorating morning walk on compact, damp sand. All of this combines to create a refreshingly private and welcome place to stay.

Outdoor Kissing

HUG POINT

A few miles south of Cannon Beach off Highway 101, watch for the signs to Hug Point.

Even when the parking lot is full, there is still plenty of room at this windswept beach to feel like you're all by yourselves. If you find yourselves at Hug Point during low tide, give in to your curiosity and permit those kids inside you to play for the duration of your stay here. The soaring cliffs along the beach are gouged with caves and crevasses of varying shapes and proportions. For the timid there are gentle tide pools and rocky fissures where you can easily observe marine life. For the more daring there are dark, ominous sea caves to hide in. When your exploring is done and the tide reclaims your playground, the grown-ups in you can finish out the day by watching the dazzling sunset over the Pacific while you hug.

Manzanita

Hotel/Bed and Breakfast Kissing

THE INN AT MANZANITA, Manzanita
67 Laneda
(503) 368-6754
Moderate

Follow Highway 101 into the town of Manzanita. Laneda is the main road through town. The inn is located one block from the ocean.

This petite, picturesque village bordering the ocean has grown a bit over the past two years, but it is still relatively undiscovered, particularly in comparison to Cannon Beach and Seaside, and it is only seven miles down the road. The town is nestled between the endless waters of the Pacific Ocean and the base of the Neahkahnie Mountains. For beach roaming, flying kites, or just an exhilarating day by the sea, this area is sheer perfection. Manzanita is close enough to Cannon Beach for you to take advantage of its dining spots and nightlife, yet far enough from the crowds there to give you a comforting sense of calm.

The inn is set amidst coastal pine and spruce and is only 200 feet from a seven-mile stretch of beach. Each unit provides the best in modern conveniences: a private fireside spa built for two, treetop glimpses of the ocean, and a wet bar with a refrigerator filled with juice and soda. The rooms boast wood interiors, cushy furnishings, and firm, cozy beds with down comforters. This could easily become one of your favorite getaways along the coast.

◆ **Romantic Alternative:** THE NEW SUNSET SURF MOTEL, Ocean and Laneda, (503) 368-5224, (Moderate), isn't much of a romantic alternative, but if you want oceanfront accommodations it is still pretty good. The efficient units have small kitchens and sitting areas, but the big attraction is the sliding glass windows that look out to the expansive ocean and electrifying sunsets beyond.

Restaurant Kissing

BLUE SKY CAFÉ, Manzanita
154 Laneda
(503) 368-5712
Moderate to Expensive

On the main street of Manzanita, three blocks from the beach.

It doesn't seem possible that a town this size can be home to two such outstanding restaurants as the Blue Sky Café and Jarboe's (see next entry), but it is and they are. In fact, outstanding is a bit of an understatement. These are culinary experiences par excellence.

The Blue Sky Café has a modest interior with well-spaced wooden tables, a large skylight in the middle of the room, and local art adorning the walls. The menu is more than tantalizing—it is downright seductive. The goat cheese layered with fresh herbs, sun-dried tomatoes, artichoke hearts, garlic, and olives is remarkable, as is the lobster salad with papaya, blood oranges, and mango dressing. The fresh ahi tuna served with coconut curry rice, and the red snapper baked in parchment with feta cheese, nicoise olives, and Sambucca liqueur are impeccable. Leave room for dessert; anything they prepare is worth the effort.

JARBOE'S, Manzanita
137 Laneda
(503) 368-5113
Moderate

On the main street of Manzanita, one and a half blocks from the beach.

This charming, exceedingly small restaurant is located just two blocks up the street from The Inn at Manzanita. The simple but homey dining room has a vaulted ceiling and white-linen-draped tables. Jarboe's is a must for an intimate, truly gourmet dinner. The crayfish bisque is perfect; the mesquite-grilled pizzetta with garlic and Asiago cheese is superb. For the main course, try the duck with lamb sausage or the ahi tuna prepared with roasted peppers and grapefruit for a memorable culinary experience, a prelude for a memorable romantic experience.

Outdoor Kissing

OSWALD WEST STATE PARK

Ten miles south of Cannon Beach, on the west side of Highway 101. Look for signs pointing the way.

Oswald West State Park is one of the most inspiring campgrounds in these parts—just ask any Northwest camping enthusiast. Its superior desirability has to do with its mode of access. In order to set up camp, you must walk a quarter of a mile down a rain forest path, wheeling a cart (provided) with your things piled on top. This short jaunt tends to eliminate featherweights and RVs, giving you and your loved one much-needed privacy. The forested setting is within arm's reach of the water, with footpaths that take you briskly down a 13-mile stretch of surging surf. The scenery to the south is a succession of overlapping mountains jutting into the ocean, making a dark jagged profile against the distant skyline. The white sand, effervescent surf, and rock-clad shore make exploring here a treasure hunt.

OCEANSIDE

Follow the signs from Highway 1 just north of Tillamook out to Oceanside, eight miles due west of Tillamook on the Three Capes Scenic Loop.

Much of the Oregon coast is heavily traveled, especially in the summer—except for Oceanside. This fairly remote village is about eight miles west of the main road on the small peninsula that forms Tillamook Bay. The drive along this section of the coast, away from the crowds, affords plenty of opportunities to stop whenever you see an inviting stretch of rugged coastline. As the mist mingles with the cry of seabirds, you will know for sure that you've left city life behind you, far, far away.

There is nothing fancy in Oceanside; the handful of accommodations range from basic to austere, and there are only two restaurants in the area. The magnificent Oregon coastline is reason enough to be here, with only yourselves and the calm of the moment to concern you.

Hotel/Bed and Breakfast Kissing

HOUSE ON THE HILL, Oceanside   ◆◆
1816 Maxwell Mountain Road
(503) 842-6030
Inexpensive

Call for directions.

House on the Hill comprises an interesting set of gray, weathered buildings that sit atop one of the highest points along the entire Oregon coast. The interiors are strictly motel quality, but they are clean and nice and they now have new linens, a welcome addition. Nevertheless, a stay here can make you feel a little closer to heaven: the view through the floor-to-ceiling windows is nothing less than awesome.

OCEANSIDE INN, Oceanside   ◆
1440 Pacific Northwest
(503) 842-2961, (800) 347-2972
Inexpensive to Moderate

In the heart of Oceanside, on the west side of the street.

This is another place that I would never recommend if it weren't for the strategic placement of the Pacific Ocean right outside your front door. As you may have guessed, the Oceanside Inn is best described as a motel. Inside and out, it is less than inspiring. The eight small units have sitting areas, kitchens, and double beds. What you will notice and be pleased with is that the building sits on a bluff overlooking the surf. A tremendous wooden staircase, with more steps than I care to count, leads straight down to the beach below. Units 1 and 8 are the best, with ringside views of the dazzling scenery.

SEA HAVEN INN, Oceanside   ◆◆
5450 South Avenue Northwest
(503) 842-3151
Inexpensive

From Tillamook follow the signs off Highway 101 to Netarts and Oceanside. Just before you enter the town of Oceanside, follow the signs to Sea Haven on the west side of the road.

This inn is not really a romantic destination, but because Oceanside is so special, and there are so few accommodations available here, I feel a responsibility to give you all the options and let you make your own kissing decisions.

The rooms at Sea Haven are very pleasant, but on the lackluster side. Although the common areas and outside deck have a wondrous view over the azure ocean and the shoreline far below, most of the rooms are at the rear of the house and have far less expansive views. The innkeeper explained (while she puffed away on her cigarette) that guests are encouraged to mingle and get to know each other, which is nice but hardly intimate. The tasty, generous breakfasts are served family-style in a dining room that looks out over endless miles of empty, mountain-framed beaches.

THREE CAPES BED AND BREAKFAST, Oceanside   ❤
1685 Maxwell Mountain Road
(503) 842-6126
Inexpensive (no credit cards)

Call for directions.

This is not a fancy bed and breakfast, yet the scenery that fills the bay windows of your homespun room can make any morning or sunset seem like a dream come true. The home is situated on the side of a hill overlooking the spectacular Oceanside shore. One of the two rooms has a private deck and private entrance. Full breakfast is served in the dining room, where a picture window offers the same overview of the sparkling sweep of horizon. The crab quiche and Belgian waffles are very good, but with that view, you might not notice anything else.

Restaurant Kissing

ROSEANNA'S RESTAURANT, Oceanside   ❤❤
1490 Pacific Northwest
(503) 842-7351
Inexpensive to Moderate

On the main road into Oceanside, just off Highway 101.

Roseanna's is Oceanside's only oceanside restaurant. A rustic interior filled with wood tables and chairs provides a casual Northwest dining environment. Healthy breakfasts, lunches, and dinners are served here, all beginning with a bewitching appetizer: the ocean, as seen through Roseanna's windows. In the evening, nature prepares another treat to accompany your meal: an ambrosial sunset for two.

Outdoor Kissing

THREE CAPES SCENIC LOOP

North of Tillamook you will see signs for the Three Capes Scenic Loop. Turn west off Highway 101, and follow the signs along this loop to Cape Meares, around and south to Oceanside, and down to Netarts.

Highway 101 is inconsistent around here. It usually offers beautiful things to gaze at and admire, but it also interrupts the view with crowded shopping areas in towns set far from the water's edge. You can avoid some of this irritation by driving on the Three Capes Scenic Loop. Even on the sunniest day in summer the throngs of tourists seem to be somewhere else, and your movement along this exquisite passage through forest and ocean beaches can be taken at a slow, cruising pace. You can stop at dozens of locations to dig for clams or go crabbing. **ANDERSON VIEWPOINT**, a precipitous mountain bluff just south of Oceanside, overlooks everything north, south, and west, and is a supreme location for a picnic. There or elsewhere, take time during your day's journey to swoon into each other's arms and toast the views you've enjoyed.

Sandlake

Hotel/Bed and Breakfast Kissing

SANDLAKE COUNTRY INN, Sandlake
8505 Galloway Road
(503) 965-6745
Inexpensive to Moderate

Call for directions and go over them with the innkeeper twice; this place can be tricky to find.

If you're traveling the coast of Oregon, you probably expect me to recommend places that take in the view or are at least conveniently located near this wonderland of nature's finest. And for the most part that is exactly what I've done... up until now, that is. The Sandlake Country Inn is one of the few inland locations along the coast that is intriguing enough to recommend.

On a side road off the Three Capes Scenic Loop is where you will find the inn. The outside is rather plain, with weathered shingles and a gravel entrance. Inside you will find affectionate detailing and immaculate surroundings. The atmosphere is decidedly homey, but with enough elegance to make it endearing. Each of the four spacious suites is appointed with dramatic floral fabrics and wallpaper, wicker furniture and antiques, and separate sitting areas. Some of the rooms have private decks, large spa tubs, and private entrances. All of them are exceedingly intimate and attractive.

A formal three-course breakfast can be served in your room at your request. Imagine waking to fresh-squeezed orange juice, grapefruit with raspberry sauce, lemon bread, and green chile soufflé with fresh salsa. The menu changes daily, making every morning an extravaganza.

◆ **Romantic Suggestion:** A few miles south of the Sandlake Country Inn is the beach at Tierra del Mar. This section of surf and sand is nothing less than gorgeous, and even on hot summer weekends it's almost empty.

Lincoln City

Hotel/Bed and Breakfast Kissing

PALMER HOUSE, Lincoln City   💋
646 Northwest Inlet Avenue
(503) 994-7932
Inexpensive to Moderate

From Highway 101 turn west on Sixth Drive and then north on Inlet Avenue.

A striking hillside location lording over the ocean is the compelling draw of this bed and breakfast set in a quiet neighborhood. There are three rooms here, all with comfortable furnishing and sitting areas. The best room is on the top level, with a fireplace, private entrance, and plenty of room. Avoid the room on the ground floor; it can feel a bit claustrophobic. Breakfasts here can be wonderful when the innkeepers take the time to display their culinary talents.

There is a common deck area for lounging and gazing at the scenery, but the scenery is marred by a huge Best Western sign plastered across an even bigger Best Western motel that blocks much of the shoreline.

Restaurant Kissing

BAY HOUSE, Lincoln City
5911 Southwest Highway 101
(503) 996-3222
Expensive

Just south of Lincoln City, immediately after you cross the bridge over Siletz Bay, look for the restaurant on the west side of the road.

Bay House is an easy place to pass by. Its weathered gray exterior, all by itself on a steep bank off the main highway, is hardly what you'd call a showcase. But you are making a major error if you neglect to have an evening meal here while you're touring the Oregon coast. First, Bay House enjoys a flawless view of Siletz Bay, the driftwood-strewn shoreline, and the flow of the calm clear blue water. Almost every table is blessed with its own share of the lovely scenery. Second, the menu is an enterprising assortment of Northwest creations that use fresh local meats and fish. Meals are consistently outstanding. The fresh halibut rolled in Parmesan and lightly dabbed with a flawless béchamel sauce is remarkable, and the filet mignon with bleu cheese butter and a cabernet demi-glace is not to be believed. Even the desserts are something to save room for.

Gleneden Beach

Restaurant Kissing

CHEZ JEANNETTE, Gleneden Beach
7150 Old Highway 101
(503) 764-3434
Expensive

From Lincoln City take Highway 101 three miles south to the Gleneden junction, where you turn west onto Old Highway 101. Chez Jeannette is a quarter mile down the road, the first house on the east side.

I discovered this superior restaurant almost seven years ago, and it was incredible back then. The only thing that has changed is that today Chez Jeannette is even more incredible. The stone-fronted, homey structure rests snugly against a vine-covered hill and has thick branches curling around its roof and walls. The interior is divinely elegant, yet remarkably cozy and warm. The small dining salon is warmed by two blazing fireplaces that illuminate the softly lit room. Velvety forest green drapery, lush carpet, regal chairs, and tables set with bone china and crystal create a romantic atmosphere that satisfies your eyes. The delectable, inventive dishes will satisfy the rest of you.

Depoe Bay

Hotel/Bed and Breakfast Kissing

CHANNEL HOUSE, Depoe Bay
35 Ellington Street
(503) 765-2140, (800) 447-2140
Inexpensive to Expensive

In Depoe Bay on Highway 101 look for Channel House signs on the west side of the road. Turn west onto Ellington Street; Channel House is at the dead end.

This bed and breakfast is one of the best kissing places anywhere along the coast. Don't let its street appearance fool or disappoint you: another world awaits inside, once you close the door of your room. Appropriately named, this towering blue frame building sits above the turbulent entrance to Depoe Bay. The rocky cliff setting and venerable coastline are visible from almost all of the 12 rooms. Some of the more desirable (i.e., *expensive*) rooms have their own private deck, where you can lie back in a steaming hot spa tub and watch the boat traffic file by. There are new wet bars in each of the rooms, and the bathrooms have all been retiled. Nice touches, but the view and hot tub are still the two major reasons for a secluded stay here; another is the handsome, oversized suites that ooze comfort and relaxation. Sit back and let the fireplace warm the sea air while you feel the stress leave your bodies.

In the morning, the three-course breakfasts are served in a terra-cotta-tiled breakfast nook downstairs. They aren't gourmet, but they are very good.

◆ **Romantic Suggestion: FOGARTY BEACH** is a short three-mile drive south from Depoe Bay.

◆ **Romantic Alternative: THE HARBOR AT DEPOE BAY**, Highway 101, (800) 635-7089, (Expensive), is a time-share complex along the coast that couldn't sell out its time and now does rentals. Their pain is your gain. These spacious two-bedroom townhomes, some with vaulted ceilings, are fairly basic, except for their front-row view of a small section of the bay.

Newport

Hotel/Bed and Breakfast Kissing

OCEAN HOUSE BED AND BREAKFAST, Newport　◆◆◆
4920 Northwest Woody Way
(503) 265-6158
Inexpensive to Moderate

Call or write for reservations and directions.

For more than eight years Ocean House Bed and Breakfast has maintained a flawless reputation along the coast as a treasured place to stay. Rain or shine, you will find many reasons to prolong your visit. Perched above Agate Beach, with a huge lawn and meticulously maintained gardens, Ocean House offers homey comforts for leisurely interludes. A private trail leads down to the beach for beachcombing or long walks (more than five miles of firm sand) at the shore. A series of cedar decks has been strategically placed along the bluff to take best advantage of sunset's magic. All of the common rooms, including a glass-enclosed atrium, share this same perspective.

The four somewhat old-fashioned rooms here are attired in '50s and '60s-style furnishings complemented with touches of wicker. All have private baths that are in need of some updating. What doesn't need to change are the windows of the upstairs bedrooms, which open toward the sea. One upstairs room has a private balcony and the downstairs room opens to an outside deck. A somewhat average, though satisfying, breakfast is served downstairs at a common table—not the best arrangement for romantic considerations, but with all these other distractions for the heart, this is easily overlooked.

NYE BEACH HOTEL AND CAFÉ, Newport
219 Northwest Cliff
(503) 265-3334
Moderate

From Highway 101 in downtown Newport, turn west on Northwest Third and follow it to the beach. Turn right on Cliff to the hotel.

The beachfront area of Newport has a unique tone in comparison to other beachfront communities along the coast. This special corner of the world still thinks it is 1967. That isn't a romantic disadvantage for some; to others it may be a warning. To some extent that has all changed with the presence of this newly constructed, polished, cosmopolitan 18-room hotel.

The Nye Beach Hotel is a rare and beautifully designed structure that sticks out like a sore thumb amidst the rough exteriors of its neighbors. The striking facade is a mixture of shingles and wood painted a deep shade of red. Inside, the banisters and lobby are hunter green with touches of taupe and cranberry. The glass-enclosed oceanfront café on the main floor is decorated with red and white tiles and is an attractive setting for lunch or dinner. The best rooms here are the ones with both a spa tub and an unobstructed view of the water. All of the rooms are nicely arranged, with wicker-cane furniture and thick comforters. This is definitely a noteworthy place to savor the coast and each other.

STARFISH POINT, Newport
140 Northwest 48th Street
(503) 265-3751
Moderate to Expensive

Just off Highway 101 on the west side of the road, a few miles north of the Newport city center.

Starfish Point has had a rather shaky history. It started out its life as a small (six units) rental condominium complex. When the tide of time-share developers hit the Oregon coast, it became a time-share complex. That didn't work, and another owner bought the entire property and made it once again available for daily rental.

Despite this muddled career, Starfish Point is still an exceptional place to stay. Each two-bedroom, two-story unit is a spacious townhome complete with everything you could possibly think of for a totally luxurious getaway: a full kitchen; sunken dining and living room; a study with bay windows; fireplace; private decks; two bathrooms, one with a Jacuzzi; and absolutely fantastic views of the ocean. A well-groomed but steep trail leads down to the outstretched shore below. Some needed renovations have been taking place, which means that as good as all this sounds it is getting even better. If the owners of Starfish Point decide to keep the property as a rental, it could stay one of the better romantic spots along the coast.

Waldport

Hotel/Bed and Breakfast Kissing

CLIFF HOUSE, Waldport
1450 Southwest Adahi Street
(503) 563-2506
Moderate to Expensive

From Highway 101 just south of Waldport, turn west on Adahi. Cliff House is a few doors down on the north side of the cul-de-sac.

Everything about Cliff House is extraordinary. A superlative renovation has turned this small seaside home, perched on a cliff overlooking thundering surf, into an intriguing retreat from the world at large. The interior is covered (and I mean *covered*) with antiques and heirlooms, plus you'll find vaulted ceilings, knotty pine walls, a grand piano, and a beach-stone fireplace. The five wonderful rooms feature plush linens, chandeliers, and comfy sitting areas. Two of the rooms have spacious private decks, and the honeymoon suite (rated Unbelievably Expensive) has its own spa tub and fully mirrored (including the ceiling) bathroom walls. Outside there is a huge deck with a 180-degree view of everything north, west, and east; a massive hot tub in the center of it has jets that move up and down your spine. Like I said—extraordinary.

◆ **Romantic Note:** The innkeepers can be overly attentive. Depending on your perspective, you may find it intrusive or the best service in town. In addition, the breakfast area, which is large enough to accommodate several small tables for a more intimate morning meal, is arranged with one medium-size table for everyone (except those in the honeymoon suite—they get room service).

Restaurant Kissing

SWEETWATER INN, Waldport
3349 Highway 34
(503) 563-5664
Moderate

From Highway 101 turn right on Highway 34 and drive three and a half miles to the restaurant.

This small, unassuming white-and-pink-trimmed building is far away from the crowded world of the Coast Highway. If you want to treat yourselves to an outstanding evening meal, do not hesitate to make this your first choice if you happen to be in the area. The night we were there, the broccoli soup was rich and thick; the halibut, lightly breaded with a hint of Parmesan, was perfect; and the salmon fettuccine was laden with moist fresh salmon blanketed with freshly made pasta. Fresh pear pie finished the meal in rare form; their chocolate offerings are too rich to describe in polite company.

Yachats

Midway along the Oregon coast.

The town of Yachats is a rare blend: a popular tourist destination that still retains the spirit and appearance of innocence—a sense of Oregon as it was before the gold rush publicity uncovered it from obscurity. Located at the midway point on the coast dividing north and south, Yachats lacks the urban sprawl that proliferates in most of the other towns along Highway 101. Some impressive bed and breakfasts and restaurants are to be found in this area. Locals hang out with tourists and there is a distinctive friendly atmosphere all about. Be sure to stop at the New Morning Café for coffee; you'll get a taste of the area and a well-prepared caffe latte or cappuccino.

Yachats is also one of the few areas where the coastal mountain range actually merges with the shoreline. The hiking here is some of the best in the area, and the beaches for the most part are remote and empty.

Hotel/Bed and Breakfast Kissing

ADOBE RESORT, Yachats
1555 Highway 101
(503) 547-3141
Moderate

In the town of Yachats, on the west side of Highway 101.

This well-known affectionate retreat is loved by its many regulars, who will stay nowhere else along the coast. You can hear the waves crash against the rocky shore only feet from your room, and watch the sunset cast wondrous colors on the sky and water. Many of the spacious rooms have spa tubs, beamed ceilings, fireplaces, and privacy. Some of the rooms have public walkways in front of them.

The restaurant at the resort has unexpectedly good food: breakfasts are bountiful and hearty; dinners have a slight French accent. The view is mesmerizing.

OREGON HOUSE, Yachats
94288 Highway 101
(503) 547-3329
Inexpensive to Moderate

Eight miles south of Yachats, directly off Highway 101 on the west side of the road.

The owners of Oregon House have made this one of the most difficult bed and breakfasts to describe, because the 10 units are so dramatically different from one another. Don't misunderstand—this is indeed a premier oceanfront accommodation, but to do each unit justice would take up quite a bit of room. Three units have rambling, family-oriented floor plans, two others are charming, comfortable cottages; two more share a delightfully romantic and spacious townhome arrangement; and one room located in the main house is run like a bed and breakfast (it's the only unit that gets a full-service breakfast in the morning) and is all done in white and floral fabrics and is as pretty as a picture. All the units, regardless of size, include a varied assortment of fireplaces, skylights, dining nooks, decks, patios, full kitchens, extremely comfortable furnishings, attractive fabrics and linens, and whirlpool tubs. All this is set on well-kept lawns dotted with trees; the piercing blue ocean is only a hundred feet away. Oregon House is one of the most captivating, nonconformist places to stay along the coast.

◆　**Romantic Warning:** It's not easy to get a reservation here, so call now for your own romantic interlude. You will thank me if you do.

SEAQUEST BED AND BREAKFAST, Yachats　　
95354 Highway 101
(503) 547-3782
Moderate to Expensive

Seven miles south of Yachats town center on the west side of the road.

This is one of those places I'd rather not tell you about, because once I do I know how hard it will be to get a reservation and I want to come back… again and again. Everything I look for in a romantic getaway is here, and much more. The 7,000-square-foot home is Oregon coast architecture at its best, and it resides a mere 50 feet from the water's edge and a rocky sand dune. Their brochure doesn't exaggerate when it claims that the beauty here will fill your soul with tranquillity and love.

Each of the five immaculate and beautifully designed guest rooms has a Jacuzzi tub, bright pastel linens and wallpapers, a private entrance, and tantalizing views. The entirely glass-enclosed dining and living room is where you will enjoy a sensational three-course gourmet breakfast and a crackling fireplace. The fresh cakes and pastries were outstanding and the croissant stuffed with eggs, cheese, and mushrooms was delicious. I never had room to sample the homemade granola and jams, but they looked incredible. The enthusiastic innkeepers are also a delight, but be clear if you want privacy—during breakfast, they are great at social introductions you may not want with the other guests. If I could award a five-kiss rating to this bed and breakfast I would, but it would drive the typesetter crazy.

SERENITY BED AND BREAKFAST, Yachats　　
5985 Yachats River Road
(503) 547-3813
Moderate to Expensive

From Highway 101 turn east on Yachats River Road, just south of town, and drive six miles.

Don't make the mistake of discounting this outstanding romantic destination simply because it is not on the ocean. It is a world of unexpected luxury and opulence, located on a 13-acre sweep of lawn lined with red alders, touched by ocean breezes and, in comparison to the coast, perpetual sunshine. The white frame country farmhouse gives no indication of what lies inside. The three guest suites here have thoroughly sensual furnishings and lavish detailing. The rooms are appointed with soft pastel-and-white fabrics, plush carpet, large white marble whirlpool tubs, hand-crafted leaded glass windows, hand-crafted king-size beds, billowy down comforters, separate sitting areas, ornate whitewashed wood-beamed ceilings, skylights, stereo and TV with VCR, and French doors that open to private decks overlooking the mountains and lawn. Sigh!

If you find it possible to leave your oasis for breakfast, you won't be disappointed. The innkeeper is known for her authentic German-style hearty farm breakfasts. You may feel too full to do much else for the rest of the morning, but you can always retire to your room, which was hard to leave in the first place.

ZIGGURAT, Yachats
95330 Highway 101
(503) 547-3925
Moderate

Seven miles south of Yachats, on the west side of the road.

After reviewing so many bed and breakfasts, it can get a bit redundant when each one describes itself as unique. After all, unique means one of a kind, and how many of those can there be? I only use that word when it is totally applicable. Having said that, believe me when I tell you that this ziggurat is beyond unique: it is an unparalleled, architecturally striking specimen of coastal escapism, a towering four-story shingled pyramid set on a sea-grass-covered bluff with a keen view of the visually potent scenery. The interior is a strange combination of homey couches and bedding, slick surfaces of gray tile and laminate, black Berber carpeting, and handsome locally crafted wood armoires and furnishings. There are three rooms here—two large rambling rooms on the lower level and one on the very top of this terraced, maze-like floor plan. Until you get used to it you can actually get lost. Although all the rooms are spacious and have wraparound windows with scintillating views, the sexiest one by far is the West Suite. The private deck and glass-block shower are wonderful. The top-floor room has a remarkable view and a private deck, but the bathroom is two flights down. A full, carefully prepared breakfast is served in the ultra-modern kitchen.

Restaurant Kissing

LA SERRE RESTAURANT, Yachats
Second Street and Beach Street
(503) 547-3420
Moderate

In downtown Yachats, just off Highway 101 on the west side of the street at Second.

La Serre Restaurant remains one of my favorite dining spots along the Oregon coast. Unlike most other restaurants along this shore, it is neither Oregon formal nor rustic American standard, but a refined, gourmet dining experience with a liberal emphasis on natural, fresh whole foods. The interior design reinforces this image with thriving greenery, oak tables, and a wood floor. The service can be slow due to the strain on the kitchen from the popularity of this place, but the wait is well worth it. A meal at La Serre will satisfy your palate, your health awareness, and your need to be close to your special someone all at the same time.

Outdoor Kissing

DEVIL'S CHURN and CAPE PERPETUA, Yachats
Two miles south of Yachats, just off Highway 101 on the west side of the road. Look for the signs to the turnoff.

If you thought the drive from Cannon Beach to Yachats was awesome, you ain't seen nothing yet. Every mile between Yachats and Gold Beach is stupendous. The coast is even more rugged and mountainous, and is bordered on the east by the Siuslaw National Forest. The vista turnoffs along this stretch of highway are all located on soaring cliffs that offer arresting panoramas of the coastline due south and north. Take your time during this drive and take advantage of every wayside opportunity for looking and kissing.

Two of the best places to take advantage of the astounding mixture of rock, sand, and shore are the Devil's Churn and the 2,700-acre Cape Perpetua Scenic Area. Your eyes and hearts will be glad you stopped. At the **CAPE PERPETUA VISITOR CENTER** you'll find hiking maps available with a diverse range of easy to difficult trails. An **AUTO TOUR MAP** is available for those who want to see the area by car; the drive is fantastic.

The Devil's Churn wayside features an overview and a steep flight of wooden stairs down to the rocky, narrow channel. The movement of water through this natural cut into the land at the exchange of tides is electrifying.

◆   **Romantic Suggestion: TILLICUM BEACH STATE PARK** and **BEACHSIDE STATE PARK**, (503) 563-3220, both offer campsites (without RV hookup) located a stone's throw from the beach. There are plenty of trees to protect your tent from the wind, so the proximity to the ocean is a sterling bonus, not a shortcoming.

Florence

Hotel/Bed and Breakfast Kissing

THE EDWIN K BED AND BREAKFAST, Florence
1155 Bay Street
(503) 997-8360
Inexpensive to Moderate

In Old Town Florence on Bay Street, just off the town center.

Without question, the Edwin K is Florence's premier place to stay. The innkeepers have a rare talent for creating luxurious yet exceedingly comfortable surroundings. This grand old white frame mansion has been lovingly refurbished. The four guest rooms, named after the four seasons, are all spacious and elegantly appointed with four-poster beds, soft pastel fabrics and linens, down comforters, and sensual designer bathrooms. Out back there is a small stone-lined waterfall that can lull you to sleep. A generous breakfast is served in the formal dining room.

There is one encumbrance to all this luxury: across the street from the Edwin K is a large parking lot for a popular dining spot. Sand dunes are next to it as well, but there is no ignoring this eyesore.

Restaurant Kissing

WINDWARD INN, Florence   ❦
3757 Highway 101 North
(503) 997-8243
Moderate

Just north of Florence on Highway 101, on the west side of the road.

It is best to see this restaurant on the inside; if you glanced only at the outside you might not give it a second look. There are four separate dining areas here—one for any dining mood you might be in. There is a traditional booth and counter set-up, not romantic but great for lighter meals; a room with book-lined shelves, wooden tables, and windows that look out on the garden; a courtyard lounge with an immense 30-foot window and a magnificent, massive antique-style oak bar; and a more formal dining area with a grand piano. Fresh pastries, breads, and desserts are the kitchen's hallmark, but the rest of the diverse menu is really quite impressive. The fresh fish is probably the most tempting. If you're near Florence, and it's almost time for breakfast, lunch, or dinner, you can find what your appetites need at the Windward Inn.

◆ **Romantic Suggestions:** OLD TOWN COFFEE COMPANY, 1269 Bay Street, Old Town Florence, (503) 997-7300, (Very Inexpensive), has the art of espresso making down to a polished science. This earthy specialty café is a breath of fresh-roasted air. Wander around **OLD TOWN FLORENCE** and browse through the shops and along the riverfront while you sip a steaming brew. For something totally different, **THE COTTAGE RESTAURANT**, 239 Maple, Old Town Florence, (503) 997-8890, (Inexpensive), serves high tea in a very quaint setting. The scones are good and the finger sandwiches are fine, but it is oh, so civilized.

Outdoor Kissing

DUNE BUGGY RIDES

The Oregon Dunes National Recreation Area is one of the most beautiful sections of this coast, and much of it is accessible only by dune buggy. Renting one of these nifty (albeit potentially dangerous) little vehicles opens the phenomenal ecosystem of the dunes to your personal viewing. Imagine 600-foot sand dunes dotted with wisps of sea grass, secret lakes, and unusual islands of trees. The area is immense. During the summer season you are likely to run into screaming kids, but depending on how you navigate your excursion, you can cleverly avoid them.

There are many dune buggy companies in this area. Two good ones are **SAND DUNES FRONTIER**, 83960 Highway 101, (503) 997-3544, and **SANDLAND ADVENTURE**, 85366 Highway 101, (503) 997-8087. The price varies depending on the type of vehicle you rent and the amount of time you spend, but the average is about $35 an hour.

Charleston

Restaurant Kissing

CAFÉ FRANCAIS, Charleston
8085 Cape Arago Highway
(503) 888-9977
Moderate

From Highway 101 follow the signs for Cape Arago and Charleston. The restaurant is in the center of town, just west of the harbor.

Authentic, classic French cuisine is a treat in this otherwise working harbor area, where the other restaurants are nondescript. The very French chef here prepares superb filet mignon marinated in cognac, snapper in a flawless shrimp sauce, and tender coquilles St. Jacques. Spend a day of discovery at Cape Arago, then enjoy this discovery *pour deux*.

Outdoor Kissing

CHARLESTON STATE PARKS, Charleston

The town of Charleston is south of Coos Bay, on a small peninsula 30 miles due west of Highway 101. This trio of state parks south of town is well marked and well worth the detour from the main road. Each of the parks has a distinctive perspective and mood, despite the fact that they are separated by only a few miles.

The first park is **SUNSET BAY**, where forest and cool sandy earth flank a small, calm ocean inlet. The second, farther south, is **SHORE ACRES**. The remains of an estate, spread on a soaring cliff high above Oregon's coast, this park is renowned for its extensive formal gardens, which are maintained to resemble their former glory. There are numerous lookouts and intriguing paths that ramble over rock-strewn beaches gouged with caves and granite fissures where the water releases its energy in spraying foam and crashing waves. The third park, **CAPE ARAGO**, has less imposing grounds and is more of an everyday picnic spot than its neighbors to the north, except for its position high above the shoreline with a northern view of the coast. It is known for its sea lions and harbor seals romping in the surf or sleeping languidly on the rocks.

Bandon-by-the-Sea

Bandon-by-the-Sea is one of the few relatively undiscovered seaside towns along the Oregon coast, although that won't last much longer. Real estate signs and new deluxe developments abound, which isn't surprising. The beach here is more spectacular and interesting than at any of the more popular sites farther north, with a multitude of haystack rocks that rise in tiers from the ocean. There are a surprising number of noteworthy restaurants in this small community, and a handful of relaxing bed and breakfasts. If you yearn to retreat from the usual, this small up-and-coming beachside community is your answer.

Hotel/Bed and Breakfast Kissing

CLIFF HARBOR GUEST HOUSE, Bandon-by-the-Sea
Beach Loop Road
(503) 347-3956
Moderate

From Highway 101 turn west onto 11th Street and then right on Beach Loop Road.
Turn left at Ninth Street, which is the driveway before the Table Rock Motel.

Cliff Harbor Guest House is set atop a cliff overlooking the Bandon
shoreline. The two guest rooms each have private bathrooms and
private entrances. One has a stupendous view, a kitchen, and a fireplace,
and is quite large; the other has a sun deck. Both are nicely done,
extremely comfortable, and extremely private. There is a feeling of
exclusivity about your location. The innkeepers take good care of
guests, and their breakfasts, made with organic ingredients, prove it.

THE GORMAN MOTEL, Bandon-by-the-Sea
1110 11th Street Southwest
(503) 347-9451
Inexpensive

Just off Beach Loop Road on 11th Street. Look for the well-marked building.

The management can be a bit gruff when they're busy, which is almost
the entire summer, but this seaside accommodation is new and comfortable and has a remarkable view of the waves thundering over the rock-
clad shoreline below. The units are sparsely furnished but modern, and
have a fresh feeling unlike most motel units along the coast.

LIGHTHOUSE BED AND BREAKFAST,
Bandon-by-the-Sea
650 Jetty Drive
(503) 347-9316
Inexpensive to Moderate

Call for directions.

There are four rooms at this genial, warm bed and breakfast. The
entire house is for the guests and the views from the living area look out
to Bandon's historic lighthouse, the ocean, and the Coquille estuary. All

of the rooms have their own private bath (some adjoining), plus a varied assortment of assets: one has a fireplace and bedside view of the scenery, one has a whirlpool tub and a bright sunny setting, and one has its own private deck overlooking the river. The owners will make your stay memorable, even though you won't see much of them while you are here, which can be considered a romantic asset.

SUNSET MOTEL, Bandon-by-the-Sea
1755 Beach Loop Road
(503) 347-2453, (800) 842-2407
Inexpensive to Moderate

The office is on the east side of Beach Loop Drive.

This is indeed a motel, and the accommodations for the most part live up to that style, but the oceanfront section built into a bluff, only a few feet above the shore, has absolutely supreme views and private decks that lord over the scenery. Centrally located on Bandon's Beach Loop Road, the Sunset has a spa on the property, some of the rooms have fireplaces, and two are wheelchair accessible. The oceanfront units are quite comfortable and attractive.

Restaurant Kissing

HARP'S, Bandon-by-the-Sea
130 Chicago Street
(503) 347-9057
Moderate

In Old Town Bandon, a half block from the water.

A small unassuming weathered building houses this superlative restaurant that serves dinner only. Inside, wooden tables and wood paneling continue the rustic theme, but the food is anything but rustic. The salmon with capers marinated in vermouth is impeccable and the halibut in a hot pistachio sauce is outstanding.

INN AT FACE ROCK, Bandon-by-the-Sea
3225 Beach Loop Road
(503) 347-9441, (800) 638-3092
Moderate

Follow the signs off Highway 101 to Beach Loop Road.

The solarium dining room at the Inn at Face Rock has a distant view of the water and OK food. Order a simple breakfast or a cocktail, then sit back and enjoy the view. At dinner the fresh fish is the safest entrée to order.

The Inn at Face Rock also has accommodations. These pretty units are set across the street from the water, but they are more like a condo complex than an inn.

LORD BENNETT'S, Bandon-by-the-Sea
1695 Beach Loop Road
(503) 347-3663
Moderate

Follow the signs off Highway 101 to Beach Loop Road.

Lord Bennett's has an excellent, fairly traditional menu and a decent view of the beach, although the windows are really too small to be all that effective. But the real reason to come here isn't the view but the food. The locals rave about the new chef, and the reviews are well deserved.

SEA STAR BISTRO, Bandon-by-the-Sea
375 Second Street, Old Town
(503) 347-9632
Inexpensive to Moderate

On Second Street in Old Town Bandon just off of Highway 101.

Ignore the sign out front that says "Youth Hostel." Sea Star Bistro is not only one of the premier restaurants in the neighborhood, it also runs a youth hostel. Confusing? Well, not to the kitchen staff, who consistently serve up the most delectable international cuisine. Try the poached salmon Portuguesa with cumin and huckleberry or the polenta crostini with prawns and gorgonzola; they are both delicious. The lingcod served with a puree of olives, sweet peppers, capers, and lemon is also a taste treat. It may not be ideal for kissing, but for savoring and relaxing it's great. The Sea Star Bistro is also open for hearty breakfasts and lunches.

Outdoor Kissing

FACE ROCK WAYSIDE, Bandon-by-the-Sea

Turn off Highway 101 at the signs indicating Beach Loop Drive.

Many sections of beach and shoreline along the Oregon coast claim to possess the most phenomenal views and the most stupendous scenery. The competition is tough, but there are no real winners because the claims are all accurate. Yet, if there must be a winner, I would vote for the beachfront at the Face Rock wayside. The rock-studded water and damp, firm expanse of sandy beach are truly without equal. Images of your time here will linger long after you've left.

Langloise

Hotel/Bed and Breakfast Kissing

FLORAS LAKE HOUSE BED AND BREAKFAST,
Langloise
92870 Boice Cope Road
(503) 348-2573
Moderate

From Highway 101 turn west on the Floras Lake turnoff, continue around for three miles following Floras Lake Road, then turn west on Boice Cope Road to the bed and breakfast.

This entry was a struggle. Should I include it? After all, it is a wonderful contemporary home with four spacious, attractive guest rooms. All have plush down comforters, two have fireplaces, and all have private entrances that open onto a wraparound deck that faces the spring-fed lake and abutting ocean in the distance. The beach is only a short walk away through sea grass, and it is gorgeous and empty. Or should I leave it out? The young innkeepers have a very active toddler, another one is on the way, and they also cater to families, which can make the common room noisy, negating any genuine romantic atmosphere. But there was one point that made it hard to leave out. Floras Lake is one of the only lakes directly next to the ocean where you can windsurf. (The proximity to the ocean is what makes the windsurfing so ideal.) The owners rent sailboards, wet suits, and give lessons. If you windsurf, this place is a kissing bonus.

◆ **Romantic Alternative:** A small campground called Boice Cope Campground is situated directly on Floras Lake, hidden by trees from the bed and breakfast. If camping is more your style, this is a secluded spot, protected from the ocean, and you can still rent sailboards and wet suits from Floras Lake House.

Port Orford

Restaurant Kissing

WHALE COVE RESTAURANT, Port Orford
Highway 101
(503) 332-7575
Expensive

On the Coast Highway in the town of Port Orford, on the east side of the road.

There is only one word for the dinners here at Whale Cove Restaurant: exquisite. The traditional French menu and flawless presentation are what you would expect to find in any big city. When you consider that the chef honed his skills at Maxim's in Paris, it isn't all that surprising. The scallops in champagne sauce, the duck breast stuffed with oysters in a lemon cream sauce, and the rack of lamb are all sheer perfection. But make your reservations soon; I heard rumors that the tourist trade isn't necessarily interested in this kind of quality dining, and that could hurt this restaurant's future. Let's prove them wrong.

Gold Beach

Hotel/Bed and Breakfast Kissing

INN AT NESIKA BEACH, Gold Beach
33026 Nesika Road
(503) 247-6434
Inexpensive to Moderate

From Highway 101, just before the town of Gold Beach, turn west on Nesika Road to the inn.

One of the last stops for romance before the California border is this newly built Victorian-style home settled on a steep bank overlooking the Pacific. Each of the four spacious and tasteful guest rooms has a ringside view of the crashing surf and brilliant sunsets, and every romantic amenity is provided. Three of the rooms have black marble fireplaces, whirlpool tubs, thick down comforters, featherbeds, lace curtains that billow in the breeze, and cozy sitting areas. The fourth room has everything but the fireplace. Breakfast is served at a common table in the formal dining room, or you can take your coffee out on the enclosed sun deck. Scones, pecan French toast, and overpuffed pancakes stuffed with peaches are some of the morning offerings you will find.

OREGON CASCADES

Columbia River Gorge

Oregon's Interstate 84 borders the south side of the Columbia River. Highway 14 runs parallel to it on the north side of the river in Washington state. Several bridges span the river between Oregon and Washington.

The Columbia River Gorge is a most fitting region to include in this kissing travelog. The 60 miles or so of scenery formed by the river carving its way through the Cascade range are a kaleidoscope of heart-stirring images. To travel this passage is to sense the magic afoot in the emerald mountains to the west and blazoned across the sunburnt mountains and grasslands to the east. This is a vast collage of all the intensely beautiful things the Northwest has to offer.

A land so richly endowed by nature is sure to figure in Native American folklore and legends, and the gorge most certainly does. There are scads of ponds, mountain lakes, and trails, but the waterfalls are undoubtedly the most remarkable natural feature. Depending on the season, they rush to earth in a variety of contours and intensities: **ONEONTA FALLS** drops abruptly off a sheer ledge for several hundred feet. **ELOWAH FALLS** sprays a fine, showery mist over deciduous forest. **PUNCH BOWL FALLS** pours into crystal-clear **EAGLE CREEK. UPPER HORSETAIL FALLS** is forced out in a jet stream through a portal centered in a wall of rock, and **WAHKEENAH FALLS** rushes over rocky steps and beds of stone. Wherever you happen to be in the Columbia River Gorge, its stunning natural pageantry will make you feel that you've found paradise.

◆ **Romantic Note:** Though this area is visually stunning, and the trails, natural wonders, and fruit-laden countryside are totally splendid, it has yet another attraction: windsurfing. This area has just the kind of reliably exciting air currents that windsurfers relish, and you can watch these enthusiasts and their multicolored sails whip across the gorge or get out there and zip over the water yourselves.

Outdoor Kissing

THE COLUMBIA RIVER SCENIC HIGHWAY

The 22-mile route starts at the Ainsworth Park exit or the Troutdale exit on Interstate 84 east of Portland.

This highway, the first paved road to cross the Cascades, was constructed in 1915 and is reported to be an engineering marvel. Once you drive this sinuous, moss-covered work of art, you will swear it was really built by wizards. There is none of the commercialism you associate with road travel; you won't be bothered by neon, billboards, super highways, traffic signs, or speeding cars. This scenic highway really accentuates the scenery. In the days when it was built, driving was called touring and cars moseyed along at 30 miles an hour. You can go a tad faster through here now, but not much, and why bother? You won't want to miss the falls, hikes, and roadside vistas that show up suddenly along the way.

◆ **Romantic Note:** During summer, when the kids are out of school, this can be a very crowded strip of road. The best time for romance here is when school is in session.

◆ **Romantic Option:** I don't generally recommend tourist attractions; the crowds associated with them usually prevent intimate moments and privacy. The restaurant in **MULTNOMAH FALLS LODGE**, Troutdale, (503) 695-2376, (Inexpensive), is indeed a tourist attraction, and if it weren't for one unbelievable feature (proclaimed in the lodge's name), this would be just another Northwest wood-and-stone dining room serving three decent meals a day. That attraction, of course, is the plummeting waterfall, spilling a dramatic 620 feet, almost in the lodge's backyard. This spectacle makes any snack or meal here a momentous occasion.

Hood River

Hotel/Bed and Breakfast Kissing

COLUMBIA GORGE HOTEL, Hood River
4000 West Cliff Drive
(503) 386-5566
Expensive to Very Expensive

One hour east of Portland on Interstate 84, take Exit 62 to the hotel.

The wide-ranging grounds of this prestigious Spanish-style villa are on a high, forested bank of the Columbia River with Mount Hood's glacial peak glistening in the distance. The restaurant's atmosphere is reminiscent of an elegant 1920s country estate, filled with fine crystal, silver, pastel tablecloths, and arched bay windows looking over the woods and river. If you plan on being in the neighborhood, you may want to consider a morning stop here. Their well-known breakfast extravaganza has lost some of its flavor over the years but it is abundant and the views are spectacular. Dinners are just average; vegetables can be undercooked, salmon can be overcooked, and the presentation is undistinguished.

The guest rooms at the Columbia Gorge Hotel have finally been redecorated and the result is rooms that are almost as attractive as the restaurant and lobby. Each suite has new Queen Anne-style furniture, floral bedspreads, and, at long last, new plush carpeting. Unfortunately, the bathrooms are still the same—not great, but not entirely awful either. It's the price tag on these accommodations that makes you expect more than what you get here. In any case, this historic landmark deserves the recognition it has achieved over the years.

HOOD RIVER HOTEL, Hood River
102 Oak Street
(503) 386-1900
Moderate

Take Exit 63 from Interstate 84 on the Oregon side of Hood River. Go straight into town and take a left on Oak Street. The hotel is on your left at the corner at the end of the block.

Visit yesteryear and spend an evening in a venerable 1913 red-brick hotel, located in the core of downtown Hood River. The lobby summons you through stylish French doors into the handsome embrace of contemporary posh sofas, myriad large potted plants, and high ceilings that allow the room to fill with profuse sunlight in the morning.

You'll know this is a vintage hotel when you take your first ride in the antique elevator with a brass door that you pull shut yourself, a time-machine-like experience. Upstairs, the hallways with high ceilings and Oriental carpet runners can be misleading, depending on your room; not all of the rooms are this nice and spacious.

None of the guest rooms escape the perpetual hum of traffic beyond, but if you can get used to this (after all, you *are* downtown; what can you expect?) you're likely to appreciate your accommodations. The third floor has several comfortable options. One is a two-bedroom suite with hardwood floors and a canopied wood bed, Oriental carpets, antique mirrors, a full kitchen, and plenty of windows. You can catch a glimpse of the Columbia Gorge, although its natural beauty is obstructed by surrounding buildings. Other options are several of the guest rooms down the hall that also have canopied beds, some with matching floral print curtains, and windows with better (but less than perfect) views of the gorge. The rooms are on the small side, pleasant but not superior, and breakfast is *not* included.

This is a nice option for those who want the convenience of a downtown hotel, but don't want to pay exorbitant prices for elegance.

Romantic Note: The **HOOD RIVER HOTEL CAFÉ** is adjacent to the downstairs lobby, and you might consider having breakfast or lunch here. The fare is light and relatively inexpensive, ranging from home-made minestrone soup served with a baguette to creamy pasta dishes.

LAKECLIFF ESTATE BED AND BREAKFAST,
Hood River
3820 West Cliff Drive
(503) 386-5918
Inexpensive

Call for reservations and directions.

Rather than staying in the costly accommodations at the Columbia Gorge Hotel, consider a sojourn at Lakecliff Estate Bed and Breakfast, only a half mile down the road from the hotel. This large, beautifully renovated country home is situated on a magnificent, enviable piece of Columbia River property. Almost every room in the house has a commanding view of the river. An outside deck at the back of the house is perfect for lounging and gazing. The rooms are spacious and totally appealing. Each one is a cozy hideaway with thick quilts, stone fire-places, and soft new carpeting. A hearty breakfast awaits you in the morning, making this bed and breakfast an easy place to call home. Sad to say, the rooms do share baths and the dining room table is family-style instead of seatings for two, but the view and the quality of the rooms make those details minor romantic inconveniences and nothing more.

STATE STREET INN, Hood River
1005 State Street
(503) 386-1899
Inexpensive

Call for directions.

This immaculate, handsomely renovated bed and breakfast is in the town of Hood River, on a hill over looking the area. The English-style house, with its gabled roof, oak floors, and leaded glass windows that look out to the Columbia River in the distance, is a bright and airy place. All the rooms share baths, but for the price, the quality, and the delicious breakfast, State Street Inn is a great alternative, especially if romance and windsurfing are high on your list of priorities.

Restaurant Kissing

STONEHEDGE INN, Hood River
3405 Cascade Drive
(503) 386-3940
Moderate to Expensive

Call for directions.

Considered one of the state's best-kept romantic secrets, Stonehedge consistently lives up to its well-deserved reputation. It is set away from the town area, up a gravel road, surrounded by dense shrubbery that gives no clue to what lies beyond. This century-old, stone-clad home is an intriguing find. The rooms have been beautifully transformed to accommodate intimate seating, and the food is classic continental with a Northwest accent. Everything is incredibly fresh and artistically presented.

Mount Hood

Hotel/Bed and Breakfast Kissing

INN AT COOPER SPUR, Mount Hood
10755 Cooper Spur Road
(503) 352-6037
Moderate

Take Highway 26 to Government Camp, where you connect with Highway 35 to Hood River. Nineteen miles past Government Camp, before you reach Hood River, turn left onto Cooper Spur Road. Follow it two and a quarter miles to the inn.

This restaurant and lodging is best described as a romantic anomaly. It definitely has all the outward signs of a provincial mountain snuggery. At the foot of a gentle, lesser-traveled slope, definitely off the beaten bath (about a half hour from the Timberline ski area), a log gateway guards a stone path leading to a charming wood cottage. Inside the restaurant there is more distinctive woodwork, and the aroma of just-baked pies dances about the room. The rooms and cabins have the same type of exterior, and the interiors are all wood, with stone fireplaces. Outside there are almost a dozen hot tubs waiting to soothe tired, over-skied muscles. (There is no privacy in the outdoor hot tubs, which all occupy the same cement slab, but they are soothing for skiers just the same.)

Who could deny how quaint and cozy all that sounds? And it is, but only up to a point. What you discover is that the homey, ultra-basic decor and furnishings and laid-back atmosphere really make this more a place for hiking or ski chums than a haven for starry-eyed lovers. Though this may not be exactly the intimate destination you were looking for, if it's ski season, the Inn at Cooper Spur has mountain hospitality aplenty and all the warmth and social activity you could want.

THE RESORT AT THE MOUNTAIN, Mount Hood ❧
68010 East Fairway Avenue
(503) 622-3101
Expensive to Very Expensive

Located off Highway 26 on Mount Hood, about an hour outside of Portland. Call for more specific directions.

Romance abounds at Mount Hood, inspired by nature's ever-present splendor, flourishing in the surrounding forests, rows of distant hillsides, rushing waterfalls, and diverse wildlife. With all of this scenery just waiting to inspire you, you need to find a place to stay, and this isn't so easy. Especially in the height of ski season, you'll need to make reservations far in advance, and even then you might be out in the cold. However, your chances are better at this resort, which offers 160 guest rooms.

Typically, I would not recommend a resort of this magnitude, not only because its size reduces your sense of privacy, but also because the grounds resemble a country club and the rooms are reminiscent of a standard hotel. Nevertheless, the setting is sublime, nestled in 300 acres of evergreen woodland in the foothills of the Huckleberry Wilderness Area of the Mount Hood National Forest. It's truly a special place to be in any season, but particularly spectacular when the grounds are covered in snow.

The resort caters to your every whim, from golf courses, tennis courts, and an outdoor heated pool and Jacuzzi, to a fitness center, hiking trails, volleyball, etc. (I could go on forever.) It's perfect for athletes, but for those of you who have come looking for some peace and quiet, I suggest taking a walk in the stillness of the woods and drinking in the enthralling mountain views. As you fill your lungs with the sweet, fresh air, you're likely to be thankful for this mountain vacation spot, even if it was your only option.

◆ **Romantic Note:** Dinner at the **HIGHLANDS**, (503) 622-3101, (Moderate), is a must. Not only is it conveniently located in the resort's complex, but it offers serene intimacy in an elegant green and peach room with a view of the evergreens and grounds beyond. Lobster bisque, seafood fricassee, and hazelnut-chicken linguine are just a few of the dishes you can relish over candlelight.

◆ **Romantic Option:** If you are still hard-put for a place to stay, I recommend the **MOUNT HOOD INN,** 87450 East Government Camp Loop, Government Camp, (503) 272-3205, (Inexpensive to Expensive). Its exterior resembles a chain hotel's, and, not surprisingly, it borders the highway, but the rooms here far exceed the Resort at the Mountain's rooms in pleasantry. Each room is tastefully decorated with matching linens, comforters, and curtains; plush new carpeting; and contemporary natural-wood furniture, not to mention the private, beautifully tiled, two-person Jacuzzis in a corner of most rooms. Given the fact that the same mountain setting is just moments away, this might even be your better option.

TIMBERLINE LODGE, Mount Hood
On Mount Hood
(503) 272-3311
Moderate to Expensive

Traveling to Mount Hood from the south, follow Highway 26 up the east side of the mountain. As you near the summit, turn onto the Timberline access road, which will take you to the lodge. From Portland, go east on Highway 26 to Government Camp, where the Timberline access road starts its six-mile climb to the lodge.

Mount Hood, like its relative to the north, Mount Rainier, stands as an overwhelming example of nature's potency and formidable genius. Appropriately, near the summit, there rests an example of human creativity, Timberline Lodge. This grand structure is endowed with character and masterful craftsmanship, evidenced in its metal filigree, stone chimneys, archways, and massive hand-hewn beams. The metal-strapped furniture, wall murals, and intricately arranged wood rafters are further testimony to this artistry. Originally built in 1937, the rooms are beautifully restored, with inviting, comfortable furnishings; some have fireplaces. This handsome lodge and the riveting countenance of Mount Hood together create a scene of rugged romance perfect for two.

◆ **Romantic Note:** In winter, when snow transforms the area into a winter wonderland, the lodge's warmth and the rush of downhill or cross-country skiing make this a sensationally sensual hideaway. But it is extremely difficult to get a reservation. This popular mountaintop destination isn't a secret and can be booked year-round.

Bend

Hotel/Bed and Breakfast Kissing

INN OF THE SEVENTH MOUNTAIN, Bend   ❂❂❮
18575 South Century Drive
(503) 382-8711
Inexpensive to Expensive

Just south of Bend, off Highway 97; follow the signs to the resort.

I am including this one for my husband. He has a rough time feeling romantic when the only thing on the agenda is romance. Given what I do for a living, he gets bored with finding hidden getaways where everything is quiet mountain seclusion or private ocean cottages with glowing fireplaces and huge doses of gentle intimacy. He likes a change of pace once in a while. He needs a trip down a coursing white-water river, challenging mountain trails, sturdy mountain bikes, a large pool where rough-housing is considered acceptable, lots of hot tubs, roller skating, horseback riding, a world-class golf course, and, of course, excellent restaurants, with a late-night disco just in case we both can't sleep. This turns him on. In fact, with options like this it's hard to turn him off. The Inn of the Seventh Mountain has all these things right at your front door, and more. And most of the rooms, whether efficiency units or suites, have views of the forest and snowcapped Mount Bachelor.

Of course, this isn't what *I* would call a romantic getaway. The numerous condo-like accommodations are privately owned and reflect each proprietor's individual tastes, which vary between "resort simplicity" to absolutely beautiful. The pace here is almost always vigorous and busy. In summer the inn becomes the scene for family vacations, and the winter months bring the ski crowd. But off-season, when kids are in school and the first snows are still a few weeks away, this place can almost be called cozy. In any season, my husband calls it heaven.

◆   **Romantic Suggestion:** VICTORIAN PANTRY, 1404 Northwest Galveston, (503) 382-6411, (Inexpensive), is a charming small restaurant, all wood and brick, that serves hearty meals for those in need of nourishment to prepare themselves for the rigors of outdoor activity.

LARA HOUSE BED AND BREAKFAST, Bend
640 Northwest Congress
(503) 388-4064
Moderate

On the corner of Louisiana and Congress.

One of the oldest homes in Bend, Lara House was built in 1910 and sprawls graciously on a residential corner, offering views of tranquil Drake Park and Mirror Pond from a large front porch and bay windows. Your hostess will welcome you with a genuine smile and offer a cup of her steaming, delicious spiced cider. The common rooms are dignified, with well-polished hardwood floors, a brick fireplace with close-by comfy armchairs, and antique sofas. A cheery, glass-enclosed sun room serves as a breakfast room.

All of the five guest rooms upstairs are equally comfortable and private, with quilt-covered queen-size beds, antique rocking chairs, bright wallpaper, and quaint vanity sinks providing all the warm touches needed to make you feel at home. Some of the rooms' color schemes and views are preferable to others.

After an ample full breakfast of stuffed French toast, fresh fruit, and almond-flavored coffee served at your private table in the solarium, you'll probably agree that although Lara House is not exceedingly elegant, it's the ideal place to let your hair down or loosen your tie, and liberate your hearts.

◆ **Romantic Option:** Another alternative is the **FAREWELL BEND BED AND BREAKFAST**, 29 Northwest Greeley, (503) 382-4374, (Very Inexpensive to Expensive). This Dutch Colonial home built in the 1920s has been entirely and lovingly refurbished, as is evident in the stunning, refined hardwood floors, new glass-and-wood furnishings, floral-printed linens, and guest rooms with tiled private baths, handmade quilts, and queen-size beds. The elegance is pervasive.

In addition, you can look forward to a full breakfast of apple pancakes or eggs Benedict the following morning. So what's the catch? The busy thoroughfare, just yards away. It's really a shame, because with a more serene setting, this bed and breakfast could be prime.

RIVER RIDGE at MOUNT BACHELOR VILLAGE, Bend
19717 Mount Bachelor Drive
(503) 389-5900
Inexpensive to Unbelievably Expensive

From Bend, follow Galveston Street, which becomes the Cascade Lakes Highway. Follow this for several miles and you will see signs for Mount Bachelor Village on your left.

Imagine a living room furnished with palatial, floral-patterned sofas, ornamented with numerous soft cushions, brand-new thick carpet, well-chosen art, and elegant wicker furnishings. High ceilings, natural-wood trim, surrounding bay windows and deck beyond, with complete views of the evergreen forest and Deschutes River below. A sparkling full kitchen, plentiful sunlight, and private outdoor Jacuzzi. Bedrooms appointed with private indoor spas, queen-size beds boasting thick paisley- and floral-printed down comforters, dressed in rich colors and adorned with a teddy bear nestled in the pillows, every corner of the room evincing utterly blissful elegance. Now imagine that it's for real, not to mention affordable. And I promise you, there isn't a catch.

The River Ridge is a condominium complex nestled in the heart of Mount Bachelor Village. This series of sprawling, two-story contemporary buildings is privately owned, but available for rent through the Village's registration office. You can choose to rent one-, two-, or three-bedroom suites, all of which are seductively sensuous. Although the one-bedroom suites don't have a spa or kitchen, they do have space for the two of you, and enough opulence and natural beauty to last you a lifetime. The one-bedroom suites are also particularly desirable, not only because they're incredibly cozy, but because of their phenomenally low prices. Book your reservations now, before they discover what a steal you're getting and raise the rent.

◆ **Romantic Note:** Fortunately or unfortunately, depending on how you look at it, the River Ridge is part of a bigger resort. This means more people in the surrounding area, but it also means that as guests you have access to all of the Village's amenities. You can bring your fishing pole and fish the Deschutes River, take a romantic walk on the nature trail that runs through the Village and next to the Deschutes, tone your muscles at the athletic club, splash in the outdoor pool in the warmer months, or, when the snow has fallen, ski Mount Bachelor, just 20 minutes away.

The Village also rents one- and two-bedroom suites in various other buildings. These are adequate and comfortable rooms, decorated individually by the owners of each unit. You have a wide variety to choose from, and you're sure to find one that's right for the two of you. Keep in mind that the one-bedroom suites, although they have full kitchens, don't come remotely close to the River Ridge, in price or decor.

ROCK SPRINGS GUEST RANCH, Bend
64201 Tyler Road
(503) 382-1957
Moderate to Expensive

On Highway 20 head toward the small town of Tumalo, 10 miles north of Bend. Immediately after you pass the town of Tumalo, look for signs that direct you to the ranch.

Ever since I visited Rock Springs Guest Ranch, I have secretly longed to return. The memories of my time there are crystal clear, and when I recall the serenity I came to know during my stay, I feel euphoric.

I got my first impression of the ranch as I drove up the dusty dirt road toward it and saw a grassy meadow full of vigorous horses playing rambunctiously. I knew that I had either truly found the Ponderosa, or these were the type of horses you could look at but not touch. I'm a city woman born and raised, and my experience with horses has been at riding stables where the animals look as if they'd rather die than be touched one more time by human hands. At Rock Springs, nothing could be further from that urban reality. These horses adored human contact. They were eager to be tended to and even more eager to challenge the trails and paths that webbed the countryside.

To adequately portray this diamond-in-the-rough location, I should probably describe the arresting scenery of mountains and rambling streams, or elaborately detail the cabins with fireplaces and the large outdoor hot tub and swimming pool. But the essence of Rock Springs Guest Ranch is not revealed by such details; rather, it is revealed when you traverse this land on horseback with someone you love, the breeze cooling your brow in fall and spring, the blush of winter cold on your cheeks or the balmy summer sun tanning your face while an eagle soars overhead.

As soon as I can get my hands on a parcel of time with my significant other, my saddlebags will be packed and I will return to one of the most inspiring escapes I have found in the Northwest.

◆ **Romantic Note:** The environment at the ranch, especially during the summer, is family-oriented. Plan a visit when school is in session for the optimal romantic atmosphere. Also, the meals are served family-style in the main lodge and are included in the package price.

Restaurant Kissing

PESCATORE, Bend
119 Northwest Minnesota
(503) 389-6276
Inexpensive to Moderate

Between Minnesota and Gasoline Alley.

Located on a side street in the quaint downtown area of Bend, Pescatore serves fine Italian cuisine at affordable prices. The blue and pink art-deco color scheme is surprisingly soothing, particularly when a pianist is lulling you with soft melodies from the white grand piano in the corner. The interior is decorated with natural wood trim and thriving plants, in addition to large windows that overlook the shops across the way. It's perfect for intimate whispers and for sharing bites of delicious food. Choose from many luscious pasta dishes, such as bow-tie pasta cooked with smoked salmon and fennel cream, and sprinkled with Parmesan cheese. Conclude with a tantalizing, creamy tirami-su, made from marscapone cheese; quite possibly the best you've ever tasted.

Outdoor Kissing

CASCADE LAKES HIGHWAY

From Highway 97 just south of Bend, turn west onto Cascade Lakes Highway and follow the signs.

Adventurous souls with, depending on the season, good snow tires can journey together on this 89-mile paved loop with stirring views of this splendid habitat. Mount Bachelor, the Three Sisters, and Broken Top will greet you overhead in astonishing panoramas. Celebrate the beauty, stopping frequently for closer looks at the numerous lakes, streams, and unique environments, all teeming with wildlife. Take a moment to bird-watch at the osprey observation area or investigate lava caves with provided flashlights. Keep your eyes open for deer, rabbits, hawks, and the other wild creatures who inhabit this heavenly place. I can't think of a more opportune spot to kiss—and to think you've got 89 blissful miles of it.

Sisters

Hotel/Bed and Breakfast Kissing

BLACK BUTTE RANCH, Sisters
Highway 20
(503) 595-6211, (800) 452-7455
Inexpensive to Very Expensive

Follow Highway 20 west toward Salem, west of Sisters. Black Butte Ranch is eight miles from Sisters, on your left.

For some, a romantic retreat consists of shutting out the world for hours or even days and focusing solely on each other. Others interpret romance to mean exploring the world actively together, side by side, or hand-in-hand. You can have the best of both at Black Butte Ranch, although it caters more obviously to those who want to see and do it all.

The ranch is set on the pinnacle of seven impressive mountains, on a flat, grassy plain sparsely covered with ponderosa pines, meandering streams, and fertile meadows. Your interlude begins in the registration lodge, an unusual three-story building with open wood beams, high ceilings, terraced landings and stairways, cozy nooks and crannies, and a live tree growing through its center. Encircling glass windows give you calming views of the nearby lake dotted with geese in the summer, distant plains, and glorious mountains. The surrounding ranch-style interior makes you feel like you've really gone out West.

You can rent one-, two-, or three-bedroom condominiums, all set in contemporary gray wood complexes with wood walkways and views of the grounds. Inside, the suites feature high ceilings, fireplaces, full kitchens, and a continued ranch-style decor that can look somewhat outdated, depending on the condominium. Neither luxurious nor elegant, Black Butte is nevertheless a favorable place to enjoy some country privacy together.

And for a taste of real ranch life, the stables are moments away. Befriend a horse, and take a guided tour on horseback in the silent, lush backwoods. Choose from various trail rides, some of which include a barbecue dinner in the barn afterward, design your own ride, or get lessons if you're a tenderfoot.

As if this were not enough, Black Butte Ranch offers the standard resort options: tennis courts, four outdoor swimming pools, bike rentals, jogging trails, sufficient restaurants, and golf course. Needless to say, these activities are not geared toward intimacy, but you never know. Life is full of surprises.

SOUTHERN OREGON

Steamboat

Hotel/Bed and Breakfast Kissing

STEAMBOAT INN, Steamboat
Highway 138
(503) 496-3495
Moderate to Expensive

Directly on Highway 138, 38 miles east of Roseburg.

Almost halfway between Interstate 5 and Crater Lake is the world of Steamboat Inn and the Umpqua National Forest. The Umpqua River rambles for miles in conjunction with the road, coursing over boulders and rocks or lingering serenely, guarded by old-growth firs towering over the waters edge. Hiking to a dozen different waterfalls, wading in the river, and, of course, fly-fishing are on the lineup of possible activities at the inn. Although the conversation in the lobby is an angler's dream, the inn itself makes steelheading seem lackluster by comparison. Well, almost.

There are seven ideal cabins (two with an extravagant price tag attached) with white tiled soaking tubs, fireplaces, small kitchens, spacious bedroom and living room areas, and large private decks. The more expensive ones also have a spectacular view of the rushing river and the forest, while the others surround a wooded meadow where the deer and antelope (and anything else that plays) search for salt licks on the lawn.

The inn is known for its Fisherman's Dinner, served family-style in the dining room around a long wood slab table. The food is basic, plentiful, and good. It isn't even vaguely romantic, but it is an event the anglers seem to take to naturally; after all, romance occasionally does take a back seat to a 15-pound steelhead.

Outdoor Kissing

CRATER LAKE

From Interstate 5 take Highway 138 east approximately 130 miles to Crater Lake.

It's hard to fathom the dimensions of this volcanic formation cut into the earth thousands of years ago by forces that make the Mount St. Helens eruption look like a firecracker on the Fourth of July. A towering border of golden, rocky earth encompasses this inconceivably blue body of water. It is an astounding spectacle to behold. You can drive around the entire perimeter, with fascinating vistas all around, or hike the trails down to the lake and embrace amidst scenery that will take your breath away. The car caravans of tourists during the summer can also take your breath away, and hamper some pretty good kissing. Springtime is the best season at Crater Lake for fine weather and privacy. Remember, this is on the east side of the mountains, so the rainfall and cloudy days occur much less frequently.

At this time there are no accommodations near the crater and the lodge is being renovated, so camping is your best option. For more information, call the visitor center at (503) 594-2211.

Grants Pass

Hotel/Bed and Breakfast Kissing

RIVERBANKS INN, Grants Pass
8401 Riverbanks Road
(503) 479-1118
Moderate to Expensive

Call for directions.

Two cabins and two large homes here share 17 acres of rambling garden. We think the three guest rooms in the main house are the most fascinating places to stay. The Casablanca Room has carved Peruvian furnishings, a brick fireplace, canopied queen-size bed, wet bar, TV and VCR, and private deck and entrance. The Jean Harlow Room is a large suite with a lovely art-deco bedroom set, velvet love seat, and French

doors that open to a private patio overlooking the river. The Caribbean
Room is the most exotic. You enter through a glass-bricked foyer into a
jungle-bath/sitting room. The stone garden waterfall/shower next to a
Jacuzzi has to be seen to be appreciated. A separate bedroom and bed
canopied with mosquito netting advances the theme.

The two simple cabins don't match the distinction of the main house,
but they are close enough to the charming side of rustic to make them
interesting places to stay. The one with a full kitchen, fireplace, and
bedroom is the most roomy; the other, decorated like a Japanese *tatami*
room, is snug but endearing. The two large, lovingly restored rustic
homes on the property are available for family gatherings or for personal
rental.

A full breakfast of fresh-squeezed orange juice, peach-and-plum
soufflé, homemade granola, and decadent French toast makes mornings
here as memorable as the nights.

Outdoor Kissing

RIVER RAFTING ON THE ROGUE

Between the coast (where the Rogue River empties into the Pacific)
and Grants Pass, there are more then 45 different rafting and boat
companies that offer all kinds of excursions down the Rogue River or the
Upper Klamath River. Some of these jaunts are totally tame, letting you
float free in the midst of towering pines and mountains, while others are
radically exhilarating, making you shoot rapids and navigate rocky
channels. Boats built for one, two, eight, or large groups are all part of
the Rogue adventure; what you choose depends on skill and your level
of confidence in yourself and each other. Trips down the Rogue might
seem touristy, but once you challenge the rapids and feel the thrill of this
waterborne roller coaster, everyone else disappears and it is only the two
of you and the river.

Many of the rafting companies offer pickup in Jacksonville and
Ashland. A few of the companies you may want to consider wherever
you are along the Rogue are: **ORANGE TORPEDO TRIPS**, (503)
479-5061 or (800) 635-2925; **JET BOAT RIVER EXCURSIONS**,
(503) 582-0800; **HELLGATE EXCURSIONS**, (503) 479-7204; and
ROGUE/KLAMATH RIVER ADVENTURES, (503) 779-3708.

Jacksonville

If you haven't visited Jacksonville before, I have several excellent reasons why you should make this a priority on your Northwest romantic travel itinerary. Four indelible seasons sweep across the area's rolling hills, distant mountains, and pristine farm country, filling them in turn with sultry warmth, stunning colors, and vigorous cold. During the summer (June through early September), the exhilarating **BRITT FESTIVAL** takes place, featuring internationally recognized musicians, bands, and dance ensembles, all performing under the stars in an outdoor amphitheater surrounded by ponderosa pines. There are first-class bed and breakfasts and restaurants to be found here, some of which are thoroughly romantic. In addition, Jacksonville is only 15 miles from Ashland and the Shakespeare Festival, and is also convenient to river rafting on the Rogue. Finally, Jacksonville is a truly charming revitalized Old West town that gives only the subtlest hint that it is a tourist attraction. You will be pleased with what a lovely escape this can be.

◆   **Romantic Note:** For more information about the **BRITT FES-TIVAL** and to receive a brochure listing the talent lineup for next year, call (503) 773-6077 or (800) 882-7488.

Hotel/Bed and Breakfast Kissing

COLONIAL HOUSE BED AND BREAKFAST,
Jacksonville
1845 Old Stage Road
(503) 770-2783
Moderate

From Interstate 5 take the Old Stage Road exit at Gold Hill and head south to the bed and breakfast.

Renovated with attention to detail, this homey Greek Revival farmhouse is now a lovely English-style bed and breakfast. The house, flanked by ancient spreading black oaks, faces a sweeping view of the Rogue Valley and mountains in the distance. The three extremely comfortable and sizable guest rooms have separate sitting rooms, king- or queen-size beds, floral fabrics, wicker furniture, and private baths. A full breakfast is served at a common table in the formal dining room or in the glass-enclosed Garden Room, each warmed by a massive crackling fireplace. Brie omelets, sausage frittatas, and eggs Creole with spicy sausage are some of the innkeepers' special morning fare. A proper, cordial high tea is also served promptly at 4 P.M. in the Garden Room.

JACKSONVILLE INN, Jacksonville
175 East California Street
(503) 899-1900
Moderate

In the heart of Jacksonville, on the main street through town.

For the most part I haven't seen great renovations of landmark hotels. They are often adequate, but lack warmth and comfort. Just the opposite is true for the Jacksonville Inn. The hotel has been fastidiously restored to a showcase blending old and new. All of the eight rooms have exposed brick walls, private baths, handsome antique armoires, comfortable beds, and a great deal of polish. One room even has a wonderful whirlpool tub—not exactly authentic, but very deluxe. Full breakfast of your choice is served in the inn's famous Victorian dining room, which is a romantic must even if you aren't staying here (the restaurant is reviewed elsewhere in this section).

OLD STAGE INN, Jacksonville
883 Old Stage Road
(503) 899-1776
Moderate

From Interstate 5 take the Old Stage Road exit at Gold Hill and head south to the bed and breakfast.

When it comes to bed and breakfasts, this one is truly state-of-the-art. The kissing potential here is fairly intense. The brilliantly renovated Greek Revival farmhouse stands atop three and a half acres of immaculate lawns dotted with maple trees, lording over an expansive view of the Rogue Valley and surrounding mountains. Inside, the superb detailing is a Victorian dream come true. Grand sitting rooms with overstuffed sofas, wing chairs, wood-and-marble fireplaces, and chandeliers are to be found on the main floor. Upstairs there are three amorous guest rooms with canopied beds, bright floral comforters, and sensual bathrooms.

Two of the rooms share a bath, which is generally a no-no in our romantic criteria, but in this case the white tiled bathroom with its large white Jacuzzi tub haloed by two candelabras is a desirable exception to the rule. Behind the main house there is a separate exquisitely remodeled cottage that also has an outrageous bathroom with a Jacuzzi tub and a shower built for two.

Breakfast is served in the formal dining room at a common table or outside in the garden, weather permitting. The full gourmet breakfast may include pears marinated in wine and served with a fresh blackberry sauce, a creamy sweet buttermilk-fruit mold, chicken crêpes, or croissants stuffed with shiitake mushrooms, eggs, and cheese.

Restaurant Kissing

JACKSONVILLE INN RESTAURANT, Jacksonville
175 East California Street
(503) 899-1900
Moderate

In the heart of Jacksonville, on the main street through town.

One of the better-known restaurants in the area, this plush, demurely lit dining room consistently gets rave reviews. I'm not sure what all the commotion is about, because part of the extensive (and I mean extensive) menu leaves much to be desired. You are better off ordering the simpler entrées, because they can be delicious. The salmon crêpes with cream sauce were mushy and the sauce was too thick; and the spanikopita was greasy and hard to chew. But the meat dishes, particularly the filet mignon and the fresh fish, were just fine and quite tender. The room itself is definitely a romantic setting for any meal—breakfast, lunch, dinner, or snacks—and this is a particularly wonderful place for Sunday brunch (champagne from local wineries is served with the meal). If you're careful, this can be a four-lip dining rhapsody. If not, well, you can still kiss.

◆ **Romantic Note:** The inn is reviewed elsewhere in this section.

MCCULLY HOUSE INN, Jacksonville
214 East California Street
(503) 899-1942
Moderate

On the main street in Jacksonville, just east of town.

Charm and gentility as well as remarkable country-gourmet cuisine is what you can expect to encounter at McCully House Inn. The entire first floor of this renovated Victorian houses the restaurant. The peach-colored living room features a fireplace, the formal dining room is done up in taupe and cranberry, a glass-enclosed sun room serves as the lounge, and, weather permitting, there is also elegant patio dining. Breakfast, lunch, and dinner are culinary treats, and the kitchen hardly ever slips. The grilled white king salmon with shiitake mushrooms served on a bed of greens tossed with blackberry vinaigrette is superb, and the plum-and-champagne soup is light and just sweet enough. Fresh-baked herb rolls and desserts are the inn's trademark, and break-fast is exceptional. There is one drawback: the staff is inexperienced, but they do try hard. Don't miss a chance to kiss here; regardless of the meal, you will do it with a satisfied glow.

Ashland

Ashland, Oregon, is a utopian world unto itself—tranquil neighbor-hoods, dynamic downtown area teeming with shops and restaurants, cosmopolitan nightlife, world-class cultural center, pristine countryside and mountainous terrain bordering fertile river valleys. Not only is the town attractive and its numerous accommodations literally among the best the Northwest has to offer, but the Ashland theater season, beginning in February and running through October, makes New York City's Broadway pale by comparison (and that is not an embellishment). It will take only one visit to make both of you sustaining members of Ashland's annual **SHAKESPEARE FESTIVAL**. If you are not a Shakespeare fan, don't let that stop you; keep in mind that Shakespearean drama is only one component of each season's theatrical offerings. This is one of the largest theater companies in the United States. You can call the Festival directly for tickets, (503) 482-4331, or phone the **SOUTH-ERN OREGON RESERVATION CENTER**, (503) 488-1011 or (800) 547-8052, a professionally run ticket agency that can also help you with your lodgings and other theatrical productions.

There is more to do in this small, quaint area than in almost any other town in the Northwest. Besides the in-town activities, there is white-water rafting down the Rogue or Klamath rivers, horseback riding, llama hikes, mountain climbing, and, during the winter, downhill and cross-country skiing minutes away on Mount Ashland. Plus, many of the bed and breakfasts offer winter rates that are very enticing. Several very useful lodging services are available in Ashland: try **ASHLAND'S B&B RESERVATION NETWORK**, (503) 482-BEDS.

Hotel/Bed and Breakfast Kissing

COUNTRY WILLOWS BED AND BREAKFAST, Ashland
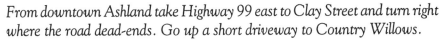
1313 Clay Street
(503) 488-1590
Moderate to Expensive

From downtown Ashland take Highway 99 east to Clay Street and turn right where the road dead-ends. Go up a short driveway to Country Willows.

Country Willows is a forested ranch estate two and a half miles from downtown Ashland. A river flows adjacent to the property and the rushing waters fill the air with soft gentle sounds. Willow trees and pasture on which proud horses graze surround the home and renovated barn. The breakfast nook, outside decks, and all the rooms enjoy this view. Each suite is large, with handsome furnishings and hand-tiled private baths, and all are brightly decorated in country fabrics and colors. There is even a huge pool out back with a hot tub that can steam away every care from your city-tired bodies. But the highlight is the newly renovated suite that I call "The Best Place To Kiss." This is a masterpiece of white-stained pinery with a secluded deck overlooking the river, a fireplace, and the most unusual built-for-two bathtub I've ever seen. Sunrise is accompanied by fresh coffee, homemade breads, and whatever creation the inspired innkeepers can think of.

COWSLIP'S BELLE, Ashland

159 North Main Street
(503) 488-2901
Inexpensive to Moderate

Take the northern Ashland exit off Interstate 5, and follow signs into Ashland. You will be on Main Street; Cowslip's Belle is on the right side three blocks north of town center.

The house may be unimpressive from the outside, but inside the attention to your needs is reassuring when things are going wrong and helpful when things are going right. The rooms provide you a great night's sleep on a firm but cushy mattress in a four-poster bed. The best rooms are in the adjacent carriage house or the newly built suite, all with private entrances. Sigh with relief as you snuggle under the softest quilts to ever touch your skin. Some of the bathrooms are beautifully done in shiny green and black tiles, and the bedroom furnishings are unique and enviable. At night, when you return from the theater, there will be homemade, hand-dipped chocolate truffles placed lovingly on your pillows. Breakfast is a fiesta of filo and cheese blintzes with sour cream cherry sauce, cornmeal pound cake in pear custard, and fresh fruit.

THE MORICAL HOUSE, Ashland
668 North Main
(503) 482-2254
Moderate

On Main Street, about one mile north of Ashland's town center.

Main Street is not the best location for a bed and breakfast, but this flawlessly renovated 1880 farmhouse is nicely hidden by a thick, towering hedge of green shrubs. The five guest rooms each have a private bath, period furnishings, and mountain views, and all are exceedingly comfortable. Out back, a considerable lawn surrounded by a veritable arboretum of trees has a putting green and space to spare for picnicking or lounging with the Cascades as backdrop. In the morning you may awake to strawberry smoothies, peach French toast, and fresh fruit.

MOUNT ASHLAND INN, Ashland
550 Mount Ashland Road
(503) 482-8707
Moderate to Expensive

Call for directions.

This massive, majestic log mansion was designed and built by the same people who created Soaring Hawks (reviewed elsewhere in this section). The building itself is an outstanding piece of design work and it's worth a stay if only to see the craftsmanship that went into constructing this mountain retreat. The inn has five rooms, some a bit on the snug side, but the mountain setting, view of Mount Shasta, and the inn itself are praiseworthy. Everything is as quaint and cozy as can be, and the full three-course breakfast is very good. You are also up in the mountains, at the heart of the Pacific Crest Trail (the inn is adjacent to it), so the hiking is excellent. Each room has a private bath, and the new suite on the lower level has its own private patio and a Jacuzzi tub with a massive stone waterfall next to it (you have to see this one to believe it.) Not at all a bad option for a bit of mountain intimacy.

PINEHURST INN, Ashland
17250 Highway 66
(503) 488-1002
Inexpensive

On Highway 66, 23 miles east of Ashland.

Along a country road, a good distance from the nearest city or village, overlooking the forested hills of the Cascade Mountains, this unassuming country inn is just about the most enchanting place to find yourselves in for miles around. The entry room is all cedar and pine, with a huge stone fireplace for luxuriant heat. Just beyond that is the restaurant, with willow furniture covered in bright floral patterns, lace tablecloths, and a rich scarlet wool carpet. At the front of the dining room is an authentic pot-bellied stove that manages to keep everything warm. From the kitchen comes innovative Northwest cuisine, with fresh ingredients and creative combinations. The menu changes with the mood of the chef and the availability of seasonal vegetables and herbs. Naturally grown beef from local ranches is a specialty, but the chef also has a light hand with fish.

Upstairs there are simple, almost austere rooms with views of the surrounding woods, and, surprisingly, each one has a private bath. These rooms aren't exactly suitable for high romance, but the entire experience is unique and serene and the breakfast is superb. If getting *away* from civilization is what you're looking for, you'll be happy at this location.

◆   **Romantic Note:** Pinehurst Inn has a summer special that includes bed and breakfast and dinner for a price that is less than inexpensive. I don't even have a price category for this romantic bargain. They also have wagon and horseback rides that start in Ashland

and end with a gourmet dinner at the inn. If your backside can stand the ride, it is a delightful summer excursion to cherish.

THE QUEEN ANNE, Ashland
125 North Main Street
(503) 482-0220
Moderate

On Main Street between Church and Bush streets.

Victorian renovations abound in Ashland, some more appealing than others. This Queen Anne is very appealing. Lovingly renovated, the bright stately exterior has well-tended gardens, a handcrafted stone waterfall, an outdoor deck overlooking the Cascades (and, unfortunately, busy Main Street), and a white gazebo. Inside, the three ample guest rooms each have lace curtains, a cozy sitting area, and private bath. All are extremely sunny and comfortable. Breakfast in the morning may include a nectarine smoothie, almond croissant French toast, strawberry and blackberry compote, and fresh-baked breads.

ROMEO INN BED AND BREAKFAST, Ashland
295 Idaho Street
(503) 488-0884
Moderate to Expensive

From Ashland's main plaza, head south on Main Street and turn right onto Gresham Street. Two blocks down, turn left on Holly and then left on Idaho. The inn is on the corner of Idaho and Holly.

The area across the street is not the best, but the inn itself is superb. The classic Cape Cod mansion rests on a manicured hillside dotted with 300-year-old ponderosa pines and stately oak trees that fill the air with a sweet, balmy fragrance. There is even a view of the Cascades in the distance. The five guest rooms are large, sophisticated, country-style suites. The Stratford Suite and the Canterbury Room will be of particular interest to those who want a fireplace, hot tub, and private entrance. Be sure to take notice of the hand-stiched Amish quilts in each room. The Cambridge Suite has a vaulted ceiling, tiled fireplace, and French doors that open onto a private garden. All the rooms have remarkably comfortable king-size beds and luxurious details. There is even a swimming pool and outdoor hot tub set amidst a well-tended garden. In the morning a generous, conscientiously prepared breakfast is served on bone china, accompanied by freshly squeezed orange juice.

◆ **Romantic Note:** Ask the innkeeper about her newly published cookbook. Her skill in the kitchen is now something you can actually take home with you.

SHREW'S HOUSE BED AND BREAKFAST, Ashland
570 Siskiyou Boulevard
(503) 482-9214
Inexpensive to Moderate

North Main becomes Siskiyou Boulevard just outside of the town center.

Perhaps it's too close to the main street to be preferred, but other details make this a great bed and breakfast. A separate cottage near the main home is where the three guest rooms are located. Each has its own private entrance; two have whirlpool tubs, king-size beds, floral fabrics, wet bars, private phones (a plus for any bed-and-breakfast traveler), and secluded porches. A sumptuous full breakfast is served to your room upon request each morning.

There is also a small but refreshing swimming pool next to the cottage for the use of the guests. It's a shame you have to look at the Safeway across the street while swimming, but the innkeepers are working on building up the garden to block the view.

SOARING HAWKS, Ashland
500 Mount Ashland Road
(503) 482-8707
Expensive

Call for reservations and directions. A three-night minimum is required; available June through October only.

Soaring Hawks is one of the absolute best places to kiss in the Northwest. The rustic home is an octagonal wood masterpiece, jutting out from the forested slopes of Mount Ashland with an unparalleled 180-degree view of the Cascades, Siskiyou Mountains, and Mount Shasta's snowy peak 75 miles to the south. The entire home is yours while you are here. Special features of the house include a vaulted living room ceiling, a gigantic rock fireplace, floor-to-ceiling windows, an outdoor hot tub with its own majestic ringside view, a bi-level deck encompassing the entire abode, and two bedrooms (one is in a separate wing of the house) with simple, almost sparse comforts. Located only 16 miles from downtown Ashland and three miles from the ski slopes, the best of all worlds is available at Soaring Hawks. By the way, the expensive price tag becomes a bargain if you're traveling with another amorously inclined couple.

WATERSIDE INN, Ashland
70 Water Street
(503) 482-3315
Expensive to Very Expensive

Call for directions.

You could call these sizable, gracious suites/apartments a home away from home, but only if you live in a stunning, designer antique-filled home. Even if you happen to be so blessed, you will still envy the style in which each room has been outfitted. The innkeeper was once a cinematic set designer, and she has used her appreciation of sumptuous, intriguing details to distinguish each suite. The suites offer dining and living rooms with plush furnishings and 20-foot ceilings, TV, VCR, stereo, incredible full kitchens, sensuous bedrooms with down comforters, overstuffed pillows and floral fabrics, a full loft, and wraparound windows facing a babbling stone-scattered creek. Two of the units have two bedrooms; both are equally elegant. Adjacent to the building is a lavish, abundant garden with a gazebo where a casual continental breakfast is served. Long relaxing hours can be spent here listening to the creek and the quiet.

◆   **Romantic Note:** If you are traveling alone the price might seem steep, but if you have another couple in tow, this is a spectacular romantic deal.

Restaurant Kissing

CHATA, Talent
1212 South Pacific Highway
(503) 535-2575
Moderate

Four miles north of Ashland on Highway 99.

This isn't a great location, but it's better than traveling to Eastern Europe for authentic Polish, Rumanian, and Hungarian ethnic cuisine. The world inside this green-shuttered country-style home is charming and casual. Every dish is hearty and sumptuous. If you haven't tasted mamaliga, bigos, or jarski obiad, you are in for a treat. Mamaliga is sautéed slices of cornmeal pancakes covered with cheddar cheese and ladled with a white wine and mushroom sauce; bigos is a hearty Polish beef and smoked pork stew. You will have to eat here yourself to discover what jarski obiad is all about. You may never get a chance to kiss in Eastern Europe, but Chata is a good substitute.

CHATEAULIN RESTAURANT, Ashland
50 East Main Street
(503) 482-2264
Expensive

On East Main Street in downtown Ashland, near Oak Street.

In the heart of Ashland is where you will find this traditional French restaurant. Inside, the subtle lighting is supplemented by flickering candlelight; lace window treatments, scarlet carpeting, and dark woodwork create a romantic milieu. The seating is intimate, with the accent on tight, almost too tight, table arrangements, particularly just before showtime. Still, the food produced by the serious kitchen is excellent.

IL GIARDINO CUCINA ITALIANA, Ashland
5 Granite Street
(503) 488-0816
Moderate

Just off Lithia Rose Park on Granite Street.

The bright interior and contemporary Italian menu make this cucina a great asset to the Ashland dining scene. The atmosphere is a refreshing blend of formal and comfortable. The pasta dishes are delicious and creative.

LITHIA SPRINGS RESTAURANT, Ashland
212 East Main Street, in the Mark Anthony Hotel
(503) 482-1721
Moderate to Expensive

On East Main Street in downtown Ashland, at First Street.

Lithia Springs Restaurant is certainly one of the most old-fashioned places to dine in Ashland. Some of the appeal can be attributed to the setting of whitewashed walls accented with floor-to-ceiling floral draperies framing tall windows. Music softly playing in the background almost completes the mood. But the pièce de resistance is the 2,000-pound crystal chandelier that hangs glistening (and I mean *glistening*) in the center of the room. This has to be seen to be believed. There are more than 1,200 separate prisms in this antique showstopper, and though it sounds overpowering it really fits the room. The food could be better, but the kitchen tries. Lunch is probably the best, and a simple breakfast is also good.

MONET RESTAURANT, Ashland
36 South Second Street
(503) 482-1339
Moderate to Expensive

On Second between Hagardine and Main.

Contemplate an exquisite French meal, with every dish more delectable than the last, and you have a firm grasp of what awaits you at Monet. A simple but immaculate large white frame building is home to the extremely elegant interior with cushioned fabric walls, pale pink and green tones throughout, and elegantly comfortable chairs. Unfortunately, the tables are a little too close for comfort and the wait staff is very young and inexperienced, but all is forgiven once the procession of delicacies begins. Standouts on the menu include salmon wrapped around a heavenly avocado puree, homemade whole-grain French bread, creamy cucumber soup artistically drizzled with sour cream, and a perfect artichoke, olive, and Parmesan fettuccine. From the appetizer to the entrée, all the portions are unexpectedly generous. The array of desserts is stellar, particularly the chocolate mousse, and worth saving room for if you can, but I'm not sure how that's possible. By the way, lunch and dinner are equally wonderful.

OREGON CABARET THEATER, Ashland
First and Hargadine
(503) 488-2902
Inexpensive to Moderate

One block off Main Street, in the town center.

Don't let the name deter you; this is not a small, crowded, smoke-filled room, nor is it a dinner theater with tired shows and food to match. Oregon Cabaret Theater is a professional (non-Equity) company doing some of the most innovative musical theater around. Many of the productions are original, some are famous off-Broadway hits, but all are delightfully entertaining. From February through December the company performs three to six nights a week, depending on the season. After several nights of Shakespeare and contemporary theater at the Festival, everyone could use a taste of musical comedy.

I almost forgot about the food, and that would be a mistake because it is surprisingly wonderful. Primavera Restaurant (reviewed elsewhere in this section) does the cooking, which explains the rich, flavorful entrées. The menu changes with each show, with clever associations to the theme of the play.

PRIMAVERA, Ashland
241-A Hargadine
(503) 488-1994
Expensive

Below the Oregon Cabaret Theater, on Hargadine near First Street.

Etched bronze pillars, exotic boldly painted frescoes, demure lighting, handsome floor-length curtains, and a baby grand piano highlight the dramatic interior of Primavera. Crystal sparkles on the white-linen-draped tables, and black-lacquered chairs add to the overall effect. The striking dining room is accented by an equally striking dinner menu. The smoked sturgeon in a rich sour cream sauce, the tender duck in a flaky pastry shell served with a fresh raspberry sauce, the pureed vegetables layered with pasta and ricotta custard, and the pasta with Brie and olives are all outstanding and beautifully presented.

◆ **Romantic Note:** Weather permitting, a terraced garden is laced with tables for dining under the stars.

THAI PEPPER, Ashland
84 North Main
(503) 482-8058
Moderate

On North Main Street near Church.

Authentic Thai cuisine—heavy on the curry and impeccably fresh—is a spicy change of pace from the European-oriented cuisines offered by most of the restaurants here. Dining outside on the patio in the summer is the best, where birch trees border a flowing stream tumbling over stones. Inside, the setting is contemporary yet soft, and the subtle lighting creates an attractive mood for dinner. Try the Red Seafood Curry, filled with every imaginable fresh fish and savory seasonings.

WINCHESTER INN, Ashland
35 South Second Street
(503) 488-1113
Expensive

One-half block from Main Street on South Second Street, in the town center.

Ask anyone in Ashland where the best food is served and they are likely to mention Winchester Inn. The restaurant is on the main floor of a renovated Queen Anne-style home where tables are placed casually throughout the library, living room, and dining alcove, with plenty of privacy space in between. The windows look out onto tiered gardens where you can also dine, and the mood is always cordial and relaxed. International cuisine is the kitchen's specialty and they do it with finesse and skill. The eggplant layered with polenta, and the chèvre and plum tomatoes in marinara sauce, are rich yet subtle. The chicken sausage, apple, and ricotta crêpes covered with a brandied cream sauce are incredible.

Outdoor Kissing

LITHIA ROSE PARK, Ashland

In the heart of the theater district is where Lithia Rose Park begins. The park comprises 100 acres of lawns, forest, ponds, trails, tennis courts, flower gardens, and a volleyball court, so there is enough space to offer you an individualized section of this lovely playground for yourselves. The immaculate trails eventually become unpaved as they wind their way up to a panoramic view of Ashland and the valley beyond.

MOUNT ASHLAND

Ashland is crowned by the 7,500-foot summit of Mount Ashland. In winter, outdoor buffs hit the more than 100 miles of cross-country ski trails that snake their way through forest, across open fields, past crystal-clear mountain lakes and flowing rivers, and over rolling hillsides. The views are spectacular. As you glide over endless stretches of white powder you can see the peaks of the Cascades to the north and Mount Shasta at 14,000 feet to the south. The terrain is steep and Mount Ashland is considered one of the most challenging downhill mountains around. These trails are equally as challenging and beautiful in the summer and fall and perfect for hiking. For information on skiing in the area, call the **ASHLAND WINTER RECREATION ASSOCIA-TION**, (503) 482-8707 or (503) 488-1590.

"When kisses are repeated and the arms hold
there is no telling where time is."

Ted Hughes

INDEX